THE UNITED STATES
AND
THE REPUBLIC OF PANAMA

THE UNITED STATES

AND

THE REPUBLIC OF PANAMA

BY

WILLIAM D. McCAIN, Ph.D.

WITH A FOREWORD

BY

J. FRED RIPPY

NEW YORK / RUSSELL & RUSSELL

1965

To

M. L. M.

ACKNOWLEDGMENTS

THE kindness and assistance of the staffs of the Duke University Library, the Columbus Memorial Library of the Pan American Union, the Department of State Archives, the Library of Congress, and the Greenville, Mississippi, Public Library are much appreciated. Valuable aid was rendered in the preparation of the manuscript by Miss Mary Elizabeth Robertson of The National Archives. The help and encouragement of William Pratt Dale II, of Duke University, inspired part of the energy that overcame the weariness of long hours of labor under the blazing summer suns of the Mississippi Delta. The author owes and tenders sincere thanks to Dr. J. Fred Rippy, without whose aid this study would not have been possible.

WILLIAM D. McCAIN.

The National Archives
Washington, D. C.
January 10, 1937.

FOREWORD

WRITERS have often dealt with the relations of the United States and the countries of the Mexican Gulf and the Caribbean without adequate concentration on fundamentals. The careful student of the subject will observe that our policy with reference to this area has been characterized by one outstanding objective: namely, that of dominating it to the extent required (or deemed necessary) to prevent its domination by any other first-rate Power. This has been the keynote of the policy of the United States for more than a century, and the national interest which has been envisaged as being at stake is that of security. The region has been most vital in our defense strategy.

At least four other motives have influenced our policy at times: land hunger; the desire to promote commerce and investments; the desire to protect the lives and property of our citizens; and something of an eagerness to help the people of the region along the road to progress. But the desire to safeguard our security, supposed to be menaced immediately or remotely by other strong Powers, has been the most constant motive—or at any rate the one most often asserted.

In its broad outlines, the history of our Gulf and Caribbean policy is well known. Its keynote was first sounded by Thomas Jefferson with reference to Louisiana and East and West Florida, when he insisted that these areas bordering on the Gulf of Mexico and so vital to our national security must either be retained by weak Spain or transferred to the United States, and that they must not be permitted to fall into the hands of a stronger Power. And Louisiana and the Floridas were eventually acquired by the United States largely for the purpose of preventing their acquisition by France or England, although the desire to give the complaining citizens of the Old Southwest access to the rivers of the region furnished another motive.

Texas was probably annexed mainly for the purpose of acquiring fertile lands. But fear that it might be seized or dominated by England was also a real factor. And, in like manner, land hunger and fear of European intrusion or domination explain the annexation of the Far Southwest and the Pacific Coast.

Although the latter regions were not a part of the Gulf and Caribbean area, their acquisition vastly increased the strategic importance of this area. Control of the Isthmian routes of interoceanic communication then became a corollary of our policy of dominating the Gulf and Caribbean region in order to prevent its domination by Europe. For the Pacific Coast and the Far Southwest had to be defended, and speedy transit across the Isthmus was vital in this defense strategy.

More than a decade before the outbreak of the Civil War, the United States began to pursue the policy of safeguarding the Isthmian routes. The government at Washington interested itself in Panama, Nicaragua, and Tehuantepec, and citizens of the United States devoted attention to all three of these routes and others as well. At that time, however, England and—to a lesser extent—France were confronted, both of whom objected to the domination of the Gulf and Caribbean by the United States; and English opposition was so effective that the contest was not resolved in our favor until the signing of the Hay-Pauncefote Treaty in 1901.

Since the Civil War, the government of the United States has been somewhat loath to acquire territory in this area. It has annexed little more than what has been deemed necessary to make effective its policy of controlling the region against the intrusion of other great Powers. It annexed Puerto Rico after the war with Spain; bought the Virgin Islands in 1916 after many years of intermittent negotiation; and acquired by lease or purchase the strips of territory necessary for the construction and control of transportation across Panama and Nicaragua. In a crisis we should perhaps feel obliged to take similar action with reference to the Colombian Atrato and the Mexican Tehuantepec routes.

And not only have we annexed territory and canal routes in the Gulf and Caribbean region; we have also placed certain limits on the sovereignty of the nations located there, and we have acquired several naval bases. In a word, we have taken any action which has seemed essential with reference to this fundamental, national security phase of our policy. It is even probable that we have gone farther than this phase of our policy has justified; but if we have done so, such action has been caused by the aggressiveness of social reformers or the pressure exerted by citizens who reside in the area or have economic interests there; or, again, the action of government may have been determined in part by nervous statesmen and congenital imperialists.

The region has not been difficult for the United States to dominate. The American states have not been strong, and the European nations have been too suspicious of each other and too busy elsewhere to offer effective resistance. A war was necessary to secure Mexico's acquiescence in the annexation of Texas, and another war was required to exclude Spain from Cuba and Puerto Rico. But the rivalry and antagonism between the United States and the other great Powers have not been so intense as to result in open hostilities, and a few Marines have been sufficient to coerce the remaining states of the Gulf and Caribbean.

The fact that this important region is not an uninhabited area, not a no-man's-land, deserves emphasis. The region was occupied long before we promulgated the policy of dominating it against Europe and even before we won our national independence. Its population was twelve or fourteen million in 1823, and the twelve theoretically sovereign nations now existing in the area have a combined population of forty million. For the most part, these people have been swept into the orbit of our destiny whether they have desired it or not. Owing to their proximity, and because of their location with reference to our defense strategy, many of these nations have been forced to become our satellites, and in respect to them the people and the government of the United States have definite and inescapable responsibilities.

The people of the area have always been, and probably will long continue to be, an important problem in our international relationships. They are not organized in model republics after the vision of a Plato. They have been, and may continue to be, turbulent and troublesome. In dealing with them our national morality has been, and will be, subjected to a severe strain, for the morality of a nation will be tested most severely at the point where it thinks it has most at stake.

Because these nations of the Gulf and Caribbean area have almost no protection save that which they may find in the public conscience of the United States, it is important that the people of the United States understand them and the nature and problems of our relations with them. Hence the significance of the present study, which deals with the intimate relationships of the United States and Panama from 1903 to 1936.

This little republic has an area of about thirty thousand square miles and a population of approximately half a million, not more than 10 per cent of which is white (the rest being Negroes, Indians, and mixtures of the three); but because it lies athwart one of the world's great highways of transportation, and owing to its position in reference to the United States, this small country is of tremendous significance to our commerce and our security. Tiny and turbulent and weak as it is, it is nevertheless one of the most important satellites of the United States.

The narrative set forth by Dr. McCain amply illustrates this fact. He has not attempted to add anything distinctly new to the accounts of the revolution of 1903 or to previous Panamanian history, but he has presented a useful sketch of both as an introduction to the thorough and judicious discussion of the events which follow, events which make up the story that he has undertaken to tell. When additional manuscript materials of the Department of State for the period after August, 1906, are made available, as well as the manuscript correspondence of the archives of Panama, certain phases of his story may be slightly modified; but it is believed that the main threads of Panamanian-American relations have been followed in a definitive manner.

Dr. McCain has not hesitated in some instances to express his views with reference to the wisdom and ethics of our policy. Whether these views are soundly based upon the facts, the reader will be free to judge. Certainly an idealist, and perhaps even a realist, will sympathize with his desire that the orbit in which the people of Panama revolve may be made as agreeable to them as possible. I do not hesitate to congratulate the author upon the high standard of his performance.

J. FRED RIPPY.

University of Chicago,
January, 1937.

TABLE OF CONTENTS

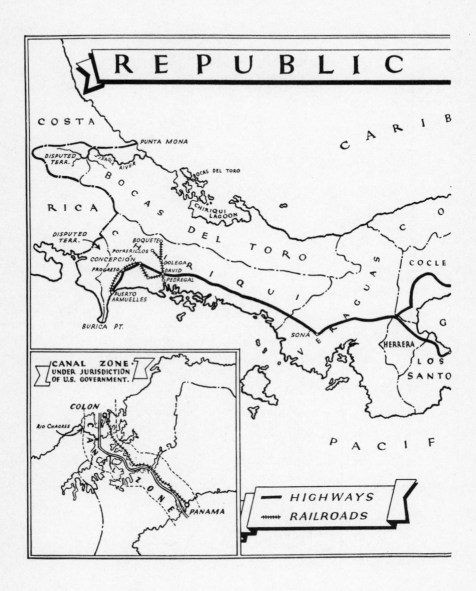

REPUBLIC

COSTA

PUNTA MONA

DISPUTED
TERR.

SIXAOLA RIVER

BOCAS DEL TORO

CARIB

B O C A S

CHIRIQUI
LAGOON

CO

RICA

DEL

DISPUTED
TERR.

BOQUETE

POTRERILLOS

CONCEPCIÓN

PROGRESO

DOLEGA

DAVID

PEDREGAL

T O R O

COCLE

PUERTO
ARMUELLES

C H I R I Q U I

BURICA PT.

SONÁ

VE R A G U A S

HERRERA

G

LOS
SANTO

CANAL ZONE
UNDER JURISDICTION
OF U.S. GOVERNMENT.

PACIF

COLON

RIO CHAGRES

C
A
N
A
L

Z
O
N
E

PANAMA

HIGHWAYS

RAILROADS

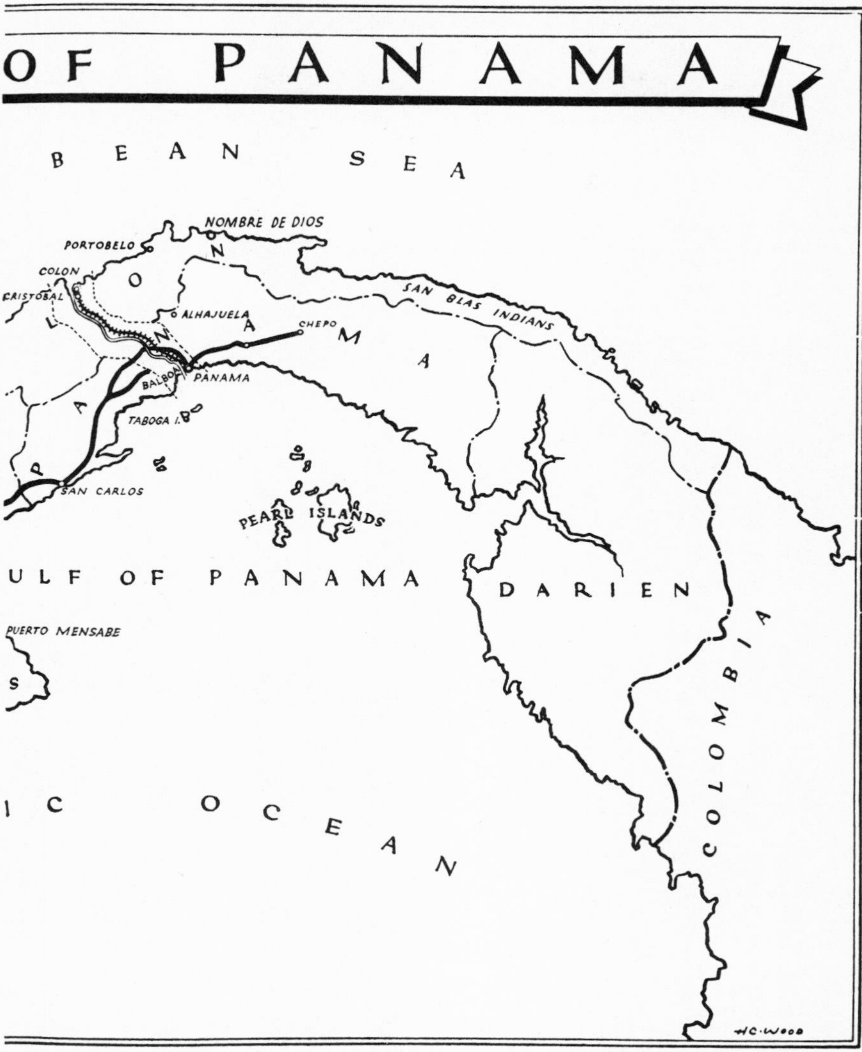
OF PANAMA
BEAN SEA
NOMBRE DE DIOS
PORTOBELO
COLON
CRISTOBAL
ALHAJUELA
CHEPO
SAN BLAS INDIANS
PANAMA
BALBOA
TABOGA I.
SAN CARLOS
PEARL ISLANDS
ULF OF PANAMA
DARIEN
PUERTO MENSABE
IC OCEAN
COLOMBIA
H.C. WOOD

CHAPTER I

FOUR TUMULTUOUS CENTURIES

THE COLONIAL PERIOD

THE FIRST European to view the Isthmus of Panama was Rodrigo de Bastidas, who explored along the coast of *Tierra Firme* in 1501.[1] During the following year Christopher Columbus reached the mainland on his fourth voyage. After resting in Almirante Bay and at Portobelo (Puerto Bello, Porto Bello),[2] he attempted unsuccessfully to establish a settlement at the mouth of the Belén River.[3] The Indians received him cordially, but became hostile. Columbus reported: "I felt very sure that peace would not last very long between us, for the inhabitants were very barbarous and our men very greedy, and so I took possession of their country."[4] Spain soon divided the new land into Nueva Andalucía and Castilla del Oro. Alonso de Ojeda was appointed governor of the southeastern province, and Diego de Nicuesa was given the peril of ruling Castilla del Oro. In 1509 Ojeda tried to settle San Sebastián on the Gulf of Darién, and Nicuesa made an effort to colonize Nombre de Dios,[5] but both failed.

Martín Fernández de Enciso soon founded Santa María la Antigua del Darién at the mouth of the Darién River, but Vasco Núñez de Balboa, a subordinate, assumed leadership and became friendly with the natives. After hearing rumors of a sea on the other side of the Isthmus, and beyond that a fabulous land, Balboa started across on September 1, 1513, to investigate. At the end of a hazardous journey he took formal possession of the South Sea on September 29. Again he and Francisco Pizarro heard of the riches of a wondrous land to the south,[6] but the discoverer soon found himself imprisoned by Pedro Arias de Ávila, the new governor and captain-general of Castilla del Oro.[7] Later released because of his distinguished service, he crossed the Isthmus to prepare for an expedition on the *Mar del*

Sur, but fell victim to the jealousy of the old governor and was executed in 1519.[8] On August 15 of that year Pedrarias officially established a Spanish settlement at the Indian village of Panama, and Nombre de Dios soon replaced Antigua. Darién returned to the folds of the tropical jungle never to be conquered by the efforts of white men. Pizarro assumed the task from which death relieved Balboa, and within a decade was plundering Peru.[9]

The first royal *audiencia*—a high judicial body with certain legislative and administrative functions—was established at Panama in 1533. Castilla del Oro had been under the jurisdiction of Española, but Panama then became the seat of government for the Isthmus and Peru. A year later Charles V instructed his officials in the New World to consider the construction of a canal, partly in the valley of the Chagres River, across the Isthmus.[10] The project was not undertaken, but the streams of Peruvian wealth caused the development of a system of transportation from Panama City to Nombre de Dios. The treasure trains, comparable to the ancient caravans of the Orient, used either the *Camino Real* the whole distance or loaded their cargo on Chagres River boats at Cruces. One witness recounted that he saw twelve hundred mule loads of precious metal leave Panama City in 1550.[11]

After Luis Columbus, the grandson of the discoverer, sold his claim to Veragua in 1556,[12] Concepción was settled and became the capital of that province. Other small settlements on the Isthmus in 1775 were Santa Fé, Meriato, Philipina, Natá, and Villa de los Santos. Panama City was an important port of four hundred houses and five hundred families. Goods from Spain were brought across from Nombre de Dios, a town of two hundred houses, which was practically uninhabited in the absence of the treasure fleet. The harbor was not protected, the surrounding country was unhealthful, the rain and heat were excessive, and the pirates and *cimarrones* (runaway Negro slaves) were troublesome.[13]

The story of Panama for the next century is a saga of the buccaneers. They were venturing up the Chagres by 1571, and in 1572 Francis Drake was repulsed from Nombre de Dios after being treated to the sight of a stack of silver reported "seventie foote in length, of ten foot in breadth, and twelve foot in hight." After harassing the Isthmus several months, he captured a train of 190 mules in 1574, as it approached the Panama gate of Nombre de Dios. So great was the treasure that he was forced to abandon about fifteen tons of silver.[14] One of his followers, John Oxenham, crossed the Isthmus in 1575 and built ships on the Pacific, but was soon seized and executed by the Spaniards.[15] In August, 1578, *El Draque* passed through the Straits of Magellan in the *Pelican,* which he rechristened the *Golden Hind.* After harrying the coast up to California, he continued around the world, being the second to circumnavigate it.[16] He was again in the Caribbean in 1595, and burned Nombre de Dios, but died on the morning of January 28, 1596, and was buried off the Portobelo Harbor.[17]

The inroads of the pirates caused Spain to send its treasure galleons in a single fleet to the Isthmus. The practice began about 1526 and was made obligatory in 1561. After the destruction of Nombre de Dios by Drake the eastern trade terminus was moved to Portobelo, where the great fair of that name arose. The fleet anchored at Cartagena to avoid the unhealthful climate of the Isthmus and did not move until the Peruvian plate ships arrived in Panama. During the fair Portobelo was thronged with thousands of sailors, soldiers, officials, and traders; houses rented at five to six thousand *pesos* a month; the remainder of the year it was practically deserted. Merchants from all parts of the Spanish world displayed their wares in the hot, humid, wretched climate of Portobelo. Hundreds of persons died during a single fair, and vessels often lost half of their crews from disease and dissipation. At the beginning of the eighteenth century the annual business was estimated to be from thirty to forty million pounds sterling, but the commerce and treasure had so declined by 1748 that the Portobelo fair was discontinued.[18] A visitor, Friar Thomas Gage, writing graphically of conditions caused by the arrival of the fleet in 1637, stated:

... what most I wondered at was to see the requa's of Mules which came thither from *Panama*, laden with wedges of silver; in one day I told two hundred Mules, laden with nothing else, which were unladen in the publick Market place, so that there the heaps of silver wedges lay like heaps of stones in the street, without any fear or suspicion of being lost.[19]

Henry Morgan sacked Portobelo in 1668 and shortly afterwards reduced Fort Lorenzo, which guarded the mouth of the Chagres River. He continued across the Isthmus and destroyed Panama City in 1671. Old Panama has since remained a ruin, a monument to the brutalities of the pirates who preyed on the Spanish Main.[20] The present city of Panama replaced it in 1674, and the story is told that its fortifications were built at such great expense that the king remarked he should be able to see them from Spain, and the government inquired whether the walls were constructed of silver or gold.[21] Lionel Wafer, the buccaneer surgeon, described the site of old Panama in 1680 as a rubbish heap, but explained that plans had been made before Morgan's raid to abandon it because of its poor harbor. New Panama appeared very beautiful from the sea, Nombre de Dios was overgrown with wild canes, and Portobelo had a "very fair, large and commodious Harbour" defended by four forts; but when the tide was out it was covered with a "black filthy Mud," which gave off a terrible odor and bred "noisesome Vapours." Other towns mentioned by Wafer were Santa María, Cheapo, Scuchadero, St. Michael, and Venta de Cruzes.[22]

The Scots resented their exclusion from the riches of the new lands across the sea and looked with envy upon the enterprises of the English. Under the influence of William Patterson the parliament of Scotland enacted a law in 1695 creating "The Company for Trading from Scotland to Africa and the Indies," generally known as the Darién Company. In 1698 a colony of about twelve hundred was established at New Edinburgh in Darién, but mismanagement, disease, climate, and the Spaniards forced its abandonment in 1700.[23]

The *audiencia* of Panama was abolished in 1718, but was restored in 1721.[24] Panama, the entrepôt of the Spanish trade in the New World, was then diminishing in prestige and wealth and was descending into a long period of obscurity. Portobelo and Fort Lorenzo were destroyed during the War of Jenkin's Ear, and Panama City suffered from disastrous fires at various times during the century. After 1748 Spain sent its ships around the Horn to its Pacific possessions.[25] Panama was placed under the government at Santa Fé de Bogotá in 1751, but a new *audiencia* was established at Panama City in 1774.[26] The Isthmus continued its decline, which was caused to a great extent by the contraband trade of South America with England.[27] By the end of the eighteenth century commerce had decreased, the mines were exhausted, Spain had lost its supremacy, and the colonies were enveloped in a general lethargy. The *Camino Real* had lost its great importance, and Castilla del Oro was almost forgotten.[28]

PANAMA UNDER COLOMBIA

The Isthmus of Panama was late in throwing off the yoke of Spain. An expedition in the patriot cause under Sir Gregor McGregor took Portobelo in 1819, but was later routed.[29] The banner of revolt was raised in Los Santos on November 13, 1821; and after the Spanish garrison had deserted, the independence of the Isthmus was proclaimed in Panama City on November 28.[30] The Panamanians united with the Republic of Colombia in 1822, but many of the people came to realize that a mistake had been made. In 1830 Great Colombia was separated into Venezuela, Ecuador, and the Republic of New Granada.[31] The Isthmians planned at that time to establish an independent nation, but were induced to remain in the *República de Nueva Granada* under the constitution of 1832.[32] The continued anarchy of New Granada caused a revolt on the Isthmus in 1840 under the leadership of Colonel Tomás Herrera. His constitution provided that Panama and Veragua should become the sovereign State of the Isthmus.[33] The allegiance of the Isthmians was regained in 1842, but the centralized government set up by the constitution of the following year was very objectionable to them.[34]

On December 12, 1846, the United States and New Granada signed a treaty that was to have a far-reaching influence in the Isthmus and which finally provided the legal excuse for the action of the Washington government in securing Panamanian independence in 1903. Article 35 of that convention stipulated:

... the United States guarantee, positively and efficaciously, to New Granada, by the present stipulation, the perfect neutrality of the before-mentioned isthmus, with the view that the free transit from one to the other sea may not be interrupted or embarrassed in any future time while this treaty exists; and, in consequence, the United States also guarantee, in the same manner, the rights of sovereignty and property which New Granada has and possesses over the said territory.[35]

On April 19, 1850, Secretary of State John M. Clayton and the British minister, Sir Henry Lytton Bulwer, signed a treaty by which their governments obligated themselves not to obtain exclusive control over any ship canal in any part of Central America. They further promised never to fortify, to occupy, to colonize, or to assume dominion over any part of Central America in connection with a canal enterprise.[36] In other words, they agreed that any canal joining the Caribbean Sea and the Pacific Ocean should be controlled jointly by the United States and Great Britain.

An event of great importance to the Isthmians was the beginning of the Panama Railroad in 1850 by Americans. This first transcontinental line was started on the Caribbean side where Colón now stands. The Americans overcame yellow fever, debilitating heat, incessant rainfall, and bottomless morasses with an appalling loss of life and the expenditure of almost eight million dollars to accomplish a most heroic engineering feat. As the tropical rain fell in torrents, two construction gangs met at midnight on January 27, 1855, and the first railway to span a continent was completed.[37] The road drew the last traffic from the remaining parts of the ancient *Camino Real*. The gold rush to California not only considerably revived the prosperity of the Isthmus before the railroad was finished, but also brought much that was undesirable. Smouldering enmity between the natives and the Americans flared into an outburst on April 15, 1856. The refusal of a traveler to pay for a piece of fruit resulted in the famous Watermelon War and the first landing of American troops to keep open the way of transit across the Isthmus.[38]

Panama continued its protests against the constitution of 1843 until another was drawn up in 1853 establishing a semi-federal system of government, but that was also unsatisfactory. An amendment was added in 1855 consolidating the provinces of Panama, Azuero, Chiriquí, and Veragua into the State of Panama, but the Isthmians were still discontented.[39] In 1858 New Granada became the *Confederación Granadina,* and the federal system was extended to all the states.[40] During the following year laws were passed infringing the sovereignty of the states, and General Tomás C. de Mosquera raised a revolt and seized the government. The United States landed troops on the Isthmus in 1860 to preserve order. The Isthmians were preparing under the leadership of Governor José de Obaldía to set up an independent nation, but Santiago de la Guardia succeeded Obaldía and was won over by Mosquera. In 1861 Panama became a sovereign state of the *Estados Unidos de Nueva Granada,* but reserved the right to discard its agreement with the Bogotá government and to annul the constitution under certain conditions. Provision was made that no public officials were to be appointed from Bogotá, that Panama was to be considered neutral in civil wars and rebellions in the remainder of the country, that the courts of Panama were to be independent of outside authority, and that troops might be sent into Panama only with the permission of its government.[41]

The Mosquera revolution was successful by 1862, and in the following year the settlement made with Panama was discarded in the sixth Colombian constitution as disturbing to the general harmony of the nation. The United States of New Granada became the *Estados Unidos de Colombia* under a government best described as organized anarchy. Each province became constitutionally independent.[42] Affairs naturally did not im-

prove; the United States intervened again in 187
years later Colombian troops invaded Panama an
Pablo Arosemena, the president of the state, and th
was thereafter at the mercy of the politicians at Bogo
fortunate Panama, geographically located in one o
situations of the universe, became the "milch cow o
federation." The income from the Panama Railroa
French canal enterprise availed little for the Isthm
tolerable conditions and political ambitions resulted ꜝ
fruitless revolution in 1885.[45] Colón (Aspinwall) w
by the insurgent, Pedro Prestán, and American fc
landed to protect the railroad and American property.
President Rafael Núñez gave Colombia its seventh cc
in 1886, the government of the Republic of Colomb
highly centralized, and Panama was made the object
ous discrimination by being transformed into the equi
a crown colony. Until 1894 the Isthmians had few
than the inhabitants of other states.[47]

After centuries of discussion an attempt to cut a ca
the Isthmus was finally begun in 1879 under the auspices of
Ferdinand de Lesseps. Work was carried on several years,
and French savings were squandered by the hundreds of millions until operations were suspended in 1888. The canal company went into the hands of the receiver on February 4, 1889,
and the New Panama Canal Company was active without appre-
ciable success from 1894 until 1899.[48]

A description of Colombian political conditions characterizes
the "maintenance of public order" as an exception and civil
war as the rule during the nineteenth century; that state of
affairs continued into the twentieth. President José M. Mar-
roquín aptly described the general situation in his inaugural
address of August 7, 1898:

Hatred, envy, and ambition are elements of discord; in the political
arena the battle wages fiercely, not so much with the idea of securing the triumph of principles as with that of humbling or elevating
persons and parties; public tranquillity, indispensable to every citizen
for the free enjoyment of what he possesses either by luck or as the

fruit of his labor, is gradually becoming unknown; we live in a sickly atmosphere; crisis is our normal state; commerce and all other industries are in urgent need of perfect calmness for their development and progress.   Poverty invades every home.[49]

The Isthmus was the scene of considerable trouble in 1900, and in November, 1901, United States forces were landed for the preservation of order.[50] The methods employed in Isthmian warfare were graphically depicted by the American consul-general.

On Wednesday [he reported] I passed over the line to Colon and returned and saw the evidence of the fighting and especially at the last named place.   The soldiers were in line on the railroad and ceased firing to permit the train to pass.   This had been arranged by Captain Perry [an American officer] with both the contending parties.   The soldiers stepped off the track for the train to pass and at once after we cleared them the fighting began again. The dead and dying were on every hand.[51]

The struggle was continued in 1902.   The soldiers stationed on the Isthmus revolted on July 24;[52] American forces landed again in September to keep the railway open; peace was concluded on November 21 on board the *Wisconsin*.[53]   Thus the stage was well set for the events of 1903 that were to lead to the independence of Panama.   The change from domination by Colombia to the domination of the *Coloso del Norte* was not far in the future.

The Independence Movement of 1903

The voyage of the *Oregon* around South America during the Spanish-American War strikingly demonstrated the need of an interoceanic canal through Central America and awakened the interest of the North Americans.   On March 30, 1899, Congress authorized an investigation of the probable canal routes, and the Hay-Pauncefote Treaty of November 18, 1901, gave the United States the right to construct a waterway across Central America without British interference.[54]   After a bitter fight the proponents of the Panamanian route, aided by Philippe

Bunau-Varilla of the New Panama Canal Company, were successful over those who favored Nicaragua.[55] On June 29, 1902, President Theodore Roosevelt signed the Spooner Bill, which provided for a canal through Panama. The French offer to reduce the price of their concession from $109,000,000 to $40,000,000 had been accepted by the American government. The State Department then proceeded to secure the permission of Colombia for the canal with the result that the Hay-Herrán Treaty was signed on January 22, 1903. The United States was granted a one-hundred-year lease on a zone of land ten kilometers wide across the Isthmus for an initial payment of $10,000,000 and an annuity of $250,000 to begin nine years after the ratification of the treaty.[56]

The Bogotá politicians were dissatisfied with the terms of the canal agreement. Publicly they claimed that the treaty was unfavorable to their government and detrimental to the national honor; privately they hoped for greater concessions.[57] United States Minister A. M. Beaupré was informed early in May that the treaty would not be ratified and that Panama, Cauca, and Bolívar would threaten secession.[58] He explained to the State Department: "Without question public opinion is strongly against its ratification, but, of course, public opinion in Colombia is not necessarily a potent factor in controlling legislation."[59] The Colombians soon demanded one-fourth of the forty million that the French were to receive, and raised the price of the land to $15,000,000,[60] but Secretary of State John Hay rejected all proposals.[61]

The Panamanian representatives to the special session of the Colombian congress for treaty consideration were not reticent in stating that Panama would unfurl its carefully preserved banners of rebellion if the treaty was not passed.[62] Senator José Agustín Arango of Panama said that he was convinced that the treaty would fail and that separation from Colombia was the only means of saving the Isthmus from ruin.[63] The Isthmians became so imbued with the idea of independence that they appeared indifferent to the fate of the treaty,[64] which was rejected on August 12, 1903.[65] No further action was taken

before the legislature adjourned on October 31.[66] In the meantime sentiment for a revolution was growing in Panama, and
the Bogotá government was not helped by the appointment of
Senator José Domingo de Obaldía as governor. He was given
the position to aid the cause of Rafael Reyes for the presidency,
but was known to favor Isthmian independence.[67]

The smouldering fires of revolution, ever ready to flame,
were being fanned cautiously by prominent Isthmians who met
secretly in the home of Dr. Manuel Amador Guerrero or at
the Panama electric light plant. Plans were being laid carefully in the hope that the Washington government would assist
in freeing Panama from Colombia. Captain J. R. Beers of
the Panama Railroad and William Nelson Cromwell, counsel
for the company, gave encouragement. Amador was sent to
the United States to determine what might be done, but Cromwell was silenced by the Colombian government.[68] Philippe
Bunau-Varilla accidentally appeared in the United States and
was placed in touch with Amador, who was ready (September
23) to give up in despair. His high hopes of gaining assistance in Washington had been dashed to earth, and the pros-
pects for a revolution were very unfavorable, but he felt that
$6,000,000 for buying ships to combat Colombia would brighten
the horizon.

Bunau-Varilla set himself to the task of solving the problem that would mean $40,000,000 for his company. He learned
by means of deduction from a chance meeting with John Bassett
Moore, one of Roosevelt's friends, that the United States
remained interested in the Panama route. On October 10 he
visited Francis B. Loomis, the first assistant secretary of state,
who happened to be one of his acquaintances. Through Loomis
an interview was secured with President Roosevelt, who was
looking forward to the election of 1904.[69] There Bunau-
Varilla deduced that Roosevelt would not be averse to a revolution in Panama. He then began to rack his brain for means
of inaugurating a rebellion without the financial aid of the
United States and without an express promise of its military
co-operation. Since Amador wanted ships to prevent the land-

ing of Colombian troops on the Isthmus, the Frenchman decided that the United States might supply the required vessels under the guise of carrying out the provisions of Article 35 of the treaty of 1846. If the United States prevented fighting along the line of the railway no hostilities would ensue, for armies could meet conveniently at no other place on the Isthmus. This, he believed, the United States would feel obligated to do under the terms of the treaty.

Bunau-Varilla proceeded to unfold a portion of his plan to Amador and procured $100,000 for bribes and other expenses of the revolution. He soon had an accidental meeting with John Hay and again was led to infer that the Washington government might fall in with his scheme. Amador left for Panama on October 20 with instructions to start the revolt by the night of November 3. The Frenchman, however, first extracted a promise that he would be appointed minister to the United States to negotiate the treaty by which the prospective Panamanian republic would grant the route of the proposed canal. On October 29 he received the discouraging news that a detachment of Colombian troops was on the way to Panama. He had also read that certain American warships were converging on the Isthmus. He knew that something had to be done or the cause would be lost; he hurried to Washington and informed Loomis that a revolution was impending. Another accidental meeting with Hay assured him that all might be well. He decided that the *Nashville* would be sighted at Colón on November 2 and cabled that deduction to Amador as a fact. The *Nashville* arrived on scheduled time.[70] Actually the *Atlanta*, the *Dixie*, and the *Boston* had been ordered on October 19 to prepare for emergencies, and on November 2 the latter two and the *Nashville* were instructed to

Maintain free and uninterrupted transit [on the railroad]. If interruption is threatened by armed force, occupy the line of railroad. Prevent landing of any armed force with hostile intent, either government or insurgent, at any point within 50 miles of Panama. Government force reported approaching the Isthmus in vessels.

Prevent their landing if, in your judgment, the landing would precipitate a conflict.[71]

The orders went astray, and a Colombian force of about five hundred landed from the *Cartagena* at Colón on November 3. Loomis became quite worried before the day was over. At four o'clock in the afternoon he cabled Consul Oscar Malmros, "Are troops from the vessel *Cartagena* disembarking or preparing to land?" Twenty-eight minutes later he asked, "Did you receive and deliver to *Nashville* last night or early this morning a message?" On receiving the information that the troops had landed, Loomis wired at 8:45 P.M., "The troops which landed from the *Cartagena* should not proceed to Panama." At 10:10 P.M. he again cabled Malmros, "An important message was sent at 6 Monday night in your care for the *Nashville*. Make all possible effort to get it."[72] Secretary Hay wired Malmros at 10:30 P.M. to inform the captain of the *Nashville* that the Colombian troops were not to be permitted to leave for Panama.[73] In the meantime Loomis cabled Consul Felix Ehrman at Panama City at 3:40 P.M., "Uprising on Isthmus reported. Keep Department promptly and fully informed."[74] At 8:15 P.M. the State Department was notified, "No uprising yet. Reported will be in the night. Situation is critical." At 9:50 P.M. Ehrman's report was received that the revolt had occurred at six o'clock without bloodshed.[75] At 11:18 P.M. Loomis instructed him to tell the captain of the *Nashville* that the Colombian force was not to proceed to Panama City.[76]

The commander of the Colombians was permitted to go to Panama City on the morning of November 3. There General Esteban Huertas of the Panama garrison seized him and his aides. The military force of about five hundred men and the fire brigade of 441 men made up the revolutionary force at Panama.[77] Undoubtedly a portion of Bunau-Varilla's $100,000 had an important influence on the attitude of the Colombian soldiers in Panama City. After the seizure of the commander, Amador proceeded with his and the Frenchman's plans. He and his associates issued a declaration of independence and waited for the United States to make it effective. Federico Boyd, José Agustín Arango, and Tomás Arias were appointed to organize the new government.[78]

On the night of November 3 the Colombian gunboat *Bogotá* fired several shells into Panama City. A peaceful and unsuspecting Chinaman, one Wong Kong Yee, a native of Hong Sang, China, was the sole victim of the Panamanian war of independence. An exploding shell snuffed out his life as he quietly dined at home, making him the single martyr of the freedom of the Isthmians.[79] The other participants in that memorable event have their monuments and eulogies, but Wong Kong Yee returns to dust unmourned, in an unmarked grave, unremembered in the annals of the heroes of Panama.

The *Dixie*, the *Nashville*, the *Atlanta*, the *Maine*, the *Mayflower*, the *Marblehead*, the *Wyoming*, the *Boston*, and the *Concord* converged on the Isthmus to protect the Panama Railroad and American interests.[80] The American officials refused to permit the Colombian soldiers to cross the Isthmus. The officer in charge threatened to kill every citizen of the United States in Colón unless the Colombians seized in Panama City were released. The *Nashville* landed a detachment, and the situation was soon well in hand.[81] On November 5 the Colombian force left for Cartagena.[82] More of the Bunau-Varilla money or the funds of the treasury of Panama had been used judiciously. The revolution was over, and Roosevelt had been saved from seizing the canal route outright. The Bogotá government was soon convinced that a reconquest of the revolters was impossible. The Colombians had no means of access to the insurgent area, for American cruisers controlled all sea routes to Panama, and the tropical jungle barred approach from land. Nature greatly facilitated the task of the Washington government.

On November 6 the United States recognized the insurgent government as the *de facto* government of Panama.[83] On November 13 *de jure* recognition was granted, and Bunau-Varilla was received officially in Washington as the minister of the Republic of Panama.[84] He and John Hay then proceeded to draw up a treaty giving the United States the right to construct a canal across the Isthmus. The Frenchman drafted the convention, and Hay speedily accepted it without important alteration. It was signed at seven in the evening of November 18, 1903, in the little blue drawing-room of Hay's residence and with ink from Abraham Lincoln's inkstand.[85]

The secretary of state must have had a guilty conscience, for he brought up the matter of compensation for Colombia. Bunau-Varilla opposed the idea, explaining to Hay on the morning of November 18 that "Any man who pays something he owes not is immediately thought to pay under the pressure of blackmail; any man who pays under the pressure of blackmail is immediately thought to pay on account of a concealed crime." Further he said: "To the demonstration which would result from such an action, that the United States admit having plaid [*sic*] that Machiavelic trick to Colombia, would be added in Spanish American hearts the incurable and bitter resentment of the insulting offer of a little money compensation for a patriotic wrong."[86]

The provisions of the Hay-Bunau-Varilla Treaty of November 18, 1903, were summarized as follows by President Roosevelt in his message to Congress on December 7, 1903:

By the provisions of the treaty the United States guarantees and will maintain the independence of the Republic of Panama. There is granted to the United States in perpetuity the use, occupation, and control of a strip ten miles wide and extending three nautical miles into the sea at either terminal, with all lands lying outside of the zone necessary for the construction of the canal or for its auxiliary works, and with the islands in the Bay of Panama. The cities of Panama and Colon are not embraced in the canal zone, but the United States assumes their sanitation and, in case of need, the maintenance of order therein; the United States enjoys within the granted limits all the rights, power, and authority which it would possess were it the sovereign of the territory to the exclusion of the exercise of sovereign rights by the Republic. All railway and canal property rights belonging to Panama and needed for the canal pass to the United States, including any property of the respective companies in the cities of Panama and Colon; the works, property, and personnel of the canal and railways are exempted from taxation as well in the cities of Panama and Colon as in the canal zone and its dependencies. Free immigration of the personnel and importation of supplies for the construction and operation of the canal are granted. Provision is made for the use of military force and the building of fortifications by the United States for the protection of transit. In other details, particularly as to the acquisition of the interests of the New Panama Canal Company and the Panama Railway by the United States and the condemnation of private property for the uses of the canal, the stipulations of the Hay-Herran treaty are closely followed, while compensation to be given for these enlarged grants remains the same, being ten millions of dollars payable on exchange of ratifications; and, beginning nine years from that date, an annual payment of $250,000 during the life of the convention.[87]

Panama, urgently pressed by Bunau-Varilla, ratified the treaty on December 2, 1903, the United States Senate acted favorably on February 23, 1904, and it was signed by Roosevelt two days later. Ratifications were exchanged on February 26, and the treaty was proclaimed in Washington on the same day.[88] Thus was Panama freed from the shackles of Colombia. Theodore Roosevelt, John Hay, and Philippe Bunau-Varilla had completed their work. As the Frenchman rode the high seas on his return to his native land to enjoy the fruits of his labors, a share of the forty millions, his reflections on the sordid deed of imperialism caused him to pen a farewell eulogy to his friend, President Roosevelt: "You have rendered to your noble country and to the world the greatest of services by cutting, at last, the Gordian knot which for centuries has paralyzed humanity."[89]

NOTES

1. C. L. G. Anderson, *Old Panama and Castilla del Oro* (Washington, 1911), pp. 117-121; E. G. Bourne, *Spain in America, 1450-1580,* "The American Nation: A History" (New York, 1904), III, 71.

2. Enríque Otero D'Costa to the editor, Apr. 30, 1934, *The Hispanic American Historical Review,* XIV (1934), 554-558; H. H. Bancroft, *History of Central America* (New York, 1882-1887), I, 216; Dominic Salandra, "Porto Bello, Puerto

Bello, or Portobelo," in *The Hispanic American Historical Review*, XIV (1934), 93-94.

3. Cecil Jane, trans. and ed., *Select Documents Illustrating the Four Voyages of Columbus, Including Those Contained in R. H. Major's "Select Letters of Christopher Columbus*, II, 72-94, "Works Issued by the Hakluyt Society" (London, 1933), LXX.

4. Columbus to the Spanish sovereigns, July 7, 1503, República de Costa Rica, *Documents Annexed to the Argument of Costa Rica before the Arbitrator Hon. Edward Douglass White* . . . (Rosslyn, Va., 1913), I, 5. Hereafter cited as Costa Rica, *Documents Annexed to the Argument of Costa Rica*.

5. Anderson, *op. cit.*, pp. 130-134; Bourne, *op. cit.*, pp. 106-107; Bancroft, *op. cit.*, I, 294-295.

6. Carlos Pereyra, *Francisco Pizarro y el tesoro de Atahualpa* (Madrid, n. d.), p. 16; I. B. Richman, *The Spanish Conquerors; A Chronicle of the Dawn of the Empire Overseas*, "The Chronicles of America Series" (New Haven, 1921), II, 74-78; R. B. Merriman, *The Rise of the Spanish Empire in the Old World and the New* (New York, 1918-1934), II, 215-216; Bourne, *op. cit.*, pp. 109-111.

7. Royal *cédula*, July 27, 1513, Costa Rica, *Documents Annexed to the Argument of Costa Rica*, I, 11-16.

8. Bartolomé de las Casas, *Historia de las Indias* (Madrid, n. d.), III, 10; C. W. Hackett, "The Delimitation of Political Jurisdictions in Spanish North America to 1535," in *The Hispanic American Historical Review*, I (1918), 46; C. R. Markham, trans. and ed., *Narrative of the Proceedings of Pedrarias Davila* . . . , "Works Issued by the Hakluyt Society" (London, 1865), XXXIV, 1-22.

9. C. R. Markham, trans. and ed., *Reports on the Discovery of Peru*, "Works Issued by the Hakluyt Society" (London, 1872), XLVII, 3-12.

10. Felipe J. Escobar, *El legado de los próceres; ensayo histórico-político sobre la nacionalidad Panameña* (Panama, 1930), pp. 6-7.

11. Anderson, *op. cit.*, pp. 264, 303-307; Bancroft, *op. cit.*, I, 415-416; II, 248-250.

12. Royal *cédula*, Dec. 2, 1556, Costa Rica, *Documents Annexed to the Argument of Costa Rica*, I, 79.

13. Report of the senior judge of *Tierra Firme*, May 7, 1575, *loc. cit.*, I, 176-183.

14. I. A. Wright, *Documents Concerning English Voyages to the Spanish Main, 1569-1580*, "Works Issued by the Hakluyt Society" (London, 1932), LXXXI, 260-319; William Wood, *Elizabethan Sea-Dogs; A Chronicle of Drake and His Companions*, "The Chronicles of America Series" (New Haven, 1921), III, 101-104.

15. Richard Hakluyt, *The Principal Navigations Voyages Traffiques & Discoveries of the English Nation* . . . (Glasgow, 1914), X, 77-81.

16. Zelia Nuttall, trans. and ed., *New Light on Drake; a Collection of Documents Relating to His Voyage of Circumnavigation, 1577-1580*, "Works Issued by the Hakluyt Society" (London, 1914), XXXIV, 24-56 [Christian Isobel Johnstone], *Lives and Voyages of Drake, Cavendish, and Dampier* (New York, 1832), pp. 53-121; L. B. Kinnaird, "Creassy's Plan for Seizing Panama, with an Introductory Account of British Designs on Panama," in *The Hispanic American Historical Review*, XIII (1933), 48-49.

17. Wood, *op. cit.*, pp. 121-148; Hakluyt, *op. cit.*, X, 236-240.

18. William Dampier, *A New Voyage round the World* (London, 1703), I, 179-185; Bedford Pim, *The Gate of the Pacific* (London, 1863), p. 18; Arthur Bullard, *Panama; the Canal, the Country, and the People* (New York, 1914), pp. 282-315; Allyn C. Loosley, "The Puerto Bello Fairs," in *The Hispanic American*

Historical Review, XIII (1933), 314-335; Antonio de Ulloa, *A Voyage to South America* (London, 1760), I, 101-104.

19. Thomas Gage, *A New Survey of the West-Indies* (London, 1677), p. 446.

20. Samuel Lewis, "The Cathedral of Old Panama," in *The Hispanic American Historical Review*, I (1918), 447-453; Ulloa, *op. cit.*, I, 113-114; A. O. Exquemelin, *The History of the Buccaneers of America* (Boston, 1856), pp. 108-160; Merritt Parmlee Allen, *Sir Henry Morgan, Buccaneer* (New York, 1931); W. Adolphe Roberts, *Sir Henry Morgan, Buccaneer and Governor* (New York, 1933); Philip Ainsworth Means, *The Spanish Main, Focus of Envy, 1492-1700* (New York, 1935), pp. 206-214.

21. Anderson, *op. cit.*, pp. 439-440; Bancroft, *op. cit.*, II, 489-517.

22. Lionel Wafer, *A New Voyage and Description of the Isthmus of America* (London, 1704), pp. 45-63.

23. F. R. Hart, *The Disaster of Darien; the Story of the Scots Settlement and the Causes of Its Failure, 1699-1701* (Boston and New York, 1929), pp. 22-95; G. P. Insh, *The Company of Scotland Trading to Africa and the Indies* (New York, 1932), pp. 17-20, 109-198.

24. Royal *cédula*, July 17, 1751, Costa Rica, *Documents Annexed to the Argument of Costa Rica*, I, 476.

25. Anderson, *op. cit.*, pp. 397-399; Bancroft, *op. cit.*, II, 588-594.

26. Royal *cédula*, July 17, 1751, Costa Rica, *Documents Annexed to the Argument of Costa Rica*, I, 476-479; Bancroft, *op. cit.*, II, 585.

27. Vera Lee Brown, "Contraband Trade: A Factor in the Decline of Spain's Empire in America," in *The Hispanic American Historical Review*, VIII (1928), 178-179.

28. Bancroft, *op. cit.*, II, 593-594.

29. W. D. Weatherhead, *An Account of the Late Expedition against the Isthmus of Darien, under the Command of Sir Gregor McGregor . . .* (London, 1821), pp. 22-68.

30. Escobar, *op. cit.*, p. 20; Sabas A. Villegas, *The Republic of Panama; Its Economic, Financial, Commercial and National Resources, and General Information* (Panama, 1917), p. 18.

31. *Ibid.*, p. 22; José Manuel Pérez Sarmiento, *Manual diplomático y consular Colombiano* (Bogotá, 1927), pp. 232-236.

32. W. F. Johnson, *Four Centuries of the Panama Canal* (New York, 1907), p. 151.

33. Ramón M. Valdés, *The Independence of the Isthmus; Its Antecedents, Its Causes and Its Justification* (Panama, 1903), pp. 4-5.

34. Johnson, *op. cit.*, pp. 152-153.

35. William M. Malloy, *Treaties, Conventions, International Acts, Protocols and Agreements . . .* (Washington, 1910), I, 312.

36. *Ibid.*, I, 659-663.

37. Villegas, *op. cit.*, p. 19; Lionel Gisborne, *The Isthmus of Darien in 1852 . . .* (London, 1853), pp. 208-209; Pim, *op. cit.*, pp. 200-204; *Sen. Doc.*, No. 429, 59 Cong., 1 Sess. (Ser. 4919), pp. 4-6; Robert Tomes, *Panama in 1855 . . .* (New York, 1855), p. 104; W. A. Reid, "Busy Days in Panama," in *Bulletin of the Pan American Union*, LXIV (1930), 58. *Bulletin of the Pan American Union* hereafter cited as *BPAU*.

38. J. Fred Rippy, *The Capitalists and Colombia* (New York, 1931), pp. 64-77; Bancroft, *op. cit.*, III, 520-521; Star and Herald, *The Panama Massacre; a Collection of the Principal Evidence and Other Documents, Including the Report of Amos B. Corwine . . .* (Panama, 1857).

39. Johnson, *op. cit.*, p. 153; José de la Vega, *La federación en Colombia (1810-1912)* (Madrid, n. d.), p. 205.

40. Vega, *op. cit.*, pp. 217-218; J. M. Henao and Gerardo Arrubla, *Historia de Colombia para la enseñanza secundaria* . . . (Bogotá, 1926), pp. 651-652; Jules Humbert, *Histoire de la Colombie et du Vénézuéla des origines jusqu'a nos jours* (Paris, 1921), p. 188.

41. Johnson, *op. cit.*, p. 155; Valdés, *op. cit.*, pp. 9-14.

42. Bancroft, *op. cit.*, III, 529-530; Johnson, *op. cit.*, pp. 155-156; Valdés, *op. cit.*, pp. 14-16; Vega, *op. cit.*, pp. 239-253; P. J. Eder, *Colombia* (London, 1913), p. 40; W. L. Scruggs, *The Colombian and Venezuelan Republics* . . . (Boston, 1900), pp. 141-142; C. Arrocha Graell, *Historia de la independencia de Panamá; sus antecedentes y sus causas, 1821-1903* (Panama, 1933), pp. 166-173.

43. Johnson, *op. cit.*, p. 175.

44. Valdés, *op. cit.*, pp. 16-17.

45. See Foción Soto, *Memorias sobre el movimiento de resistencia a la dictadura de Rafael Núñez, 1884-1885* (Bogotá, 1913), 2 vols.

46. J. B. Sosa and E. J. Arce, *Compendio de historia de Panamá* . . . (Panama, 1911), pp. 274-280.

47. Scruggs, *op. cit.*, pp. 142-143; Valdés, *op. cit.*, p. 21; Vega, *op. cit.*, pp. 272-293; Graell, *op. cit.*, pp. 174-177.

48. Philippe Bunau-Varilla, *Panama; the Creation, Destruction, and Resurrection* (New York, 1914), pp. 28-154.

49. Valdés, *op. cit.*, p. 26.

50. H. A. Gudger to John Hay, U. S. secretary of state, Nov. 24, 1901, Department of State, Consular Letters, Panama, XXIV.

51. Gudger to David J. Hill, assistant secretary of state, No. 227, Dec. 2, 1901, *loc. cit.*

52. Gudger to Francis B. Loomis, assistant secretary of state, No. 438, July 27, 1902, *loc. cit.*, XXV.

53. Gudger to Hill, No. 376, Nov. 24, 1902, *loc. cit.*, XXIV.

54. *Sen. Doc.*, No. 474, 63 Cong., 2 Sess. (Ser. 6582), pp. 292-294.

55. Bunau-Varilla, *Panama*, p. 250.

56. *Sen. Doc.*, No. 474, 63 Cong., 2 Sess. (Ser. 6582), pp. 277-288.

57. Baupré to Hay, May 4, 1903, *Sen. Doc.*, No. 51, 58 Cong., 2 Sess. (Ser. 4587), p. 15.

58. *Idem* to *idem*, May 7, 1903, *loc. cit.*, p. 16.

59. *Idem* to *idem*, Mar. 30, 1903, *loc. cit.*, p. 5.

60. *Idem* to *idem*, June 10, 1903; July 9, 1903, *loc. cit.*, pp. 22, 35.

61. Hay to Beaupré, July 13, 1903, *loc. cit.*, p. 36.

62. Beaupré to Hay, July 5, 1903, *loc. cit.*, p. 30.

63. W. C. Haskins, *Canal Zone Pilot* . . . (Panama, 1908), p. 233.

64. Beaupré to Hay, Aug. 15, 1903, *Sen. Doc.*, No. 51, 58 Cong., 2 Sess. (Ser. 4587), p. 56.

65. *Idem* to *idem*, Aug. 12, 1903, *loc. cit.*, p. 51.

66. *Idem* to *idem*, Nov. 2, 1903, *loc. cit.*, pp. 91-92.

67. *Idem* to *idem*, Aug. 30, 1903; Aug. 31, 1903; Sept. 11, 1903; Oct. 21, 1903; Nov. 2, 1903, *loc. cit.*, pp. 62, 65, 86, 92; Felix Ehrman, U. S. vice-consul-general, to Loomis, No. 454, Sept. 7, 1903; No. 458, Sept. 21, 1903; Consular Letters, Panama, XXV.

68. Johnson, *op. cit.*, p. 167.

69. Rippy, *The Capitalists and Colombia*, p. 91.

70. Bunau-Varilla, *Panama*, pp. 288-335.

71. *Papers Relating to the Foreign Relations of the United States* (1903), p. 267.   Hereafter cited as *For. Rel.* (1903).

72. Loomis to Malmros, Nov. 3, 1903, *loc. cit.*, p. 236.

73. Hay to Malmros, Nov. 3, 1903, *loc. cit.*, p. 237.

74. Loomis to Ehrman, Nov. 3, 1903, *loc. cit.*, p. 231.

75. Ehrman to Loomis, Nov. 3, 1903, *loc. cit.*, p. 231.

76. Loomis to Ehrman, Nov. 3, 1903, *loc. cit.*, p. 231.

77. Malmros to Hay, Nov. 3, 1903, *loc. cit.*, p. 235.

78. Ehrman to Hay, Nov. 4, 1903, *House Doc.*, No. 8, 58 Cong., 1 Sess. (Ser. 4565), p. 105.

79. Ehrman to Loomis, Nov. 9, 1903, No. 463, Consular Letters, Panama, XXV.

80. Johnson, *op. cit.*, p. 179.

81. Malmros to Hay, Nov. 5, 1903, *For. Rel.* (1903), p. 237.

82. *Ibid.*, p. 238; E. Taylor Parks, *Colombia and the United States, 1765-1934* (Durham, 1935), pp. 395-426; Joseph C. Freehoff, *America and the Canal Title* . . . (New York, 1916), pp. 138-213; Ismael Ortega B., *La jornada del día 3 de noviembre de 1903 y sus antecedentes* (Panama, 1931).

83. Hay to Beaupré, Nov. 6, 1903, *Sen. Doc.*, No. 51, 58 Cong., 2 Sess. (Ser. 4587), pp. 97-98.

84. Bunau-Varilla, *Panama*, pp. 364-366.

85. Hay to Mrs. Payne Whitney, Nov. 19, 1903, W. R. Thayer, "John Hay and the Panama Republic . . . ," in *Harper's Magazine*, CXXXI (1915), 173.

86. Department of State, Notes from the Panamanian Legation, I.

87. *For. Rel.* (1903), pp. xli-xlii.

88. *Sen. Doc.*, No. 474, 63 Cong., 2 Sess. (Ser. 6582), p. 295.

89. Bunau-Varilla to Roosevelt, Mar. 10, 1904, Notes from the Panamanian Legation, I.   See the Roosevelt side of the affair in *I Took the Isthmus; Ex-President Roosevelt's Confession, Colombia's Protest and Editorial Comment by American Newspapers on "How the United States Acquired the Right to Build the Canal"* (New York, 1911); Theodore Roosevelt, "How the United States Acquired the Right to Dig the Panama Canal," in *The Outlook*, XCIX (Oct. 7, 1911), 314-318.

CHAPTER II

THE FIRST MAJOR CONTROVERSY

THE UNITED STATES hardly had taken formal possession of the Canal Zone when the first major dispute
arose with the Republic of Panama. The exercise of sovereignty by the Washington government in the establishment of
ports of entry, custom-houses, tariffs, and post-offices in the
Canal Zone aroused a storm of protest that required five months
of careful diplomatic negotiation and finally the presence of
Secretary of War William H. Taft on the Isthmus. On June
24, 1904, Taft issued an order opening the Canal Zone to the
commerce of friendly nations and dividing the territory into
two customs districts. Cristóbal at the Atlantic terminus of the
Canal and Ancón on the Pacific were designated as ports of
entry. Duties on importations were to be levied in conformity
with the tariff then in force in the United States. Sections eight
and nine of the order, which were not made public by Governor
George W. Davis, contained the following provisions:

The governor of the canal zone is authorized to enter and carry
out an agreement with the President of the Republic of Panama for
cooperation between the customs service of the canal zone and that
of the Republic of Panama and to protect the customs revenues of
both Governments and to prevent frauds and smuggling.

The governor of the canal zone is hereby authorized to enter
upon negotiations and make a tentative agreement with the President of the Republic of Panama respecting reciprocal trade relations between the territory and inhabitants of the canal zone and
appurtenant territory and the Republic of Panama; also a readjust-
ment of the customs duties and tariff regulations so as to secure uni-
formity of rates and privileges and avoid the disadvantages resulting
from different schedules, duties, and administrative measures in
limited territory subject to the same conditions and not separated by
natural obstacles.[1]

On the same day the postmaster-general of the United States announced that the domestic rate of postage would apply in the Canal Zone. Nine towns and stations were designated as post-offices, and agents of the Panama Railroad Company were appointed postmasters.[2] Tomás Arias, the Panamanian foreign secretary, was notified and requested to supply for temporary use postage stamps of the republic surcharged with the words "Canal Zone." The Panamanian government complied, but the sale of its stamps was discontinued by the Canal Zone government on July 17, after the arrival of stamps from the United States.[3]

These actions were based principally upon Articles II and III of the Hay-Bunau-Varilla Treaty. By Article II the Republic of Panama granted to the United States "in perpetuity the use, occupation and control of a zone of land and land under water for the construction, maintenance, operation, sanitation and protection" of the proposed Canal "for the width of ten miles extending to the distance of five miles from the center line" of its route, but with the provision that the cities of Panama and Colón and their adjacent harbors were excluded from the grant. Article III transferred jurisdiction over the Canal Zone to the United States as follows:

The Republic of Panama grants to the United States all the rights, power and authority within the zone mentioned and described in Article II of this agreement and within the limits of all auxiliary lands and waters mentioned and described in said Article II which the United States would possess and exercise if it were the sovereign of the territory within which said lands and waters are located to the entire exclusion of the exercise by the Republic of Panama of any such sovereign rights, power or authority.[4]

The meaning of these articles, as well as various other provisions of the treaty, has caused much disagreement. In any consideration of the Hay-Bunau-Varilla Treaty the fact must be noted that it was negotiated and signed within fifteen days after Panama declared its independence; that the Panamanian negotiator was a citizen of France who was primarily interested

in securing the not insignificant sum of $40,000,000 for the
stockholders of the New Panama Canal Company, of which
he was a prominent member;[5] and that its ratification was
probably necessary for the survival of the new-born republic.
Much futile disputation might have been prevented if Philippe
Bunau-Varilla had not changed the word *leases* in Article II
of the preliminary draft to *grants* in the finished treaty.[6]
Panama would have had a much better foundation for its
thirty years of protests if the United States had only leased
the Canal strip. The Washington government apparently believed that it was given the right to use the Zone as if it were
the territory of the United States, while the Panamanian government has held the opinion that the full sovereignty over the
Zone was not surrendered. The outcome seems to have been
that the United States has exercised sovereign authority and
Panama has retained "titular" sovereignty.[7]

The first protest against the fiscal measures of the United
States in the Canal Zone, which was to be followed by a storm
of disapproval, was raised on July 9, 1904, in relation to clearing the Chilean steamer *Loa* by the Canal Zone authorities at
La Boca, port of Ancón. Arias wrote Governor Davis that La
Boca was a part of and adjacent to the city of Panama and subject to the complete jurisdiction of the Republic of Panama.
He pointed out that La Boca had never been considered as a
port for international commerce, but solely as a place of access
to the Canal. Since it was the only location in "the Bay of
Panama and close by the city of the same name" which offered
shelter and anchorage for shipping, Panama City would be
without a port and its maritime commerce would be ruined.
Arias thought it "hardly credible that the American Government could contemplate the idea of inflicting such a serious
injury" on Panama. He called attention to Article XIII of the
treaty, which, he claimed, clearly determined that the United
States did not intend to exercise jurisdiction over the ports of
access to the Canal Zone. He then requested Davis to give
orders suspending the further dispatch of vessels from La Boca

wharf without appeal to the Panamanian authorities and without compliance with Panamanian law governing such matters.[8]

On July 15 the chamber of commerce of Panama City presented a memorial to President Amador protesting against the establishment of ports, custom-houses, and tariffs by the United States in the Canal Zone. The business men claimed that neither the spirit nor the letter of the treaty empowered either of the contracting parties to establish such within the Zone. If the custom-houses were instituted, all merchandise and produce except that of the United States would be excluded from the Canal Zone to the complete ruin of the Panamanian republic. The protest concluded with a dismal picture of the future:

Commerce, agriculture, and the cattle business would be strangled, and the Government of Panama, which should derive its revenues from these sources, would suffer the same fate.

Disaster would be general and all would be forced to emigrate. By Article I of the treaty, the independence of the Republic of Panama is guaranteed by the United States. By the proposed establishments the Republic of Panama would be reduced to the worst kind of dependence and servitude that exists, that of starvation.[9]

In transmitting this appeal to the Washington government, the American chargé cryptically commented: "In spite of all these criticisms published and spoken, I have seen nor heard nothing which would lead me to suppose that there exists any intention to advise the return of the $10,000,000 gold, already paid."[10]

The situation became more serious toward the end of July. President Amador protested in reply to the presentation address of Minister John Barrett against the tendency of the American government to violate the spirit as well as the letter of the treaty by the imposition of the Dingley Tariff within the Canal Zone and the establishment of ports of entry at Ancón and Cristóbal. Barrett reported that the people were greatly stirred and that there was much danger of the growth of a disposition to distrust the United States and of opposition to granting its wishes in other matters unless steps were taken for placating the Panamanians and for modifying the conditions created by the enforcement of the order of June 24.[11]   On July 26 Barrett telegraphed the State Department that agitation was increasing and that the situation was critical.   The dispute, he believed, was of highest importance because it involved the "whole issue of sovereignty in the Zone."   The chief trouble still was the entrance and clearance of vessels at La Boca.   He was inclined to agree with Governor Davis that the order of June 24 was in accordance with the treaty and that its enforcement was "absolutely essential for the successful administration of the Zone."   He did not believe the United States could retreat safely from its position, and informed the State Department that the "whole trouble might have been avoided if either in Washington or here [Panama] the President's Order had been carefully discussed through diplomatic channels before it was promulgated and enforced."   Had this sensibly been done, Panama "would eventually have accepted the treaty interpretation of the United States without this present excited feeling."[12]

In spite of the strong objections of the Panamanian government, vessels were reported arriving and departing daily.   The State Department was advised that tension was growing and that something must be done to end the trouble.   Nine ships had entered the port of Ancón up to July 26.   The Panamanians had confined their activities to protests, but at that time threatened to arrest and fine the captain and agent of the Chilean steamer *Limari* unless it left port or complied with Panamanian regulations.   Governor Davis, on being appealed to by the agent, decided that the movement of ships at La Boca should not be subject to interference.   The situation became almost intolerable for shipping interests.   Barrett recommended that a temporary adjustment be made "in order to prevent some unfortunate incident that might endanger the relations of the Panama Government and the canal zone administration."[13]

In view of the paralysis of business, excited public opinion, and tension between Panamanian authorities and shipping officials, the two governments agreed to a *modus vivendi* on July

27, limiting the action of the republic to filing a protest pending final settlement.[14]   The understanding, which was oral at the request of Arias, stipulated that the Panamanian government should not interfere with shipping before final adjustment was made.[15]   On the same day Arias lodged a formal protest against the establishment of ports of entry, custom-houses, tariffs, and post-offices in the Canal Zone.   He stated that the opening of the ports must have been due to an erroneous interpretation of the treaty of November 18, 1903, which was "really a bond of perpetual union between the two Nations," and that he was making "a most courteous but solemn and energetic" declaration of opposition.   He admitted that the United States had been given the right of exercising certain functions of sovereignty over the territory granted in the treaty to the exclusion of the exercise of sovereign rights, power, and authority by the Republic of Panama, but claimed that certain other rights indispensable to its existence had been reserved by his government.

Arias pointed out that Panama had retained the cities of Panama and Colón by Article II of the treaty and that the evident object of this was to safeguard the very life of the nation.   The right of levying and collecting maritime taxes on the Isthmus had been invariably a prerogative of his government, and he vigorously claimed it except on importations for Canal use.   He explained that the sovereign power of levying taxes within the Canal Zone did not appear to have been surrendered by any provisions of the treaty, but that it had been acknowledged explicitly by Articles X and XIII.   Therefore the exclusion of the Panamanian postal tariff and postage stamps from the Zone was "to say the least, improper."   The Republic of Panama demanded an "acknowledgment to the full extent of its economical and fiscal sovereignty within the canal zone," not only because of its rights under the treaty, but also because its very existence and future depended upon it.   He concluded: "The fact stands, therefore, that Panama, being the original owner of the canal zone, clearly reserved what it did not expressly surrender."[16]   The contention of Panama was, in brief, that only so much of its sovereignty over the Canal Zone had

been relinquished as was necessary for the construction, maintenance, operation, sanitation, and protection of the Canal.

On August 2 Barrett reported that the tension was relieved
somewhat and that excellent progress was being made toward
calming both public and official opinion. The tone of the press
had changed because of his frank discussions with the editors.[17]
A week later he believed that the friendly attitude of the
United States, which he had demonstrated, had greatly improved the situation. The people were confident that a settlement would be reached acceptable to both nations. Although
the surface was tranquil, the minister was apprehensive of the
undercurrents, for he explained to the State Department:

I am not, however, over hopeful, because I appreciate the delicacy
of the situation where both the Canal Commission on the one hand
and the Panama Government on the other are convinced that each
is right and that neither can surrender to the main contention of
the other.

Despite, therefore, my efforts to pour oil on the troubled waters,
there may be another tempest of excitement if the Commission under-
takes to conduct its own negociacions [sic] with the Panama Government without regard for diplomatic means of settlement, which the
latter seeks to invoke.[18]

On August 9 Barrett called the attention of the Panamanian
government to sections eight and nine of the executive order
of June 24, which unfortunately had not been made public by
Governor Davis who wished to discuss them with Panamanian
officials before their publication. He stated that these provisions clearly indicated that the United States wished to respect
the true interests of Panama, that they provided for an agreement for the protection of the fiscal and economic system of
the republic, and that they opened the way to a satisfactory
adjustment of the principal issue between the two governments.[19]

On August 11 José Domingo de Obaldía, the Panamanian
minister at Washington, addressed to the secretary of state a
long memorial which was mainly an elaboration of the views

of Arias, but much better stated. He cited both the Hay-Herrán and the Hay-Bunau-Varilla treaties as proof that no expression was used "implying transfer of absolute dominion over the [Canal Zone] territory, much less transfer of sovereignty" to the United States. He claimed that the legal relation between the two nations was that of lessor and lessee, and stated that if the Republic of Panama had had any intention of absolute cession of sovereignty of the Canal Zone only two articles would have been necessary in the treaty: "one specifying the thing sold and the other expressing the price of the sale." Obaldía called attention to the fact that sovereignty was mentioned only in Article III of the Hay-Bunau-Varilla Treaty which stated that the United States was to exercise rights, power, and authority as "if it were sovereign in the territory." This conveyed the idea that the United States was not sovereign in the Canal Zone. The statement of the article that the United States was to have rights, power, and authority "to the entire exclusion of the exercise by the Republic of Panama of any such sovereign rights, power, and authority" was an obvious contradiction of the first declaration and had to be interpreted "in accordance with other subsequent articles of the agreement which demonstrate[d] the real intention of the contracting parties."

Obaldía stated in reference to Article VI, which provided for a mixed commission for the adjustment of claims resulting from damages inflicted by the United States to property rights and private persons in the Canal Zone: "If the United States [had] possessed the sovereignty over the Zone to the absolute exclusion of the Republic of Panama, this clause would be inexplicable." Article X denied Panama the right to levy taxes on certain specified property of the United States and its employees, and from this he deduced that Panama reserved the right to levy and collect on all persons not named in the exception. Panama agreed by Article XII to permit the immigration and free access of persons connected with and in search of work in the Canal enterprise and to exempt them from military service. Article XIII gave the United States the privilege of importing supplies for Canal construction, maintenance, operation, sanitation, and protection into the Canal Zone duty free. All necessities for Canal employees and their families were to bear no import tariff. Therefore Panama could tax all other importations into the Canal Zone. Finally, Article XXIII permitted the United States to use land and naval forces for the protection of the Canal Zone and to construct fortifications for that purpose. Obaldía continued:

> None of these stipulations which I have enumerated would have any raison d'être if the Republic of Panama had renounced the dominion over the zone and her rights of sovereignty absolutely; but her intention never was to renounce these rights, nor was it the purpose of the United States to acquire them, for the latter, quite to the contrary, has declared that it does not wish to increase its territory at the expense of Colombia or of any other republic of Central or South America, and there is nothing to justify the most remote suspicion that this declaration is not sincere.[20]

The Panamanian reached the conclusion that the idea of the contracting parties was "obscure in everything relating to these delicate questions of dominion and sovereignty," but that a careful examination brought the conviction that the "two countries exercise[d] conjointly the sovereignty over the territory of the canal zone," and that the United States was delegated the use of that right in certain cases "expressly specified in the Hay-Bunau-Varilla treaty." The rights of the republic remained "unalterable and complete" in all matters concerning which the treaty was silent. Certainly the Panamanian government reserved part of the judicial power within the Canal Zone.

Obaldía went directly into the irritations caused by the order of June 24 by observing that the establishment of a port for international commerce was "a right inherent in the sovereign of the territory" and that the United States could not open the ports of Ancón and Cristóbal because it lacked that authority. He contended that La Boca was a part of the port of Panama City and that Cristóbal was a mere ward of Colón. Thus neither was in the Canal Zone nor within the jurisdiction of the

United States because Article II of the treaty excluded the cities of Panama and Colón and their adjacent ports from the Canal strip. His government could not accept the situation which it considered contrary to the spirit and letter of the Hay-Bunau-Varilla Treaty. Bitterly he complained that the United States did not have the right to establish custom-houses in the ports of Panama and Colón or to place in operation the Dingley Tariff. Such power was vested in the sovereign of the territory, and he believed that he had proved conclusively that the United States did not possess that absolute sovereignty which carried the prerogative of setting up a fiscal system. He continued:

The portion of its sovereign rights that the Republic, on considerations of a high order, has granted to the United States has reference to all that may be necessary or expedient to afford effective protection to the canal, in peace and in war, to maintain it open and free to the commerce of the world, and to prevent its being improperly used by any foreign power. The Republic of Panama has also granted the exercise of its rights for the establishment of a public administration that would maintain order within the canal zone, so that the works should not be interrupted or the service impaired after the completion of the canal, but it has never entered the mind of either party that the United States should turn the canal zone into a source of revenue by enforcing high customs tariffs, even against the Republic of Panama, which is the lord of the territory and still holds over it rights that it has not relinquished.[21]

The minister was of the opinion that several articles of the treaty implicitly contained the will of the contracting parties that neither should enforce customs tariffs in the Canal Zone, but that it should be open and free to the commerce of the world. Article IX prohibited the levying of customs tolls, tonnage, lighthouse, wharf, and other dues by Panama on vessels passing through the Canal and gave the Panamanian government the right to collect charges upon merchandise for consumption in the republic. Article XIII exempted certain importations of the United States and its employees from duties. He alleged, however, that if any customs duties might be imposed "at the ports of Panama and Colon; that is to say the entrances of the canal," on articles of trade destined for use in the Canal Zone, his government only could levy them.

The establishment by the United States of post-offices in the Canal Zone, which for foreign mails made use of stamps differing from those of Panama, was highly objectionable. The postage rate on letters from the Canal Zone to the United States was two cents in comparison with the five-cent charge from Panama to the United States.[22] The Panamanians bought their stamps and mailed their correspondence at the American post-offices, thereby causing serious loss to the republic. This was especially true in Panama City, where the Ancón office was practically across the street. Obaldía held that the United States might conduct a domestic mail service within the Canal Zone, but could not forward mails to foreign countries.

After exhausting his legal argument the Panamanian made an eloquent appeal to the imaginary altruistic ideals of the Washington government:

I am well aware that sentiment has no part in negotiations of this character, but even looking at the matter in the light of the most selfish expediency, what interest can the United States have in the financial ruin of the Republic of Panama, in the disappearance of its fiscal resources which would make its pecuniary position untenable, and in seeing it finally incapacitated for the proper discharge toward the world of the inherent obligations of a free and sovereign nation? Is it not rather to the interest of the United States to foster the development of the Republic of Panama and to contribute to its prosperity and aggrandizement?[23]

Obaldía predicted dire consequences for the Isthmian republic if the policy of the United States was not altered immediately. The principal cities would lose their importance as places of transit. Their revenues from international commerce would vanish. Commerce and industry would disappear. The people would emigrate, and the cities would be deserted ruins. The Panamanians would be in a worse condition than before the signing of the treaty, "in which they founded their hopes of improvement and progress." He wailed that the prospect held before his country was "one of weakness, poverty, and retrogression instead of the bright future which the United States intended to achieve for it when it extended its generous hand in its hour of trial." In conclusion, he requested the Washington government to exercise only the administrative powers conferred upon it by the treaty and asked that orders be given suspending the ports, custom-houses, tariffs, and post-offices in the Canal Zone until agreement could be reached respectful to the common interests of both nations.[24]

A great amount of excellent argument was wasted, for John Hay must have smiled at the allusions to the intentions of the Republic of Panama in reference to the treaty. He knew that the Panamanians had no part in the formulation of the stipulations of the document which they were trying to interpret in such high-sounding phrases. Poor misguided Isthmians were attempting to tell him what he and Philippe Bunau-Varilla meant when they signed that pact at seven o'clock in the evening of November 18, 1903, just two hours before the Panamanian negotiators put in appearance.

The calm was almost shattered about the middle of August by the continuance of the tactlessness of Zone officialdom. Admiral J. G. Walker, who was in charge of the Canal Zone during the absence of Governor Davis, bluntly told Arias that the United States would make no concession in regard to the ports. He stated that this was the determined attitude of the Isthmian Canal Commission and would be supported by President Roosevelt. Barrett thereupon informed the State Department that the people felt that Walker was going over his head in disapproval of his friendly and pacific measures. For this reason he requested that the Canal Commission be instructed to act through the legation instead of directly with the Panamanian government. Even Arias had complained that he was being subordinated to the Isthmian Canal Commission. Public opinion was again aroused. The anti-administration press in the United States would have another opportunity to assail Roosevelt's policy and play up the "big stick." Barrett commented

that Walker might have been depicting the real attitude of the
United States, but that his statement had been made at an in-
opportune and unfortunate time, for public feeling was "in no
state to trifle with, and nothing unnecessary should be done to
irritate it." His capacity as minister had been taxed to assuage
the injured dignity of Secretary Arias.[25]

On August 18 Hay sent Obaldía a copy of a letter written
by Bunau-Varilla on January 19, 1904,[26] when the treaty was
under consideration in the American Senate. Some controversy
had arisen over the meaning of the pact in regard to terminal
ports for the Canal. The Frenchman explained, in his capacity
as Panamanian minister, that the harbors of the cities of Panama
and Colón were completely "separated from and independent
of the harbors of the canal, of the harbors situated at its two
entrances and which ships going through the canal will have to
use." He also added that if trouble arose the United States
would have adequate protection in Article II of the treaty.[27]
In other words, the United States could take the land and water
necessary for terminal ports if Panama claimed that the treaty
did not provide for their establishment. Obaldía immediately
replied that he was aware of the Bunau-Varilla statement, but
that he based his views on no document other than the treaty
of November 18, 1903. He bluntly commented, "The motives
that actuated me in taking this course can not escape your saga-
cious perspicacity."[28] Barrett presented a copy of the Bunau-
Varilla letter to Secretary Arias,[29] and reported that the Panamanian government was not cognizant of its existence. However, after a search of the archives Arias found a copy of the
communication and the reply of the *junta* of the provisional
governing approving it.[30] The general effect of this development was depicted as follows:

There is indignation in certain circles against the original position taken by Bunau-Varilla and criticism of the junta of that time
for allowing their ministers to write such a letter, but they recognize
that it commits the Panama Government and that it absolves the
United States Government from blame for alleged arbitrary interpretation of the treaty.[31]

The note apparently settled the port question conclusively. The Panamanian government, however, was not ready to concede this officially, for it hoped that all disputed points might be dealt with in subsequent negotiations. Barrett advised the State Department that Arias had admitted informally that the port trouble was concluded, but wished to make no public statement because of local political contentions. The opponents of President Amador's administration were making great capital of the controversy. The matter had become "one of protection of revenues and not sovereignty" to the Panamanian government. Public attention had turned from the United States to the *junta,* to Tomás Arias and Francisco V. de la Espriella, and to party differences. An anonymous pamphlet was circulated accusing the *junta* of a secret understanding with the United States in regard to the ports and threatening that if "certain hundreds of American dollars" were found to have been received in payment for this act of treason the "unworthy traffickers in National Dignity" should "make ready their heads." The pamphleteers sarcastically explained to the populace:

I do not incite you to armed rebellion, because the Article "Amador Guerrero," No. 136 of the Constitution, has apparently suspended the sword of Damocles over our heads by reason of American intervention, a great piece of cleverness to sustain the Chief Magistrate who well knew the secrets now being brought to light in the Government.[32]

In the meantime the diplomats had considered the remaining differences. One of the first points settled was the manner in which negotiations were to be carried on in reference to sections eight and nine of the order of June 24. Arias claimed that, in requiring him to transact business directly with the government of the Canal Zone, the United States was not respecting the Republic of Panama as an independent nation. He wanted Minister Barrett to be present at all conferences and to sign all agreements.[33] On September 14 Barrett was instructed to attend and take participatory and consultative share in all negotiations between Canal Zone officials and Panamanian authorities.[34] Still no satisfactory arrangement could be reached because Arias wanted to wait until Hay had answered the Obaldía memorial. Local politics, always prominent in Panamanian relations with the United States, delayed matters. Arias explained that the Liberal or opposition party and the masses would criticize the administration if it started negotiations on tariff and trade relations before showing "beyond question or doubt that the United States refused to admit the contentions of the Panama government in regard to the interpretation as outlined in Minister Obaldia's memorandum."[35]

Matters progressed slowly, as they usually do when Panama and the United States are concerned. Barrett began to prepare late in September to visit the United States, and Arias requested him to discuss the whole affair with the State Department.[36] President Roosevelt grew tired of the dilatory methods of diplomacy by mail and telegraph and decided to send Secretary of War William H. Taft to the Isthmus to terminate the controversy. On October 18, 1904, he instructed Taft to proceed to the Canal Zone and the Republic of Panama in order to settle the vexing questions that threatened to shatter comity and peace between the two republics. The Panamanians were assured:

We have not the slightest intention of establishing an independent colony in the center of the Republic of Panama, or of exercising the functions of Government to a greater degree than was necessary to place us in a position to construct, protect and benefit by the canal, in accordance with the rights given to us by the treaty, and the last thing that we desire is to obstruct the commerce and prosperity of the people of Panama.[37]

The wheels of government moved slowly at Washington, but Hay finally assembled enough argument to reply on October 24 to the Obaldía protest. He asserted that the United States was justified in opening the Canal Zone to the commerce of friendly nations, in imposing customs duties on merchandise brought into the Zone, and in establishing post-offices and postal service in the Zone for domestic and foreign mails. These rights, he contended, were dependent upon the authority of the

United States to exercise sovereignty over the Canal Zone; and whether the United States had that power was to be determined by the treaty of November 18, 1903. Hay stated that "the plain and obvious meaning of Article III was the one originally intended by the parties to the treaty," and cited Articles IX, X, XII, and XIII, four of the Obaldía points of refutation, as proof that the United States was sovereign in the Canal Zone. He carefully explained that Articles XII and XIII did not apply to the Canal territory but to the Republic of Panama. He pointed out that neither was the harbor of Ancón adjacent to Panama City nor was Cristóbal in the same relation to Colón, for the Pacific entrance was five miles by shore line from Panama and the Atlantic mouth was one-half mile across the bay from Colón. Attention was called to sections eight and nine of the order of June 24 as means of settling the tariff question.

The Panamanian government, Hay thought, was trying to interpret the treaty as if dealing with the French canal company, a private enterprise, instead of the United States of America. No doubt existed in his mind of the right of his government to exercise sovereignty in the Canal Zone, and he stated decisively that it was acting within the spirit and letter of the treaty. In regard to Obaldía's reference to the disavowal of the United States of any intention of increasing its territory at the expense of Central and South American republics, Hay explained at the outset:

The policy thus announced did not originate with the proposed treaty with Colombia. It is the long-established policy of the United States, constantly adhered to; but said policy does not include the denial of the right of transfer of territory and sovereignty from one republic to another of the western hemisphere upon terms amicably arranged and mutually satisfactory, when such transfer promotes the peace of nations and the welfare of the world. That the United States may acquire territory and sovereignty in this way and for this purpose from its sister republics in this hemisphere is so manifest as to preclude discussion.[38]

The contents of the communication revealed that Hay considered the United States the sovereign of the Canal Zone and thus completely justified in using that territory as it deemed fit. His conclusion was, in effect, that the United States held permanent sovereignty over the Canal strip, but he hoped for an amicable settlement in accordance with sections eight and nine of the order of June 24. However, he appeared to have summed up his opinion of the annoying protests of the Panamanian government when he informed Obaldía:

If it could or should be admitted that the titular sovereign of the canal zone is the Republic of Panama, such sovereign is mediatized by its own acts, solemnly declared and publicly proclaimed by treaty stipulations, induced by a desire to make possible the completion of a great work which will confer inestimable benefit upon the people of the Isthmus and the nations of the world. It is difficult to believe that a member of the family of nations seriously contemplates abandoning so high and honorable a position, in order to engage in an endeavor to secure what at best is a "barren scepter."[39]

Panamanian opinion on the Hay note was lost amid the acclaim that greeted the Roosevelt order directing Taft to visit the Isthmus for the purpose of safeguarding Panamanian interests.[40] The government invited Taft to be a guest of the nation and offered him the entire second floor of the Hotel Central in Panama City. The people appreciated the honor and prepared to exert themselves to the utmost for their guest.[41]

Taft sailed from historic Pensacola on November 22 for more ancient Panama. His party of distinguished statesmen and soldiers traveled on the cruiser *Columbia*, accompanied by the *Dolphin*. Colón and the first of many cheering throngs were reached on Sunday morning, November 27. Taft immediately boarded his special train for Panama City and a greater ovation.[42] A few hours later he was welcomed officially by President Amador. The American lost no time in informing the Panamanians that their interests were to be cared for in the coming parley:

. . . the Government of the United States has no intention in being in this Isthmus to do other than to build a canal which shall connect the two oceans and thus bring great benefit, not only to your country, but to the United States and mankind. It has no desire to exercise any power except that which it deems necessary under the treaty to insure the building, maintenance, and protection of the canal.[43]

Negotiations were initiated and carried on daily. William Nelson Cromwell, one of Panama's godfathers, acted as intermediary.[44] The Panamanians neither hurried nor worried. Tomorrow, the next day, perhaps the next week—*mañana*— would bring an adjustment. The end was envisaged in the brilliant banquet given on December 1 at the Hotel Central in honor of the American emissary. An assemblage of wealth, talent, power, and beauty of the interoceanic republic met and entertained the cream of North American political, engineering, and military genius. The decorations, the food, and the spirit of friendliness that pervaded the atmosphere proved the proud hospitality of the Panamanians. When coffee and cigars were served, Foreign Secretary Santiago de la Guardia arose and welcomed the guest of honor. He spoke slowly and impressively of the vital interest of his countrymen in strengthening cordial relations between the two republics. Taft then addressed the eager and waiting company. His giant figure created an impression of dominating power as he began to praise the Panamanian nation and people. He indicated that justice should be done to Panama and that justice, order, and stability would be required of the Panamanians. The confidence and goodwill of his hosts were increased by the explanation:

This visit has been one of intense interest and of the pleasantest surprises to me; the truth is that the people of Panama, and the country of Panama, have not been done justice.

And it is a pleasure for me to correct the impression which the slanderers of your country have made upon my mind, and I am sure, upon the minds of those who have not looked closely into the facts.[45]

Taft continued amid an outburst of applause by admonishing the Panamanians against tyranny and turbulence. He referred to the imperative necessity for an orderly and stable government devoid of revolutionary movements and warned: "Stability of government is absolutely impossible unless there is implanted in the breasts of all your people who take part in the government as voters, a profound respect for the law and the constitution which you yourselves have founded." This was greeted with a burst of heartfelt and sincere "applause that bore no resemblance to mere perfunctoriness." Taft concluded:

You must have a government in which the minority shall enjoy equal rights with the majority. A government in which the minority, upon the election by the majority, retires from the borders of the country in exile, only to await the result of the next successful revolution, is not a government at all. It is a tyranny. You can have a despotism as complete by a majority of the people as by one man, and unless you respect the rights of each individual in your community you will have no government worth supporting.[46]

That was plain talk and, in view of the history of neighboring countries and the recent revolutionary activities of General Esteban Huertas, it was also salutary. Cheering interrupted the speaker three times in these last four sentences. The speech implied no intention of retrocession or consideration of retrocession, but still it was greeted with "spontaneity and manifest earnestness." Taft resumed his seat amid a veritable torrent of cheering. Round after round of applause echoed in the spacious banquet hall.

The American was followed by Pablo Arosemena, who aroused his audience to the highest pitch with his "vehement and torrential eloquence." Next came William Nelson Cromwell, who made a very tactful and practical speech calculated to assist in smoothing over the difficulties that had caused the occasion. He called attention to the fact that the six million dollar constitutional fund that Panama had created in the United States from the Canal payment and the three hundred million dollar investment of the United States in the heart of the young republic must be protected. Last arose the stormy veteran, Belisario Porras, with his "rhetorical periods" that fittingly concluded that outstanding social event—a banquet creditable to a city of far greater size and opulence—in the history of Panama.[47]

The Liberals who then formed the opposition attempted to mar the visit with a demonstration against Taft, for they feared that an amicable adjustment of the Panamanian grievances would strengthen the administration for the approaching municipal elections. Panamanian hospitality, however, overcame political ambition, and the demonstration amounted to nothing.

The news leaked out at a dinner given by Barrett for Taft on December 3 that an agreement had been signed. On the following day the visitors were given an excursion to the Pearl Islands. They returned in the afternoon to find pamphlets containing the text of the settlement being distributed throughout the city. All day Monday, December 5, invitations were spread for the people to gather that evening in the Cathedral Plaza. A grateful nation was to pay homage to its illustrious benefactor. They were all there, "aristocracy and rabble, rich and poor, white and black, Conservative and Liberal," to pay their tribute of respect. The vast assemblage was greeted by Taft and the government officials from the balcony of the Hotel Central. The popular *Alcalde* Francisco de la Ossa briefly introduced the distinguished personages. "Then Dr. Pablo Arosemena roused the enthusiasm of the throng with another of his passionate orations, in which words flowed so swiftly that even the trained Panamanian ear was taxed to catch them all." Taft responded with his last and best speech, his "stalwart figure dominating the whole scene and his resonant voice reaching the fartherest confines of the square." He commented on the blessings of an orderly constitutional government and congratulated the Panamanians that their *junta* had set up no dictatorship and that they had chosen civilians rather than soldiers for their important government posts. Probably remembering the successful resistance of the authorities against the machinations of the Liberals and their pawn, General Huertas, Taft warned, "In a republic, and in a peaceful republic, the army must always be the instrument of civil power." He was gratified that the

Panamanians had indicated no intention of being governed by the sword but by reason and law. This sentiment was "acclaimed with a universal frenzy of enthusiasm, until the fronds of the towering palms and the gray façade of the old Cathedral seemed to vibrate together with its tumultuous stress." A similar outburst followed the "straightforward and manly acknowledgement that a mistake had been made" in issuing the order applying the Dingley Tariff to the Canal Zone against the Republic of Panama—a mistake that had been rectified and for which Taft did not hesitate to assume responsibility. A third swell of wild cheering greeted Taft's concluding vibrant cry: *"Viva la República de Panamá."* Then it was over.[48]

The settlement that produced this celebration was set forth in an executive order of December 3, 1904, and was partly clarified by another three days later. The United States agreed that no goods, wares, or merchandise should be entered at Ancón or Cristóbal except those necessary for Canal use described in Article XIII of the treaty, those in transit across the Isthmus, and fuel for sale by the United States to passing ships. Panama bound itself to reduce the ad valorem duty on general imports as described in class two of the tariff law of July 5, 1904, from 15 to 10 per cent and not to increase other duties except on wine, liquors, alcohol, and opium.[49] Article 38 of the Panamanian constitution which prohibited official monopolies, as modified by Article 146 which protected the legal monopolies existing at its adoption,[50] was to remain in force and "unchanged so far as the importation and sale of all kinds of merchandise" were concerned. All consular fees and charges in respect to the entry of vessels and imports into Panama and Colón were to be reduced to 60 per cent of the rates then in force. Goods brought into Panama and Colón destined for or consigned to the Canal Zone were to be exempt from all imposts and taxes.

In view of the imperative necessity for entrances to the Canal Zone and the Bunau-Varilla letter of January 19, 1904, the United States retained the ports of Ancón and Cristóbal. Provision was made, however, that ships entered at or cleared from Panama and Colón might use the docks and other facilities of Ancón and Cristóbal, and Panama granted reciprocal rights to vessels from the Canal ports. These privileges were to be given when "not inconsistent with the interests" of the grantor and were not to affect the jurisdiction of the two governments over their ports and harbors. Ships entering and clearing the port of Panama might anchor, lade, and discharge cargo by lighterage at the usual anchorage in the vicinity of the islands of Perico, Flamenco, Naos, and Culebra, although these were included in the Ancón harbor by the provisional delimitation of June 15, 1904,[51] which was to remain provisionally in force. "All manifests and invoices and other documents in respect to vessels or cargoes" cleared from or consigned to the ports of Panama and Colón were to be made by Panamanian officials, while authorities of the United States were to perform the same duty in regard to the Canal ports.

The application of the Dingley Tariff to the Canal Zone against the Republic of Panama was revoked, a step which removed the outstanding complaint and a just grievance of the Panamanians. Panama, in return, assented to free importation of goods, wares, and merchandise and free passage of persons from the Canal Zone into the Republic of Panama. All Canal Zone mail-matter carried through Panama to the United States or to foreign countries was to bear Panamanian stamps surcharged with a mark of the Canal Zone government and was to have the same rates as those imposed by the United States, "exactly as if the United States and the Republic of Panama for this purpose were common territory." The stamps were to be purchased from Panama at 40 per cent of their face value. Panama agreed to arrange with American postal officials for the transportation of mails between the post-offices of the Isthmus and those of the United States at the same rates charged for domestic postage in the United States.[52]   All franked mail pertaining to the business of the American government was to be carried free by Panama and the Canal Zone. Mails between the United States and the Canal Zone might be placed in sealed pouches not to be opened by Panamanian officials, provided the Canal Zone government bore the costs of transportation. Finally, Panama promised to execute the currency agreement made between its fiscal agents and Secretary Taft in Washington on June 20, 1904,[53] and to abolish the one per cent tax on exports of gold coin.[54]

Thus the first of many "unfortunate difficulties" between the Isthmian republic and its great northern benefactor and oppressor was terminated. The Panamanian government immediately indicated its concurrence in the order and expressed its appreciation for the "happy solution of the differences" that had marred the amicable relations of the two governments.[55] Ten days later Minister Barrett reported that the new system had been inaugurated successfully and that he was assisting Governor Davis and Secretary Guardia in perfecting details.[56] Panama soon issued a decree fulfilling its share of the agreement.[57]

The Republic of Panama by no means gained all that was desired. The competition of the commissaries of the Isthmian Canal Commission was beginning to cause ill-feeling. They were retained as indispensable for the existence of Americans on the Isthmus and would produce more than a generation of agitation and controversy. The Panamanians, however, were apparently unanimous in the belief that they had received more than they had expected from the United States.[58]

NOTES

1. *For. Rel.* (1904), pp. 586-587.
2. *Sen. Doc.*, No. 401, 59 Cong., 2 Sess. (Ser. 5097), I, 713-714.
3. *House Doc.*, No. 226, 58 Cong., 3 Sess. (Ser. 4853), pp. 83-84.
4. Malloy, *Treaties*, II, 1350.
5. Bunau-Varilla, *Panama*, chap. xxix.
6. Draft of Article II, Nov. 17, 1903, Notes from the Panama Legation, I.
7. "Panama," in Foreign Policy Association, *Information Service*, III (1928), 358; Escobar, *op. cit.*, p. 94; O. M. Pereira, *Mi contestación al Dr. Alfredo L. Palacios* (Panama, 1926), p. 3.
8. Arias to Davis, July 9, 1904, *For. Rel.* (1904), pp. 589-591.
9. Chargé Joseph W. J. Lee to Hay, July 18, 1904, *loc. cit.*, p. 585.
10. *Idem* to *idem*, No. 116, July 18, 1904, Despatches, Panama, II.
11. Barrett to Hay, July 25, 1904, *loc. cit.*
12. *Idem* to *idem*, No. 4, July 26, 1904, *loc. cit.*
13. *Idem* to *idem*, July 26, 1904, *For. Rel.* (1904), pp. 587-588.
14. *Idem* to *idem*, July 27, 1904, *loc. cit.*, p. 588.

15. *Idem* to *idem*, Aug. 9, 1904, *loc. cit.*, p. 595.

16. Arias to Barrett, July 27, 1904; July 28, 1904, *loc. cit.*, pp. 591-593.

17. Barrett to Hay, Aug. 2, 1904, *loc. cit.*, p. 594.

18. *Idem* to *idem*, No. 14, Aug. 9, 1904, Despatches, Panama, II.

19. *Idem* to *idem*, Aug. 9, 1904, *For. Rel.* (1904), p. 597.

20. Obaldía to Hay, Aug. 11, 1904, *loc. cit.*, p. 601.

21. *Ibid.*, p. 604.

22. *Sen. Doc.*, No. 401, 59 Cong., 2 Sess. (Ser. 5097), I, 713-714; Johnson, *op. cit.*, pp. 256-257.

23. Obaldía to Hay, Aug. 11, 1904, *For. Rel.* (1904), p. 606.

24. This discussion is found in Obaldía to Hay, No. 6, Aug. 11, 1904, Notes from the Panama Legation, I; *For. Rel.* (1904), pp. 598-607.

25. Barrett to Hay, No. 16, Aug. 16, 1904, Despatches, Panama, II.

26. The question arises as to the reason why Hay did not quote Bunau-Varilla to Loomis, Jan. 15, 1904. Possibly it was lost, for the original is bound between Obaldía to Robert Bacon, Jan. 15, 1906, and Obaldía to Elihu Root, Jan. 22, 1906, Notes from the Panama Legation, I. The letter is as follows:

"I read in the papers this morning that some question has been raised in the Senate Committee about the harbors *adjacent* to the towns of Colon and Panama.

"The *Canal harbors* are not adjacent to the towns of Panama and Colon.

"There is no confusion possible about the Colon Canal Harbor and the actual Harbor *adjacent* to the township of Colon.

"The Canal harbor has not even any contiguity with the *actual* or *adjacent* harbor.

"The very same thing exists on the Panama side.

"To suppose a confusion is to ignore the material state of things. A look at a plan would clear all confusion."

27. Bunau-Varilla to Hay, Jan. 19, 1904, *For. Rel.* (1904), pp. 608-609.

28. Obaldía to Hay, Aug. 19, 1904, *loc. cit.*, pp. 609-610.

29. Barrett to Arias, Aug. 16, 1904, República de Panamá, Secretaría de Gobierno y Relaciones Exteriores, *Memoria*, 1906 (Panama, 1907), pp. 235-236. Title varies. Hereafter cited as Panama, Sec. R. E., *Memoria*, 1906.

30. Arias to Barrett, Aug. 23, 1904, enclosed with Barrett to Hay, No. 31, Sept. 6, 1904, Despatches, Panama, III.

31. Barrett to Hay, Aug. 20, 1904, *For. Rel.* (1904), p. 610.

32. *Idem* to *idem*, No. 25, Aug. 23, 1904, and enclosures, Despatches, Panama, II.

33. *Idem* to *idem*, No. 22, Aug. 20, 1904, 'loc. cit.

34. Alvey A. Adee, assistant secretary of state, to Barrett, Sept. 14, 1904, Department of State, Instructions, Panama, I.

35. Barrett to Hay, No. 43, Sept. 20, 1904, Despatches, Panama, III.

36. *Ibid.*

37. Roosevelt to Taft, Oct. 18, 1904, Panama, Sec. R. E., *Memoria*, 1906, pp. lxv-lxvi.

38. Hay to Obaldía, Oct. 24, 1904, *For. Rel.* (1904), p. 614.

39. *Ibid.*, p. 615. This discussion is found in Hay to Obaldía, No. 12, Oct. 24, 1904, Notes to the Panama Legation, I; *For. Rel.* (1904), pp. 613-630.

40. Lee to Hay, No. 58, Oct. 25, 1904, Despatches, Panama, III.

41. *Idem* to *idem*, No. 64, Nov. 11, 1904, *loc. cit.*

42. Barrett to Hay, No. 71, Nov. 29, 1904, *loc. cit.*; Gudger to Loomis, No. 531, Dec. 4, 1904, Consular Letters, Panama, XXV.

43. *For. Rel.* (1904), p. 632.

44. Barrett to Hay, No. 71, Despatches, Panama, III.

45. *For. Rel.* (1904), p. 633.

46. *Ibid.*, p. 634; Johnson, *op. cit.*, pp. 261-262.

47. *For. Rel.* (1904), pp. 632-640; Johnson, *op. cit.*, pp. 259-264.

48. Johnson, *op. cit.*, pp. 264-265.

49. República de Panamá, *Gaceta oficial*, July 12, 1904. Under general classes were three divisions. Number one listed all undutiable goods, three enumerated all articles subject to special taxes, all other imports were covered by two which levied a 15 per cent duty on the invoice.

50. *Sen. Doc.*, No. 208, 58 Cong., 2 Sess. (Ser. 4591), pp. 7, 24; República de Panamá, *Compendio estadístico descriptivo de la República de Panamá con los datos sinópticos del comercio internacional de 1909 a 1916* (Panama, 1917), pp. 116, 140,

51. Panama, Sec. R. E., *Memoria*, 1906, pp. 195-198; *Sen. Doc.*, No. 348, 67 Cong., 4 Sess. (Ser. 8167), III, 2752-2754.

52. Panama, Sec. R. E., *Memoria*, 1906, p. lxxxviii.

53. *Ibid.*, pp. 253-254.

54. *For. Rel.* (1904), pp. 640-642.

55. Amador Guerrero and Guardia to Taft, Dec. 4, 1904, *loc. cit.*, p. 643.

56. Barrett to Hay, Dec. 13, 1904, *loc. cit.*, p. 643.

57. Panama, Sec. R. E., *Memoria*, 1906, pp. 244-255.

58. Barrett to Hay, No. 71, Dec. 6, 1904, Despatches, Panama, III.

CHAPTER III

PANAMA LOSES ITS ARMY

THE REPUBLIC OF PANAMA scarcely had celebrated its first independence day when it was called upon to determine whether it was to have a stable civil government or to be subject to military revolutions. A choice in favor of the former was made in the beginning, for the president was not a general in the army but the leading physician of the country, and the other important officials were business and professional men. This might have been due in part to Panama's gaining freedom from Colombia without bloodshed and without the use of an army that might have produced a figure of dictatorship calibre.

The original government was in a measure a coalition of men of all creeds. In time antagonisms developed in and out of the Amador administration. The Liberals felt that they had a majority of the electorate, but had minority representation in the government.[1] Agitation for cabinet changes was carried on in newspapers, pamphlets, speeches, and addresses to the president. Tomás Arias, secretary of foreign affairs and war, and Nicolás Victoria J., secretary of public instruction and justice, were especially odious to the Liberals. Failing to have these men dismissed by peaceful political means, the opposition leaders, chiefly the followers of Belisario Porras, reached the conclusion that force might be more effective. They sought and acquired the co-operation of General Esteban Huertas, the commander-in-chief of the Panamanian army.

As early as December, 1903, the newspapers of Panama were pointing to the fact that the army was a menace and that the money spent for its maintenance was needed for interior development. The suggestion was made that the soldiers, who were idle and of little use to the nation, be incorporated into a police corps because the existing force was inadequate.[2] Less than a month later Minister W. I. Buchanan wrote the State Department that the army should be disbanded and formed into a *guardia rural* after the ratification of the Hay-Bunau-Varilla Treaty. The men should be armed only with revolvers and spread over the republic in order that no faction might use them collectively to intimidate the government. He believed that the importation and possession of firearms should be prohibited, and recommended that Panama store its arms and ammunition in the Canal Zone for delivery only to the existing government.[3]

General Huertas was the idol of the army and a man highly esteemed by the people for his services as commander of the *Batallón Colombia* in the revolution of November 3, 1903—or rather his lack of service for the Colombian government.[4] He was a man of ability and of a peculiarly attractive and engaging personality,[5] but he was unable to withstand the flattery of the Liberals. Nor was he averse to accepting the numerous drinks offered by these not disinterested friends. Perhaps the suggestion that posterity would rank him above Bolívar, Washington, and Napoleon produced in his imaginative mind the grandiose illusion of ruling Panama with bullets rather than ballots, if necessary. Possibly the ego of the general was somewhat inflated by his free trip to Europe, but a $50,000 grant from the National Assembly for an European tour and entertainment by royalty might have turned the heads of worthier men.[6]

The national independence holidays, declared in honor of the first natal day of the republic, were drawing near, and political agitation was steadily increasing. Although fear existed that the celebration would produce some ill-feeling, the prediction was made that it would be exhausted in torrents of words. Chargé J. W. J. Lee informed the State Department that a warship should have been near the Isthmus to furnish a band for the festivities, for the Panamanians would have appreciated such a courtesy from the American government.[7] On October 29 Huertas sent President Amador a letter "couched in the most extraordinary terms, commingling almost inconceivable egotism, extravagant affection for the President whom he was trying to bully, and bitter hatred" for Arias and Victoria.[8] Amador was reminded that he and the general, "joined by the indissoluble bonds of honest methods," had founded the Isthmian republic and were fathers of the Isthmian people. Now they must uphold and improve the fatherland, even at the risk of their lives. Huertas promised the unquestionable loyalty of the army to the executive, but demanded that heed be given the opposition by correcting the administration with an honorable personnel. A new government was needed that would shed a brilliant luster upon the country which, notwithstanding its extreme youth, suffered "tortures already from a choking iron collar."

The president was assured that neither he nor the general was disliked by the masses, but was informed that a great portion of the people found themselves "removed from the direction of Public Affairs in order that rapacious spirits, which gobble up everything, . . . [might] be sustained in office to the disgrace of the National dignity and to your disgrace as Chief Magistrate and to my disgrace as faithful executor of the Divine Will cooperating with you in the formation of our Nation." Little did the sufferings of the enemies of the country matter if it might save itself from its "sorrowful road." "Let us," the general plead, "make a holocaust if possible of all that is most precious to us, in order to make sure, when God wills, the happiness of this land for its children."

Huertas said that he judged Amador to be an honorable man and hoped that he would stand by him to save the nation, for he did not believe that the president wished him and his weak soldiers to take up the burden alone. If necessity demanded, the general would purge the republic or die in the attempt. Finally, Huertas indicated the means of preventing the predicted decadence and eventual collapse of his country by stating: "I therefore recommend and I demand the removal of Don Tomas Arias and Don Nicolas Victoria J., who by their methods are affecting the country's interests; lessening your authority and mine, and accumulating the hate of the people upon us, with grave detriment to our National and personal dignity."[9]

President Amador was an old man in awe of his troops. He did not deal with the refractory general in an energetic manner. Arias and Victoria tendered their resignations on being notified of the letter. The president sent for Chargé Lee, and the American found him "un-nerved and vacillating."[10] Lee attempted to persuade him to delay acceptance of the resignations until after the celebration.[11] The chief executive laid the trouble to the "itch for the $6,000,000" invested in the United States. The army had become a "Frankenstein" to him, and he volunteered the opinion that Panama had no need for it, but that he was unable to find a way to disband the men. Lee pointed out that the good name of Panama, which was held in high opinion among the rulers of the universe, would suffer disastrously at having the first independence day marred by revolution. The republic would be dragged from its high pedestal, and the world would know that it was lapsing into the conditions from which it had separated a year previously and to which civilization did not expect it to return. The attention of Amador was directed to his authority to meet the situation, and he made an effort to maintain peace until after the celebration.

Lee was soon visited by Belisario Porras and another Liberal chief who spoke in peaceful terms, but for the evident purpose of discovering the attitude of the United States toward a revolution. The chargé called their attention to Articles VII and XXIII of the Hay-Bunau-Varilla Treaty and to Article 136 of their constitution, all concerning the right of the United States to use force to preserve order in the Republic of Panama. They were informed firmly that the United States would countenance no revolutionary activities and that changes in the Panamanian government should be made either at the ballot box or by voluntary resignations. The Liberals were impressed, and promised to remain quiet during the festivities, but stated that they would expect the acceptance of the resignations of Arias and Victoria immediately after the celebrations.[12]

Lee informed the State Department that the Panamanian army would be a continual menace to the republic, that it would always be a "handy tool" for either party, and that it would be an unceasing source of unrest until abolished. The two hundred and fifty men who composed the force did not measure up to high standards. Among them were twenty to thirty boys, some of whom were no more than eleven years of age. Since the opposition had used the army to force Amador's hand once, Lee felt that the same weapon would be employed soon to accomplish other and similiar results. He stated that he would not be surprised if the Liberals demanded the resignation of the president. The more substantial citizens were much perturbed. Again Lee suggested that a man-of-war with a good band was urgently needed for the celebrations, for the offer of music by the United States would be considered a compliment and would be morally opportune. In submitting a copy of the Huertas letter, he bluntly commented, "It is a rare and curious document and comment is unnecessary," and explained that the general had been made to believe he was a second Napoleon, and, therefore, would not be a safe element in the future life of the nation.[13]

Amador shortly repeated his belief that the political disturbances in Panama arose from the desire of the opposition to gain access to the golden plum of six millions invested in American mortgages, and expressed the hope that President Roosevelt would save the young republic.[14] However, the situation was outwardly calm, and the festivities began in a quiet and orderly manner.[15] The outlook was more tranquil than since October 27, but "a strong spirit [was] abroad, bred of misunderstanding and covetousness," and one false step might have produced embarrassing circumstances for both governments. The morning of November 3 started auspiciously with a solemn *Te Deum* in the Cathedral. The president, the cabinet, the diplomatic and consular corps, the Canal Zone governor and staff, and General Huertas and aides were present. In the afternoon Amador held a brilliant reception at the government house. The city was profusely decorated, and the American flag was much in evidence. Practically the whole army remained in its barracks.[16]

On the same day Huertas issued to the army and the people a flamboyant proclamation in the form of an order of the day. It was a mixture of adulation for himself and praise for the Panamanians for their performances of November 3, 1903, as well as because of their consent to his recent insubordination. The republic, he stated, needed an expert pilot or it would be swallowed in the "frightful waves" eager to devour it. Where was such a leader to be found? Bolívar had passed away; Washington was dead. Huertas himself, "a weak bit of chaff in the desert of life," possessed with the protection of God the "efficiency indispensable to the solution of the great problem." The general explained that he had been ignorant of his exalted mission and merely had devoted himself indefatigably to his duties and obligations. Confident ever in "the goodness of the Supreme Being," he had risen gradually in the glorious career of arms.

But [he stated] if neither my right nor my illustriousness is enough to explain to me the portentous result achieved by me and the Army with the decisive consent of the Isthmian people, however, I succeeded in comprehending the high moral and material responsibility which has fallen to my lot, so as to know how to preserve that which the Maker has given to us, and to that end were directed all my forces, in the hope that those who collaborated in the beginning would know how to sacrifice themselves upon the altars of the most exalted Patriotism in order that our beloved Country should never run the risk of being involved in the indignity of bastard ambitions nor vile and ruinous methods.[17]

Thanks to the tact of President Amador and to the judicious warning of Chargé Lee that revolution would be frowned upon, disturbance was averted; but Santiago de la Guardia was chosen to replace Arias, much to the displeasure of the Liberals. Guardia was then Panamanian minister to Costa Rica, and had spent thirty-five years away from his native land and once had been Costa Rican secretary of war.[18] Not only was he considered a foreigner, but he was a staunch conservative, an ambitious presidential possibility, and a friend of the United States.[19] The *fiesta* closed on November 6, and soon the news of the re-election of President Roosevelt was received with general rejoicing. The Amador administration was strengthened, for the policy followed by Lee evidently would not be altered. The approaching visit of Secretary Taft had a salutary effect, but the spirit of revolution was not quenched. A week later Huertas addressed another letter to Amador more amazing in terms than the first. He was highly dissatisfied with the appointment of Guardia and more displeased that Victoria was still in office. Victoria, a stranger to dignity, honor, gratefulness, and decency, and a fraud in whose "jaundiced features" hypocrisy and perfidy were seen clearly, had to be dismissed.[20]

It is not surprising that a plot to seize Amador and Guardia was soon discovered. At midnight of November 13 Chargé Lee was awakened by *Alcalde* Ossa and Raúl Amador, the president's son, with the information that Amador and Guardia were to be arrested at six o'clock the next morning at a military review in honor of the latter. Huertas had written the president demanding his presence at the ceremony. Following Lee's advice, Amador decided to remain at home the next morning, but he feared that the general might send for him. The chargé reassured the old man with the news that the *Bennington,* an American war vessel, was due to be sighted at any moment. The president spent an anxious night and at five-thirty the next morning sent a request to Lee for a force of marines from the Canal Zone. The American refused, but warned Huertas that Article 136 of the constitution permitted the United States to intervene in Panama to preserve order and that he considered it "high time" for such proceedings as the general contemplated to cease. Lee also assured Huertas that he was positive that he had the best interests of the republic at heart and had no desire to stain its fair name. Guardia attended the review and inspected the troops alone and unmolested.

On the same day the chargé cabled the State Department that the *Bennington* should remain in Panamanian waters. He reported that the army became more dangerous daily and that the general, surrounded with flatterers who treated him with "greatest adulation" and plied him with drink, considered himself almost a dictator. Once more Lee advised that the army be disbanded and four or five bands stationed in Panama City to furnish diverting music. Concerts would amuse, interest, and occupy the minds of the Panamanians and also save money for the government. He suggested that Taft make some concession during his visit in order to obtain the disbandment of the military force. He warned that this unsuccessful attempt to overthrow the government would be followed speedily by another. The situation was likely to be embarrassing, for the opposition planned to effect a coup d'état and then say to the United States, "What are you going to do about it?"[21]

Later in the day Lee wrote that the *Boston* and *Bennington* were in the Panama Harbor and that the *New York*, commanded by Rear Admiral C. F. Goodrich, had anchored off Taboga Island. Amador had asked that one vessel remain near, pending settlement of the Huertas trouble. The moral effect of the ships was plain, and Lee thought their retention advisable since Taft and a congressional committee were shortly to visit the Isthmus.[22] On the following day the State Department instructed the chargé to offer assistance if the president desired it and to advise all naval and marine commanders immediately.[23]

Minister Barrett returned to Panama on November 16 and took charge of the situation with a firm hand. He promptly called upon Amador to present his compliments and to get his version of the state of affairs. Amador explained that the crisis had to end in retirement, resignation, or leave of absence for Huertas. He suggested that Panama would benefit by abolishing the army, and asked Barrett to arrange for the retention of a war vessel until the difficulties were adjusted.[24] On being interrogated by Amador as to means of treating the rebellious general and army, Barrett advised that Huertas be forced to resign and that the army be disbanded. Since the marines in the Canal Zone were competent to maintain order in the republic, only a military force sufficient to meet statutory requirements should be maintained.[25] The minister, however, stated that his advice was not mandatory and that Amador should follow the dictates of his own mind. The cabinet was gratified that the American had assisted in stiffening the resolution of the aged president, and a decision was made to call for the resignation of Huertas and to disband the army.

On November 17 Barrett and Goodrich visited Amador and conveyed the welcome news that all American forces on and near the Isthmus would be used to maintain order and that one ship would remain in Panamanian waters as long as necessary. Amador then notified Huertas that his resignation would be expected that day or early the next morning, and warned him that the United States would co-operate in preventing disturbances by the soldiers. Goodrich then ordered a company of marines to Ancón, from which any point of Panama City could be reached in fifteen minutes. This manoeuvre and the proximity of the naval squadron "had a most excellent effect on the city and precluded any efforts at revolution." Huertas visited Amador that afternoon and promised to send in his resignation if the president desired it, but left in such an angry mood that the administration again became alarmed. He had so much to say of the casting out of his "poor soldiers" that Amador feared he would not resign and might inspire the men to insubordination. During the night Barrett got in touch with Huertas through a mutual friend and informed him that it was hoped that no indiscretion would be committed that would require the intervention of the United States as provided in the Hay-Bunau-Varilla Treaty and in the Panamanian constitution. Even though advised to resist by his friends and followers, the recalcitrant evidently saw the folly of prolonging the struggle and prepared a long letter tendering his resignation.[26]

The "Irrevocable Resignation" was written in the flamboyant style of his former utterances. The general stated that he was far from being dazed by exaltation, but had preserved his inherent modesty and humility and had no wish to dash to pieces the republic that he had created. He denounced the action of the government in calling for his retirement as being dictated by "foreign and interested designs," and because of its obvious lack of confidence he tendered the irrevocable resignation of his high position. He also announced the retirement of the whole army, for none of its men wished to tarnish their glorious careers by serving after their offended commander had resigned.[27] On the morning of November 18, in the presence of Lee, Amador signed a decree accepting the resignation and placing Huertas on the retired list with a pension of $500 per month.[28] He then wrote the general a personal letter expressing esteem and affection, but explaining that the republic was not to be subjected to a military hierarchy.[29] On the same morning the president visited Goodrich and was further strengthened in his determination to be firm.[30]

General Huertas scornfully declined the stipend and declared to Secretary Guardia that his resignation involved the retirement of the entire army. He explained that the acceptance of money for services lent in the cause of independence would be an enormous blot that would rest upon his dignity and honor as an "indelible stigma" and threatened a violent demonstration if his terms were not accepted implicitly. Guardia met the situation with firmness[31] and informed Huertas that the government had no intention of disbanding the army at that time. The general was reminded that he was aware that troops never had any voice in their retirement. The officers might resign, but no insubordination of any kind would be tolerated. The recalcitrant was told that in refusing his pension he had interpreted erroneously an "act of justice and magnanimity" of the government and that it would be paid.[32]

That afternoon Barrett and Lee conferred with Amador and Guardia concerning the proper steps for ridding the country of the army. The president had promised the men sixty days of pay at their discharge. The American minister suggested paying half at their release and the remainder a week later on condition of good behavior, for he believed this would lessen the chance of disturbance. Amador agreed and also decided to close the saloons for three days in order that the men might not be tempted to get drunk and thus become more susceptible to excitement. The opportunity for removing the menace was deemed propitious, and Barrett recommended the immediate dismissal of the men while the naval force was in the Bay of Panama and the marines were at Ancón. Arrangements were made finally to have the soldiers call at the government house the next afternoon at one o'clock for the first installment of their pay.

After another night and morning of anxiety President Amador was prepared to have the army paid off and disbanded. None of the militia had appeared at one o'clock. At two none had come. The president sent for the American minister to learn what was best to do. He feared that the soldiers might have decided to resist, especially since friends of Huertas had been trying to instigate insubordination. When Barrett arrived at the government house he advised waiting another half-hour. A North American was advising a Panamanian to wait! Barrett promised that if the men had not appeared by then he would send Lee with Guardia to the barracks to ascertain the situation. Thereafter they would act as conditions demanded.

Just before the expiration of the time the first detachment of some fifty men marched up to the government house followed by a motley throng anticipating an exciting afternoon. The soldiers halted and sent word to Amador that they would not accept his terms, but would have all their pay at once. The president was much disturbed, and turned to Barrett for advice. The minister advised him to yield in no way, for the men had been guilty of gross insubordination and in the United States would have been court-martialed and shot without delay. Amador was informed that this was no time for temporizing. After being told that no change would be made in the plans, the soldiers persisted in their position and began to mutter threats against the chief executive.

Barrett looked the situation over and decided that further delay was dangerous. He immediately took Guardia and went downstairs and out on the sidewalk in front of the unarmed militiamen. Briefly he instructed Guardia to tell the soldiers that the United States supported the government in this crisis and that they could accept the terms or the consequences. They were warned that if they refused to acquiesce or if they engaged in any acts of insurrection, riot, or mutiny they would be dealt with in a summary manner. The naval forces in the bay and the marines in the Canal Zone would be used to maintain order. Those responsible for turbulence of any kind would receive the severest punishment possible. The warning had the desired effect, and the men declared that they would accept the plan of the government. All were paid and released within two hours except three men and twenty officers who were loyal and whose retention fulfilled the legal requirements for a standing army. Thereafter "absolute quiet" prevailed and the general feeling was that the crisis had passed. The interest of the people had died down by the time the second installment was disbursed the next Saturday afternoon.[33] General Esteban Huertas, the self-styled Bolívar of Panama, retired on November 21 to his plantation home near Aguadulce.[34]

The business community and the government were reported as being most grateful for the attitude of the American legation and military officials. Barrett was of the opinion that he had taken no part in the events that was not warranted or inspired by President Amador. The forces of the United States had not interfered, but the threat of their use had been the determining factor in quelling the disturbance. The minister explained to the State Department: "While all these events may seem very small at Washington, they have completely absorbed the attention of this community and have been the most stirring that have occurred in its small limits since the revolution of one year ago."[35]

On December 13, 1904, Barrett asked that one company of marines be stationed permanently in Ancón instead of Empire. He explained that the distance was too great from Panama City for the marines to be effective immediately in quieting disorder. He stated:

I do not apprehend further trouble in Panama or any efforts at insurrection, but it must be remembered that the masses of people are schooled and experienced in all kinds of uprisings, agitations, and popular excitements, and great harm might be done on some occasion if there were not a force, like a company of marines, convenient at Ancon, the effect of whose moral presence, even if they did not participate in preserving order, would maintain quiet or protect property.[36]

The Panamanian government soon abolished the remainder of its army. Its arms and ammunition were stored in the Canal Zone. Even the grim cannon were dismounted from the sea wall of Panama City. Battlements that had defended the capital of the Spanish Main for centuries became memories. Thus the Republic of Panama passed through its first political crisis. A repetition of the disorders of hundreds of years on the Isthmus was avoided, but the fires of revolution were to lie smouldering and threatening for another generation. The hand of the Colossus of the North had been too heavy for the tempestuous recalcitrants who could not understand the use of simple pieces of paper called ballots and preferred to use rifles instead.

NOTES

1. Lee to Hay, No. 61, Nov. 1, 1904, Despatches, Panama, III.
2. *Star and Herald* (Panama), Dec. 6, 1903, enclosed with Malmros to Loomis, No. 145, Dec. 8, 1903, Consular Letters, Colón (Aspinwall), XIX.
3. Buchanan to Hay, No. 14, Jan. 4, 1904, Despatches, Panama, I.
4. Callejas B. Santander, *Resumen político de la administración del Dr. Manuel Amador Guerrero, 1904-1908* (Panama, 1933), p. 38.
5. Johnson, *op. cit.*, pp. 238-239.
6. W. C. Haskins, *op. cit.*, p. 432.
7. Lee to Hay, No. 58, Oct. 25, 1904, Despatches, Panama, III
8. Johnson, *op. cit.*, p. 239.
9. Huertas to Amador, Oct. 28, 1904, enclosed with Lee to Hay, No. 61, Nov. 1, 1904, Despatches, Panama, III.
10. Lee to Hay, No. 61, Nov. 1, 1904, *loc. cit.*
11. *Idem* to *idem*, Oct. 29, 1904, *loc. cit.*
12. *Idem* to *idem*, No. 63, Nov. 8, 1904, *loc. cit.*
13. *Idem* to *idem*, No. 61, Nov. 1, 1904, *loc. cit.*
14. *Idem* to *idem*, Nov. 2, 1904, *loc. cit.*
15. *Idem* to *idem*, Nov. 4, 1904, *loc. cit.*
16. *Idem* to *idem*, No. 62, Nov. 8, 1904, *loc. cit.*
17. Proclamation by Huertas, Nov. 3, 1904, enclosed with *idem* to *idem*, No. 62, Nov. 8, 1904, *loc. cit.*
18. Santander, *op. cit.*, pp. 37-38.
19. Lee to Hay, No. 65, Nov. 14, 1904, Despatches, Panama, III.
20. Johnson, *op. cit.*, p. 247.

21. Lee to Hay, No. 66, Nov. 14, 1904, Despatches, Panama, III.

22. *Idem* to *idem*, No. 67, Nov. 14, 1904, *loc. cit.*

23. Loomis to Lee, Nov. 15, 1904, Instructions, Panama, I.

24. Barrett to Hay, Nov. 17, 1904, Despatches, Panama, III.

25. Isthmian Canal Commission, *The Civil Code of the Republic of Panama and Amendatory Laws Continued in Force in the Canal Zone* . . . (Washington, 1905) does not show what this was.

26. Barrett to Hay, No. 70, Nov. 22, 1904, Despatches, Panama, III.

27. Johnson, *op. cit.*, p. 250.

28. Barrett to Hay, No. 70, Nov. 22, 1904, Despatches, Panama, III.

29. Johnson, *op. cit.*, p. 251.

30. Barrett to Hay, No. 70, Nov. 22, 1904, Despatches, Panama, III.

31. Santiago de la Guardia, *La intervención fiscal Americana en Panamá* (Panama, 1917), p. 2.

32. Johnson, *op. cit.*, p. 252.

33. Barrett to Hay, No. 70, Nov. 22, 1904, Despatches, Panama, III.

34. W. C. Haskins, *op. cit.*, p. 432.

35. Barrett to Hay, No. 70, Nov. 22, 1904, Despatches, Panama, III.

36. *Idem* to *idem*, No. 72, Dec. 13, 1904, *loc. cit.*

CHAPTER IV

THE MAINTENANCE OF PUBLIC ORDER

ONE OF THE foremost causes of dissension and agitation on the Isthmus has been the intervention and potential intervention of the United States in the affairs of the Republic of Panama for the preservation of public order. The interference of American forces insured Panamanian independence in 1903 and has served to restrain the Isthmians from bloodshed ever since, but not from discontent and political disorder. The sending of American soldiers into Panamanian territory for the supervision of elections and the prevention of rioting and possible revolution has been based on Article 136 of the Panamanian constitution, which confers the right of intervention in any part of the republic for the preservation of public peace and constitutional order,[1] and on Articles I and VII of the Hay-Bunau-Varilla Treaty by which the United States guarantees the independence of Panama and is given the privilege of interfering in Panama City and Colón and their adjacent territories should the Panamanian government be deemed unable to maintain public order.

When the stabilizing hand of the United States first made itself felt on the Isthmus, long years of turbulence had made Panamanian industrial and agricultural development practically impossible. The people had a generally accepted tenet that production was foolish because a revolution would soon start and one band of the insurgents or the other, often both, would despoil the owner of the fruits of his labor.[2] Minister Buchanan undertook to place a check on the stormy spirits of the Isthmus by devoting his efforts to securing constitutional permission for the United States to intervene in Panama for the preservation of order. The State Department indifferently permitted him to use his discretion, and he was successful in the face of bitter opposition from many Panamanians.[3] Article

136, considered by Buchanan the strongest part of the constitution, was finally accepted after much caustic debate among the Isthmians. One pamphlet circulated in Panama City characterized it as a "great and everlasting shame and insult" which would be handed down with a "blush of shame" to all future generations.[4] The article provided:

The Government of the United States of America may intervene in any part of the Republic of Panama to reestablish public peace and constitutional order in the event of their being disturbed, provided that that nation shall, by public treaty, assume or have assumed the obligation of guaranteeing the independence and sovereignty of this Republic.[5]

SUPERVISION OF ELECTIONS

In September, 1905, Pablo Arosemena, looking forward to the elections of 1906, stated in a public address that the Panamanian government was morally bound to guarantee free suffrage and that if it failed to do so the Liberals would raise a cry of protest that would be heard by the stars above. He doubted if the United States would unsheathe its sword to uphold an administration that forfeited its prerogative by fostering fraudulent elections. The aged Isthmian appealed to American sentiment by declaring:

It is the sword that Washington brandished in the battle of Yorktown during the war of independence; the sword which Grant flourished at Petersburg for the liberation of the slaves; the same sword which in the battle of San Juan, fighting for the emancipation of Cuba, was borne by the glorious Rough Rider Theodore Roosevelt.[6]

The question of the citizenship of Belisario Porras, a Liberal leader and a prospective candidate for president, had then been brought before the supreme court, allegedly by the Conservatives. The Liberals called a mass meeting for October 1 to protest against this persecution; and Secretary Guardia warned Charles E. Magoon, the American minister and governor of the Canal Zone, that his government feared rioting, and requested Magoon to act according to his discretion. The Panamanian stated: "You can tell when and how a meeting of this kind among our people will open, but no one can tell when and how it will end." The minister gave no assurance of aid, but prepared to bring troops from the Canal Zone into Panama City and gave a reception on September 30 at which he dropped a few hints to several prominent Liberals. The assemblage passed quietly.[7]

On November 5, 1905, Pablo Arosemena, Belisario Porras, Francisco Filos, Eusebio A. Morales, and General Domingo Díaz presented a memorial to Magoon for transmission to the secretary of war. They contended that a majority of the Panamanians belonged to their party, and that the Conservatives illegally prevented them from exercising their power at the polls. The Liberals believed that they must permit the approaching elections to be a farce or face American intervention if they offered resistance. They wanted the following questions answered by Secretary Taft:

1. Does the American Government guarantee public order and constitutional succession in this Republic?

2. Is a government which violates the constitution and laws and attacks the first right of the citizens—that of free suffrage—within the pale of such protection?

3. Granted the possibility—to us an absolute certainty—that in the coming elections all manner of outrages will be committed against the people, will the Government of the United States look on with indifference at the spectacle of a defenseless people at the mercy of those who trample on their rights?

4. Is it not preferable for the United States to adopt while there is yet time such a course as to avoid appearing before the eyes of the world as the champions of outrage and oppression?[8]

On December 4 Secretary of State Elihu Root answered the first question in the negative, thus practically disposing of the others, and instructed Magoon as follows:

The Liberal party should be informed that the Government of the United States, while guaranteeing the independence of the Republic of Panama, does not propose to interfere with that independence. It is the earnest wish of the United States that there shall be a fair, free, and honest election in Panama, because it considers such an election necessary to the peace and prosperity of the country and the stability of its government. As between the two parties, the United States stands in an attitude of perfect impartiality and will do nothing to help either the party in power or the party of opposition. The United States will exercise its rights under the treaty for the maintenance of order in Panama, Colon, and upon the Canal strip, and will not permit any interference with the peace and order of either of those cities or of that territory which can be prevented by the exercise of its treaty rights, and it will not go beyond its treaty rights.[9]

The Liberals received this statement with glee, interpreting it to mean that the United States would not intervene outside of Panama and Colón.[10] Many openly declared that if conditions became intolerable they would organize a revolution in the interior.[11] But first they attempted to gain a place in the government through the mediation of Magoon. Their leaders requested him on December 18 to inform President Amador that, in order to allay political strife, they wished to reach an agreement on the distribution of offices. The Conservatives were agreeable, being somewhat chastened by the Root note, but the Liberals wanted equal representation in the National Assembly, while the Conservatives demanded eighteen of the twenty-eight members. Both desired control in order to elect the *designados* (vice-presidents), for Amador was not likely to live to the end of his term.[12] On that issue the negotiations foundered.

On December 29 President Amador invited the United States government to appoint observers for the approaching election. He explained that he did not fear revolution, but that the prospect of disorder would retard internal development. If the United States did not preserve order, Panama would have to re-establish its army. Amador contended that he desired fair elections, but added:

I tell you candidly that it is quite impossible to change in a day a people who have for years been practicing the election methods heretofore prevailing under the Colombian administration of affairs. I have done and will do all that is possible for me to do in order to make these people understand the value of honesty in politics and political methods, but the political strife in each locality is intense and men anxious to promote their own candidacy and interests will do a great many things which are not right. This is true of both parties, but so far as I am able to prevent it, it will not occur.[13]

In reporting this communication, Magoon stated that Secretary Guardia had informed him that carrying the elections would not be difficult. Since men customarily voted for the party that placed them in office, the government could gain doubtful districts by appointing additional policemen. At the same time the minister wrote Root of the good effect of the answer to the Liberal memorial. The propertied class, which previously had been disposed to depend entirely upon the United States, had been made to realize that it must exert some effort to prevent the growth of revolutionary sentiment. Also a few loud talkers who were inclined to revolutionary utterances because they were sure someone would "hold them" had been silenced. The general feeling had been that Article 136 of the constitution and Articles I and VII of the Canal treaty had authorized the United States to intervene in any part of Panama and that the Washington government had accepted that responsibility. Root had disturbed that belief, and Magoon advised that if the State Department would announce that it would intervene at the request of the recognized constitutional authorities, the government and an overwhelming majority of the inhabitants would be gratified.[14]

On February 21, 1906, Root advised Taft that the United States was bound to assume that Panama would conduct its elections legally, but if any considerable number of persons should assemble for the purpose of violating the election laws or overthrowing the government, the United States would have to consider whether the independence of Panama was imperiled, whether public order was disturbed in the cities of Panama and Colón and their adjacent territories, whether the Panamanian government was able and willing to deal with the emergency, and whether Canal construction and Canal Zone government were endangered. Since these were military questions, Taft was requested to instruct Magoon as to the time and conditions under which the forces of the United States might be used to re-establish peace and order in the Republic of Panama. Root reminded his colleague, however, that Articles I and VII did not relieve the Panamanian government of responsibility nor place it upon the Washington government.[15]

Party feeling became increasingly bitter and serious disorder was predicted.[16] One orator declared at the Santiago Liberal convention: "You must remember, gentlemen, that the stronghold of the Government was Article 136 of the Constitution, and that the reply of the United States to the Liberal memorial has annihilated this stronghold, as the Japanese projectiles destroyed the haughty fleet of Russia," and warned the government that if it obstinately persisted in its preference for a body of myrmidons rather than a National Assembly of independent men, and resorted to fraudulent elections, the Liberals would appeal to their last resource—revolution—against their deep-rooted desire to maintain internal peace.[17] In March the *Star and Herald* printed an open letter by J. D. Arosemena, accusing Root of being a "powerful contributor" to the fact that war on the Isthmus was being spoken of as the most natural thing on earth. Previous to the emission of the note of December 4, no one had thought of armed conflict because of fear of the American legions. After the note, trouble was being fomented because of the belief that the United States would not interfere outside of the cities of Panama and Colón.[18] Late in the month Guardia informed Chargé W. F. Sands that he had threatened to repress with severity any attempts of the Liberals at disorder. Especially would he have no mercy on Porras and Morales. He regretted that the State Department had not declared plainly that the right of revolution to which the Liberals so often alluded was not recognized, and he could not understand the answer, which had worked so much harm to the administration, of Root to the Liberal memorial. Sands opined that the people of Panama had not yet understood the policy of the United States.[19]

On April 26 Taft instructed Magoon that the note of December 4 was not intended to restrict the rights of the United States, but was meant to emphasize the dignity and sovereignty of Panama and to impress upon it the duty of maintaining its own peace and good order. He bluntly dismissed the fears and hopes of revolution by stating:

I have no hesitation whatever in saying that in my judgment an insurrection in any part of the Republic would disturb order in Panama and Colon and adjacent territory, and would greatly increase the difficulties that the United States would have in constructing the canal; and while, of course, the forces of our Government ought not to intervene until it is established that the Republic of Panama can not maintain order in its own territory, I think the United States may properly, under the clauses of the treaty construed in the light of the provision of the constitution of Panama . . . and to prevent its inevitable interference with the work of canal construction, suppress any insurrection in any part of the Republic. Of course, such action taken with respect to an independent government, even with its consent given in its fundamental law, ought not to be lightly taken, or until all the circumstances are known, until it is fully established that the Government of Panama is not able to maintain itself. Of this, a request by the President of Panama for our intervention to suppress an insurrection would be the best evidence. If this fact does not appear, then the duty of our Government will be plain.[20]

This despatch and the Root note of February 21 were transmitted to the Panamanian government on May 9,[21] and both were carried on the following day by the Isthmian press. Their publication caused the administration great elation and gave the opposition corresponding disappointment and chagrin.[22] The government expressed appreciation that the position of the United States had assured the maintenance of peace in the republic.[23]

The Liberals then sent Pablo Arosemena, Belisario Porras, Eusebio A. Morales, and General Domingo Díaz to Washington to induce the American government to intervene. Through an influential friend they obtained an appointment with Root and Taft. According to the highly colored version of Porras, the Panamanians arrived first on the appointed day in the reception room of the State Department. Root, a cold serious man without the slightest smile or the faintest facial expression, immediately appeared. He was followed a moment later by the kindly looking Taft. Soon the Panamanians were laughing at the witty remarks of Taft and were thinking of the wonderful character of the Americans. Root "remained silent, serious, cold, his lips tight shut, his eyes expressionless. . . ." Arosemena, the spokesman, began to tell of the tyranny of the Amador administration, of its cruel persecution of political enemies, of its violation of the law and the rights of citizens, and of voting lists full of the names of dead men. He painted the atrocities of the Amador régime in such vivid colors that his companions were confident of success. When he had concluded, Root looked at him blankly and fixedly. Arosemena became disconcerted. The secretary turned his gaze to Díaz, who blushed. Morales offered resistance, but succumbed. Porras, the fourth victim, felt that the glance of Root penetrated his very soul. Taft smiled and looked quietly at the Panamanians. Root then returned to Arosemena, indicated that he believed his story, and remarked that conditions were indeed deplorable. Again he stared intently at the committee. Taft continued to smile and look kindly. Root explained that despite the best wishes of the United States for an orderly republic the Panamanians would have to solve their own difficulties. He stared again, and Taft smiled with the greatest kindness. Root continued:

The day when the Government of the United States appoints citizens of this country as its agents in the territory of the little Republic of Panama and pays them from its Treasury and gives them instructions to intervene in whatever debates about the electoral or civil right the Panamanian citizens have, in order that such agents may solve them, on that day you will have lost your sovereignty.[24]

The Americans then withdrew for conference, but soon returned for the response of the committee. Arosemena made another effort to bring up the abuses, but Root interrupted: "Then the remedy lies with you yourselves. Offer civic resistance and you will prevail in the end." While Taft smiled in a mischievous manner, the Panamanians arose to leave. As they went out, "Taft was about to burst out laughing, but the great Elihu Root remained serene, calm, cold, [and] impassible."[25]

The return of the committee to Panama on June 20 was partly responsible for a request from the Amador administration that three hundred marines be moved nearer from Camp Elliott to Corozal and that 250 rifles and 50,000 rounds of ammunition be released from storage in the Canal Zone. Fifty American police were stationed in Cristóbal, and the *Columbia* was in the Colón Harbor. The Liberal demonstration at the railway station passed quietly.

Minister Magoon was constantly moving around in Panama City on June 24, the day of the municipal elections. During the morning Pablo Arosemena made an excited protest that the government was having its police vote repeatedly. Magoon spoke soothing words to the men at the police headquarters, visited the polling places, and received numerous Liberal complaints. All was tranquil until the afternoon when a Liberal received a Conservative bullet in return for a blow over the head with a cane. The Liberals began to cry that their opponents had drawn first blood, and many went home for their guns. The American minister met them marching in great excitement from Santa Ana to Cathedral Plaza. They were shouting that the government had robbed them and that they had voted in vain. Arosemena tried to speak from the Cathedral steps of the chicanery of the administration. Ramón Arias, immediately calling him a liar, was promptly knocked down by a Liberal. Arias was removed from the scene by Canal Zone police dressed in plain clothes. The excitement quieted, but after the polls were closed at four o'clock the Conservatives began to taunt the defeated Liberals. An ugly crowd started gathering in Santa Ana Plaza. Magoon hurried there, receiving the plaudits of the people as he passed. He stopped at the police station and asked that no force be sent out until he returned. At different points on the Plaza he found General Díaz and *Alcalde* Ossa and requested them to disperse their partisans. He felt that trouble could be averted if the mass scattered, but prompt action was not obtained.

The throwing of stones by street urchins soon started a fight, Ossa attempted to separate the combatants with his riding crop, and a Negro Liberal leader struck him. Ossa ordered the police to clear the square. As they came upon the scene, they were fired upon from the home of Porras, who was absent in the interior. The firing continued about an hour; three were killed and twelve wounded. Magoon reported that he received his first knowledge of hostilities when he "was given a realizing sense that rifle bullets were coming down the Central Avenue in an opposite direction" and that he returned to his office by side streets.[26]

On the following day the American minister attempted to effect a compromise between the two parties, but the leaders were too angry to entertain any suggestion. He then instructed military officials to make a conspicuous tour of Panama City and Colón. They let it be known that they were reconnoitering in anticipation of bringing in the marines for the next election. Toward the end of the week both sides were ready to agree, and decided that each should elect three members from the province of Panama to the National Assembly. However, time was insufficient to arrange fusion tickets in the other provinces. The election passed quietly. Many Liberals refused to vote, and the Conservatives obtained twenty-five of the twenty-eight places in the national legislature.[27]

An intense political campaign in 1908 led to the first American supervision of Panamanian elections. Following charges of fraudulent registration made by the *Coalición Republicana*, composed of Liberals and Conservatives, against the *Constitucional* party,[28] Foreign Secretary Ricardo Arias appealed to the United States on May 15, 1908, for aid in holding fair elections. Each party had accused the other of fraud. He pointed to the

vast interests of the United States in the Canal Zone that should
not be disturbed by election disorders. The Washington government was invited to appoint members to a joint commission for
investigating complaints. The Panamanian government promised to correct any abuses that might be discovered.[29] The
United States immediately accepted the invitation and named
two commissioners for each of the seven provinces.[30] The regular electoral machinery continued its functions; the commission
was merely to hear complaints.[31] While the party in power
technically requested supervision, a cabinet officer charged that
the interference resulted from the efforts of the opposition and
had become a "sorrowful episode" and a humiliation to Panama.[32] So bitterly did the administration resent the intervention that it refused to go to the polls. President Amador did
not attend the inauguration of his successor, José Domingo de
Obaldía, on October 1, 1908.[33]

In 1912 excitement and party spirit ran high in the Republic
of Panama. A fierce presidential contest arose between the
Unión Patriótica, composed mostly of the Conservatives in
power who backed Pedro A. Díaz, and the Liberal opposition
which supported Belisario Porras. The Liberals appealed to
the United States to supervise registration and the municipal
and national elections of June 30 and July 14.[34] A similar
request alleging that the Liberals were padding the voting lists
followed from the *Unión Patriótica* and from President Pablo
Arosemena.[35] The Washington government agreed on May 10
to supervise registration and both elections.[36] American officials and representatives of both parties then perfected plans.[37]
Thirteen army officers were assigned to register the voters.[38]
They discovered numerous instances of law violation and were
much berated by the government.[39] The United States subsequently provided nearly two hundred soldiers and Canal Zone
employees for overseeing the voting.[40] In spite of all the
efforts of the party in power, the Porras candidates were successful in the municipal election.[41] The defeated party vehe-
mently charged that the Americans favored the Liberals. The
supervisors reported that without their services the adminis-

tration would have imposed its candidates.[42] Minister F. Percival Dodge stated that the allegations of the government were untrue and based on its inability to control the election.[43] Soon the *Unión Patriótica,* confronted with certain defeat, issued a long manifesto accusing the American supervisors of fraud and partiality and withdrawing its candidate.[44] Porras was then elected in an orderly and satisfactory manner.[45] Consequently intense bitterness was aroused against the supervisors and to some extent against Americans in general.[46]

In 1916 the factions of the Liberal and Conservative parties which supported Rodolfo Chiari, the opposition candidate for president, asked for electoral supervision similar to that of 1912. On May 6 Minister William Jennings Price informed the Panamanian government that the United States was disposed to superintend the elections if the administration desired it.[47] President Porras rejected the offer on the grounds that supervision was neither necessary nor justifiable at the time and that it strengthened the opposition and encouraged it to menace the authorities and threaten public peace. The government called attention to the charges of fraud in 1912 against the American supervisors, expressed appreciation for the interest of the United States, and definitely refused its intervention.[48] Despite the assurance of Porras that the election would be fair, the opposition refused to attend the polls. A riot marred the election of June 25, but the massing of American forces on the boundary line probably prevented further trouble.[49] Ramón M. Valdés, the government candidate, was elected president without opposition.[50]

The question of supervision arose again in 1918. President Valdés died on June 3, and Ciro L. Urriola, the first *designado,* succeeded him.[51] The new administration probably feared that it would be unable to gain a majority in the National Assembly, and issued a decree postponing the municipal and the national elections.[52] The Washington government expressed doubt as to the constitutionality of the decree and, invoking Article 136 of the constitution, asked that it be withdrawn.[53] Conditions had been so grave for weeks that American soldiers were forbidden to visit Panamanian territory.[54] Urriola claimed that the elections had been postponed beause of the turbulent state of affairs in the country; the opposition protested that they should be held without delay.[55] On the afternoon of June 28 American troops marched into the cities of Panama and Colón and assumed control under Article VII of the Hay-Bunau-Varilla Treaty.[56] Urriola cabled Woodrow Wilson: "I protest this interference, which violates the sovereignty of Panama without any justification, inasmuch as the Government of Panama has sufficient means to maintain public order in these cities, and I decline to share with Your Excellency's Government the responsibilties so grave an action implies."[57]

The municipal elections of June 30 were held without disorder.[58] After the United States agreed to supervise the national election without expense, the government repealed the decree on July 2.[59] The American legation then announced that army officers from the Canal Zone would act as observers at the request of both parties.[60] The opposition gained a majority in the National Assembly, but the government contested a number of decisions and requested that the American electoral commission decide the disputes. Toward the end of August the American chargé gave a partial report of the findings of the committee and urged the National Assembly to elect Ricardo Arias president. The final judgment was that the government had won a majority of the National Assembly.[61] Belisario Porras was elected first and Pedro A. Díaz second *designado*. Díaz assumed the presidency on October 1 and was succeeded by Porras, as soon as he returned from the United States, on October 12.[62]

President Porras resigned in January, 1920, to run for re-election to the regular term beginning October 1. He was replaced by *Designado* Ernesto T. Lefevre.[63] Ciro L. Urriola opposed Porras and appealed to the State Department for intervention, claiming that his opponent was not eligible for the office and that unfair elections were likely. When no favorable response was received from Washington, the *Urriolistas* were instructed to ignore the election. Urriola charged that the *vota-*

ción would be a ridiculous farce, and Porras replied that Urriola was acting foolishly. Porras was elected almost unanimously in one of the quietest elections in the history of the republic.[64]

In preparation for the presidential contest of 1924 *El Tiempo* printed on March 20, 1923, a long note addressed to the Washington government through the American minister and the Canal Zone governor. Attention was called to the fact that Porras had obtained only twenty thousand votes in 1920 as a proof that a great number of the people were prevented from exercising their suffrage, the systems used to evade the electoral laws were described minutely, and complaint was made that after Porras attained power he had refused to alter the laws so that citizens might vote without hindrance. The United States was entreated to use its influence to bring about a modification of the atrocious Panamanian electoral methods and was warned:

Bear in mind, Sirs, that if the Government of the United States of America does not recognize in the proud and patriotic people of Panama the right to resort to revolution, which is the last means of obtaining justice, then that Government cannot and should not leave at liberty and even surround with security those who preside over the destinies of this country so that they might strangle the will of the people with the help of an iniquitous election law evidently drafted for that purpose.[65]

As the election approached, Jeptha B. Duncan and Papi Aizpuru went to Washington on matters pertaining to intervention. Minister Alfaro reported, after an interview with the chief of the Latin American division of the State Department, that the United States neither desired nor intended to intervene.[66] The Washington government remained aloof and permitted the Panamanians to manage their own affairs. Rodolfo Chiari, the Liberal candidate, defeated General Manuel Quintero V., the commander of the Panamanian army at Coto and the leader of the opposition, for the presidency in an election of *orden perfecto*.[67]

On December 15, 1927, Minister Horacio F. Alfaro accompanied Belisario Porras on a visit to the State Department, where Porras requested that the United States supervise the elections of 1928, and filed documents in support of his supplication. Alfaro also left a note asking information as to the attitude of the Washington government in regard to supervision or interference in the internal affairs of the Republic of Panama. His government wished to know if the Root notes of December 4, 1905, and February 21, 1906, and the Taft declaration of April 26, 1906, continued to be the policy of the United States.[68] Secretary of State Frank B. Kellogg answered on December 23 as follows:

In reply I am pleased to inform you that the policy outlined in the communication referred to above continues to be the policy of this Government. As stated in substance by Secretary Root, the primary duty to maintain order and to enforce the election laws devolves upon Panama. As between the two parties, the United States will maintain absolute impartiality and will not, directly or indirectly, lend support to any candidate for president or any other office. The United States will, of course, carry out its treaty obligation guaranteeing to maintain the independence of Panama, and will exercise the treaty right to maintain order in Panama, Colon and the territories and harbors adjacent thereto but it does not intend to supervise the election in Panama. Of course, it is the earnest wish of the United States that there shall be a free, fair and honest election in Panama, as such elections are necessary to the peace and prosperity of the state, but the United States cannot assume the primary obligation of supervising the election.[69]

Jorge E. Boyd, the *Unión Coalición* or *Porrista* candidate for president, sailed for the United States in June. His opponents claimed that his purpose was to ask the intervention of the American government, but Boyd explained that he was accompanying his wife on a visit with her family.[70] Whatever the quest of the Panamanian in the United States, Kellogg stated on July 27 that interference was unwarranted, reminded Panama of its obligation to conduct a fair and free election, and pointed out that Alfaro had promised that his government would administer the electoral laws in a scrupulously impartial manner. He concluded:

The opposition party has stated that unless there is intervention by this Government revolutionary activities will ensue. The Department sincerely trusts that such counsel will not prevail. Nevertheless, should such a lamentable situation arise, the Department believes the Panama Government will be able to preserve public order. Should this, unfortunately, not be the case, the United States would be compelled to exercise the power granted under the treaty and the Constitution to maintain order.[71]

Boyd stated from Washington that this declaration meant that the American government would become the sponsor and underwriter of the group then in power and of their self-designated successors and warned:

The new policy which the Secretary of State is taking toward my country bodes ill for the future of Panama. Another four years of extravagance and gross corruption such as characterizes the present regime can only lead to National bankruptcy. We may be faced, not with American good offices, but with full-fledged intervention for the purpose of protecting American bondholders.[72]

After the government had arrested a number of important members of the opposition,[73] Porras issued a manifesto withdrawing the candidacy of Boyd and stating that the refusal of the Washington government to intervene was beyond his comprehension.[74] The election passed quietly on August 5. The Liberal candidate, Florencio H. Arosemena, supported by the Chiari administration, was elected almost unanimously with over forty thousand votes.[75]

None of the three parties which named presidential candidates in 1932 sought the intervention of the United States. In fact, American interference seems to have become odious to all factions and parties. For the first time the use of intervention as a campaign issue probably received no serious thought. The extent of American participation was the sale by the Canal Zone government to the republic of some worthless dye for coloring the index fingers of the Panamanians as they voted in order that they might not absent-mindedly exercise the privilege of suffrage more than once.[76]

INTERVENTION TO SUPPRESS OTHER DISORDERS

Aside from the attempts of the United States to preserve order during Panamanian elections, the Washington government has held continually, or been forced to hold, the threat of intervention over the Isthmians to prevent rioting and revolution from other causes. The brutality of the Panamanian police during the early years of the republic; the disorderly conduct of Canal Zone employees and American soldiers and sailors; and the turbulent spirit, born of centuries of conflict and confusion, of the Isthmian people have caused incessant trouble. The Panamanian and American governments were able to rid the republic of its army in 1904, but found no practical way to provide an efficient police force composed of Panamanian citizens.

On May 25, 1904, the United States and the Republic of Panama signed a general extradition treaty covering all crimes except those of a political nature. This was necessary because the territory of Panama bordered on the Canal Zone on both sides and would have provided a refuge for its criminals. However, prisoners were being extradited by courtesy before ratifications were exchanged on April 8, 1905.[77]

The Panamanian government co-operated with the United States in preventing disorder during the Panama Railroad strike in 1904.[78] On April 27, 1905, an American foreman called the Panamanian police to subdue two hundred Jamaicans who refused to work because of the poor quality of their food, and the result was an attack upon the defenseless Negroes by fifty armed policemen. Minister Barrett believed that both sides were at fault, but requested the Panamanian government to take steps to prevent a recurrence of the brutality.[79] On October 1, 1905, the Panamanian police assisted the Canal Zone police in forcing a group of Martinique Negroes, frightened witless by the prospect of vaccination and other rumored horrors, to disembark from the *Versailles* which had brought them to Panama for Canal construction work.[80]

Early in 1905 Samuel Davis, an American, was engaged as police instructor by the Panamanian government with the hope that he might improve the police force, which was characterized as a band of guerrilla fighters. Davis soon succumbed to yellow fever and was succeeded by George W. Jiménez, formerly of the New York police.[81] Both men tried earnestly to build an efficient police corps, but were hampered by the "ignorance, ill-will, and worse" of Panamanian officials. The chief difficulty that confronted Jiménez was *Alcalde* Francisco de la Ossa, who was reported to have opposed any attempt to substitute law for his despotic and arbitrary rule of Panama City. Since Ossa was related to President Amador, Jiménez was unsuccessful.[82]

In 1906 Chargé Sands reported a noticeable tendency of the Panamanian police to use unnecessary violence in making arrests. He believed that leniency should be shown the Panamanians, but that Panama should be required to give Americans every security and advantage afforded by model republics. He thought neither the police nor the courts more than poor excuses, but explained that the conditions were more or less natural because of years of violence and corruption. The low pay attracted police only from the poorest class, and both men and officers had been trained to arrest for political reasons or no cause at all. Neither the police nor the people thought anything of arbitrary imprisonment. Sands advised that the United States should exert pressure before the police became such a menace as the army had been.[83]

Early in June, 1906, the Colón police perpetrated a brutal attack on three sailors of the United States cruiser *Columbia*.[84] The men perhaps were unjustly arrested in the *luz roja* (red-light) district and were severely beaten in a general mêlée at the police station. They were charged with attacking an officer,[85] but the facts in the case did not seem to justify the brutality of the ignorant and ill-trained policemen. The American officials had considerable difficulty in getting the men released and in having the charges against them in the Panamanian civil courts dropped.[86] After a thorough investigation the State Department demanded indemnity for the injured men, and for the policemen responsible punishment so severe as to prevent future attacks.[87] At the request of Minister Magoon,[88] three officers

and six men of the Colón force were transferred to the interior
and their places filled with English-speaking men from Panama
City. The American inhabitants of Colón and Cristóbal were
then reported to be in a much better frame of mind.[89]

Magoon explained that the attack was not due to anti-
American feeling, but that Central Americans were prone to
exhibitions of sudden and uncontrollable rage. He admitted,
however, that considerable friction existed between the Americans of Colón and Cristóbal and the Colón police. Their
natural racial antipathy had been intensified because most of
the Americans were Southerners who made no distinction between Panamanians and Negroes. The Americans were not
wholly to blame for the animosity, because the Colón police
were far enough away from the restraining influence of Panama
City to be devoid of discipline. The outbreak had been smouldering for some time, and the attack on the sailors was only a
culmination of the general ill-feeling.[90]

During an altercation between sailors of the *Buffalo* and
citizens of Panama City on September 28, 1908, Charles Rand
was killed and Joseph Cieslik was seriously wounded. The
American government charged the police with maltreatment and
brutality and claimed that Rand's death was caused by their
negligence.[91] As a result of this and previous difficulties, the
Washington government demanded assurance from the Panamanian government that American sailors would be protected
in the future from abuses and disorders. Since conditions required the American fleet to visit Panama and the cruiser squadron would be there November 12, the republic was warned that
if the guarantee had not been made by November 11 the
president of the United States would

. . . consider it his duty to direct the officer in command of the
fleet to land from his ships a sufficient force, under arms, to maintain
order in the city of Panama and anywhere else on the Isthmus where
necessary, to protect the men while in transit or on shore leave in
the exercise of the authority assured to the United States by the terms
of the treaty between Panama and the United States.[92]

Finally, in 1908, Panama gave the United States permission to establish patrols in the cities of Panama and Colón for the purpose of preventing clashes between American service men and Panamanians.[93] This action helped in the preservation of order, but has not prevented occasional riots. The patrols have even been attacked.

The State Department continued to press the indemnity demand for the *Columbia* affair and added greater claims for the outrages against the sailors of the *Buffalo*. Eventually on July 31, 1909, the Panamanian government paid $5,000 for the *Columbia* crime, $8,000 for the death of Rand, and $1,000 to assuage the healed wounds of Cieslik.[94] That $14,000 would have been a far better investment if it had been devoted to the improvement of the Panamanian police force.

On July 4, 1912, a riot occurred between Americans and Panamanians in Cocoa Grove, *un distrito de luz roja de Panamá*, in which one American was killed and nineteen injured. The Washington government again charged the police with brutality and demanded the dismissal of the chief and the inspector general, who were "responsible for the personnel and consequent dangerous character of the force."[95] The Panamanian government was reluctant to comply with the demands of the State Department and delayed until August 31, when Minister Dodge called for the immediate discharge of the two officers and delivered the following ultimatum:

... unless the Panaman police is so reorganized as properly to insure in Panama City, Colon, and the harbors and territories adjacent to them the maintenance of public order, the Government of the United States will find it necessary to consider the immediate measures which must be taken by it in connection with the duties, obligations, and rights which appertain to it in this matter.[96]

The United States further demanded indemnity for the wounded and especially for the death of Ralph W. Davis, a civilian.[97] The Panamanian government was informed that the conclusion had been reached that the brutal and criminal conduct of its police was responsible for the deplorable affair.

Foreign Secretary Ernesto T. Lefevre indignantly demanded proof of this charge.[98] Minister Price continued to seek payment of the damages, explaining that the families of the victims and their congressmen were more insistent. He stated that the United States had been patient and indulgent, but had waited long enough.[99] The Panamanian government reached the conclusion that the disorder was caused by drunken American soldiers and sailors, and absolved its police force.[100] Price expressed surprise at this and called attention to the fact that his government had made its demands without passion and after a careful investigation. The dilatory conduct of Panama had created the disagreeable impression that the republic did not wish to comply with its international obligations. The decision that the Americans were responsible for the riot was characterized as a denegation of justice and an indication that Panama was unwilling to treat the matter fairly and justly.[101]

Negotiations dragged on until April, 1915, when Panama offered to place American policemen in charge of the *distrito de luz roja* of Panama and Colón to prevent future trouble,[102] and to submit the question of indemnity to any diplomatic agent accredited to Panama that the United States might designate.[103] The resistance of the Panamanian government was broken down finally, and a protocol was signed November 27, 1915, naming W. L. F. C. van Rappard, the minister from The Netherlands to the United States and Panama, to decide the amount of the damages.[104] Accordingly, a total of $12,350 was awarded on October 20, 1916, for the death of Davis and injuries of sixteen others.[105] Panama closed the disagreeable episode by paying the award on December 9.[106]

Before the riot of 1912 was settled, several clashes occurred to clutter diplomatic channels between the two nations. After a minor fray between sailors from the *Terry* and Panama City police on January 23, 1913, the Panamanian government reminded the American legation that the ship had neglected to abide by Panama's request that patrols be supplied when forces of the United States disembarked on its territory.[107] After brawls between American soldiers and Panamanian police on

May 23 and May 27, 1914, the Panamanian government asked the Washington government to compel its soldiers to obey the law while on Panamanian soil.[108]   Minister Price replied that the national police neither had nor merited the respect of Americans and that their lack of ability, discipline, and coolness was the principal cause of numerous disorders in Panama and Colón.[109]

Another serious clash occurred in Cocoa Grove in the early hours of the morning of February 14, 1915. About twenty American soldiers and a similar number of Panamanians were wounded. Price explained that the trouble was caused by the ignorance, excitability, and lack of control of the police.[110] This affray had hardly quieted when a riot broke out in Colón on the afternoon of April 2. About twelve hundred American soldiers were attending a baseball game there between two American teams. Trouble started on the streets between soldiers and a Negro. A policeman was struck with a swagger stick; an attempt was made to arrest a soldier; he and his comrades resisted; the police shot two privates. Later as the men left the ball park, Negroes again caused disorder. The American officers immediately got the men in hand and marched them to their special train, but the police were aroused sufficiently to begin indiscriminate firing. Another man was wounded, and Corporal Charles M. Langdon was killed, while in charge of an American patrol.[111] The action of the police was described as unjustifiable, reckless, and unprovoked, and the Panamanian government was warned that, unless settlement was made for the outrage and action taken to prevent its repetition, the United States might take over the police forces of Panama and Colón. Secretary Ernesto T. Lefevre protested that such action would deprive the Republic of Panama of its sovereignty.[112]   Price reported that he was convinced that Panama would use its usual dilatory tactics and that the offenders would not be prosecuted if the United States did not threaten to occupy Panama and Colón.[113]

Negotiations customarily dragged on, and the Panamanian government indicated no desire to punish the two policemen arrested in connection with the death of Langdon. The United States demanded $15,000 for his heirs and $1,000 for each of the wounded. On August 20, 1917, Price was still trying to collect,[114] and Secretary Garay stated that his government had an equal right to demand indemnity for the Panamanian victims of the mêlée. He claimed that Panama could not be held responsible because the American patrol had been insufficient to prevent the outbreak.[115] On October 8, 1918, Price repeated a demand for $10,000 for damages arising from the Cocoa Grove brawl of February 14, 1915. He again gave a long account of the affair and called special attention to the fact that the police were armed with rifles and bayonets.[116] Negotiations were pressed until Panama agreed to submit both cases to arbitration.[117] Neither affair was settled until 1933, when, under the claims convention of 1926 as amended on December 17, 1932, $2,000 was paid for the death of Langdon and $14,500 for the Cocoa Grove trouble.[118]

The Washington government was not satisfied with demanding the punishment of offenders and the payment of indemnities. On August 15, 1915, Price was instructed to urge the Panamanian government to disarm its police of high-powered rifles and to enforce the law prohibiting the bearing of concealed weapons.[119] Governor George W. Goethals advised that the rifles be stored in the Canal Zone,[120] but the Panamanians promised that the guns would no longer be used in municipal service and in no circumstances where Americans were concerned.[121] The Panamanian government was bitterly opposed to the idea of surrendering the rifles, and Lefevre stated that the United States might come and take them, but that no voluntary compliance could be expected.[122] Price reported that Lefevre

. . . felt that Panama was being imposed upon; that little by little their sovereignty was being usurped or appropriated by our Government; that if their dignity and rights would not be respected they would better yield up to a superior power their entity as a government and make known their cause to the world; that they had given up their army several years ago and that the bearing of larger arms by their police was the only symbol of the military retained by them; that he did not suppose we would claim the right to forbid them to organize a small military force or army, who could carry rifles, if they should be taken from the police; that the attitude of their political opponents and the capital they might make of it should be taken into consideration by us, if they should yield to our demands; that Panama was willing to submit this matter and other important matters pending between our respective Governments to representatives of the A. B. C. Alliance for arbitration or determination.[123]

The State Department postponed action until a police patrol armed with rifles attended a fire in Panama City on January 12, 1916.[124] This incident provided a fulcrum for a general demand for the immediate disarmament of the police of the cities of Panama and Colón of high-powered rifles. Panama was again advised to store the weapons in the Canal Zone for delivery only in cases of necessity. If the American military authorities did not object, a few guns might be retained for the presidential guard of honor.[125] The Panamanian government demurred, and on May 12 the State Department cabled Price: "You will immediately inform the Government of Panama that this Government expects immediate compliance with its demand for the complete disarmament of the police in Panama and Colon of high-powered rifles."[126] On the following day Lefevre indicated that the weapons would be delivered and requested that the Washington government be notified that this was done under protest and because Panama was unable to resist. The outcome caused a mild sensation in Panama City, but no ugly incidents.[127] One hundred rifles were retained for prison service until the arrival of 125 shotguns ordered by Governor Goethals. The Panamanians wanted 120 rifles for the presidential guard, then 50, but were refused more than 25. Delivery was completed by May 15, 1916,[128] and the guns were disposed of later in the United States.

After a clash between service men and Panamanians in Colón on May 27, 1917, Panama suggested that the number of sailors landing at one time be limited.[129] The United States was further requested to establish a *cuartel* in the *Barrio Rojo* of Colón similar to the one in Panama City.[130] The Washington government refused to place police in the *Barrio Rojo* on the grounds that the Canal Zone police and soldiers in Cristóbal were sufficiently near.[131]

In connection with the general disorder and the occupation of the cities of Panama and Colón, and because of the belief that American lives and property were endangered, the United States sent troops into the province of Chiriquí in July, 1918, and did not withdraw them until August 16, 1920.[132] Panama protested bitterly that the continued occupation of Chiriquí was a violation of its sovereignty, and claimed that the Canal treaty only authorized interference in Panama and Colón. The United States was asked to remove the soldiers after the new administration supposedly provided adequate protection for foreigners.[133]   The State Department announced on February 18, 1919, that a careful study failed to show that the removal of the troops was warranted, but that they would be removed as soon as the local government insured the protection of Americans and other foreigners. Attention was called to the rights conferred by Article I of the Hay-Bunau-Varilla Treaty and Article 136 of the Panamanian constitution to show that the occupation was legal.[134]

Panama contended that Article I of the treaty only provided protection from foreign invasion and that Article 136 did no more than authorize its president to ask American co-operation. Would the State Department please advise as to the meaning of public peace and constitutional order and state the reason for American troops in David?[135]   The reply was that troops were in Chiriquí because of the lack of protection to American citizens and their property and because foreigners had received little or no protection there.   Again the promise was made that the soldiers would be retired as soon as adequate safeguards were provided.[136]   The Panamanian legation immediately requested the name of any American citizen being offered little or no protection.[137]   In refutation of the claim that the occupation of Chiriquí was justified by Article I Chargé José E. Lefevre called attention to the meaning of the word "independence" as given by *Webster's International Dictionary*, and reiterated the contention that the treaty only authorized intervention in the cities of Panama and Colón.[138] The State Department remained adamant.[139]

Soon a new source of complaint arose. After another outbreak between Americans and Panamanians, the officer in charge of the troops posted a notice asserting that as long as certain named culprits refused to recognize and obey the law the American soldiers would remain in Chiriquí, whether this be one year, ten years, or forever.[140] When a protest against the action of the officer made no impression, Panama began to complain that the soldiers were disorderly, that their sojourn in Chiriquí was affecting their morals and discipline, and that they were setting bad examples for the natives.[141] A report was circulated that the soldiers broke into the post-office at David and opened the mail pouches to get their mail. Their excuse was that the postal officials did not provide prompt and efficient service.[142] The act cannot be condoned, but may be better understood in the light of the saying in Panama that no one need call for mail if the postmaster is sitting down.[143] Repeated requests for the removal of the troops, allusions to the friendship and co-operation of Panama with the United States, and the attempts of Panama to improve conditions finally resulted in the withdrawal of the American soldiers from Chiriquí on August 16, 1920, after an occupation of more than two years.[144]

The second intervention of American troops in Panama City resulted from a reported statement of President Porras in 1921 that war with Costa Rica over the land on the Pacific involved in the boundary dispute would be an absurdity. The country was in a fever of excitement over the attempt of Costa Rica to occupy the area around Coto. A committee of citizens visited the president on February 28 and unsuccessfully demanded his resignation.[145] Later in the day a mob gathered before the presidential palace. The American minister was in conference with Porras, and apparently at his oral request called for troops from the Canal Zone. The palace was attacked before the soldiers arrived; but they speedily restored order and, despite a demand for their immediate withdrawal, guarded the president throughout the night in accordance with the provisions of Article VII of the Hay-Bunau-Varilla Treaty.[146]   The Panamanians were soon united in their attempt to repel the invader, the necessity for intervention passed quickly, and the American troops were retired within two weeks.[147]

In 1921 the Republic of Panama made an effort to limit the power of the United States to intervene in its territory. The alleged right of the Washington government to occupy Panamanian territory under Article I of the Canal treaty was attacked.   Secretary Garay stated: "If the United States had the right to occupy the territory of the Republic without the authorization of our Government, the guarantee in the treaty would not be of independence but of absolute subjection."[148] After a controversy with the Canal Zone governor in 1922 the Panamanian government declared that the United States could not invoke Article VII of the treaty until disorder had actually occurred.   The State Department was asked for a written interpretation of its meaning.   Secretary Charles E. Hughes answered that the clause was difficult to interpret in advance, but that the Washington government would believe public order had not been maintained in Panama and Colón if a situation should arise which might endanger the tranquility of the Canal Zone or the lives and property of foreigners within the two cities.[149]

The Republic of Panama contends that under Article I of the Hay-Bunau-Varilla Treaty the United States may intervene only to protect it from foreign aggression; the United States claims that it may intervene to protect the independence of Panama even against its own citizens.   Panama holds that Article 136 of its constitution is not an international agreement and that it merely authorizes the president to invite intervention in cases of necessity.   Panama maintains that under Article VII of the treaty the United States may interfere only after the actual outbreak of disorder, whereas the Washington government interprets that article to mean that it is privileged to intervene at any time the public peace is threatened.

In February, 1925, the San Blas Indians went on the warpath, and it appeared for a time that the United States would have to quell the uprising. The abuses of Negro policemen among the natives were partly responsible for the outbreak that claimed the lives of more than a score of police, several Indians considered traitors, and a number of *zambo* children.[150] Approximately thirty thousand Indians inhabited the disturbed area,[151] and the Panamanian government charged that they were being incited to rebellion by an American adventurer, Richard O. Marsh.[152] Minister J. G. South accompanied officials of the republic to the seat of the disturbance on the cruiser *Cleveland* and witnessed the signing of a peace pact on March 4, 1925.[153] The American agitator took refuge on the vessel, and for that reason the Panamanian government was unable to bring him to justice.[154]

The first formal request for American occupation of Panamanian territory arose from the rent riots of Panama City in 1925. Probably the possession of a large part of Panama and Colón by the Panama Railroad Company played some part in creating unfavorable conditions.[155] The workers of Panama City, allegedly led by radical agitators, demanded lower rents, and their activities culminated in serious and bloody rioting on October 10 and 11. After a conference between President Rodolfo Chiari and American officials the Panamanian government formally requested the aid of troops from the Canal Zone.[156] On the afternoon of October 12 about six hundred soldiers marched with fixed bayonets into Panama City. Conditions had become so turbulent by that time that traffic was suspended, practically all business houses closed, and the streets were filled with disorderly masses. A large mob was speedily dispersed, and the efforts of the strikers to cut telephone lines laid by the troops and to shut off the water supply were frustrated. The square before the government buildings was soon commanded by American machine guns, and the situation was well in hand within a few hours. Most of the soldiers were withdrawn on October 15 and the remainder on October 23.[157]

After the United States refused to interfere in the election of 1928 Florencio H. Arosemena was chosen president almost by default. Discontent rose steadily during his administration, and considerable trouble was caused by Secretary of Public Instruction Jeptha B. Duncan in 1930.[158] Out of charges of fraud, gross corruption, extravagance, and illegal attempts of the Arosemena government to perpetuate itself in power sprang a revolution in the early hours of the morning of January 2, 1931.[159] Notwithstanding the warning of Secretary Kellogg in 1928 that the Panamanians would be permitted no revolutionary privileges, which drew from one American commentator the remark, "Thus, the State Department is playing its old game of underwriting abuse, and the honest citizens of Panama are simply knocking their heads against a stone wall,"[160] the *Acción Comunal*, composed of several hundred young men, stormed and carried the police station and the presidential palace about 2:30 in the morning of January 2. By daylight Arosemena and most of the important government officials had been seized, and Panama City was quiet before nine o'clock. The only American casualty was a newspaper man, Hartwell F. Ayers, but a party of American congressmen who were on the Isthmus gained some first-hand information on Latin American insurrections.[161]

Minister Roy T. Davis and Canal Zone officials were awakened at four o'clock, and began to cast about as to their procedure; but only a few soldiers were sent into Panamanian territory, and they were to guard the American legation. The insurgents carefully refrained from injuring property of aliens and even placed guards before the Chase National and National City Bank buildings. A committee of the revolutionaries visited Davis early in the morning, and he immediately conferred with Arosemena who indicated his desire about noon to resign. At 2:30 that afternoon the president and his cabinet were taken before the supreme court which announced that the 1930 election of vice-presidents was illegal and that those of 1928 were still in office. Therefore Ricardo J. Alfaro, the minister at Washington, would be called as first *designado* to fill the unexpired term of Arosemena. Justice Hector Valdés further explained that the president had appointed Harmodio Arias as secretary of government and justice in order that he as premier should occupy the presidency until the arrival of Alfaro. After considerable wrangling this was agreed to, and the supreme court proceeded to its quarters and entered an order accepting the resignation of Arosemena.[162] The president and his family then went to the Hotel Tivoli in the Canal Zone.[163] Alfaro accepted the presidency at midnight.[164]

The State Department vigorously denied having any knowledge of the impending revolution, denied it so vigorously that one wonders. Arias expressed deep appreciation for the "neutral actions" of Minister Davis in risking his life to be of assistance to the Panamanian people.[165] The American government awaited developments and hoped to extricate itself from the embarrassing situation. After an interview with State Department officials Alfaro stated on January 5 that he was confident that the United States would view his assumption of the presidency as a constitutional transfer of power.[166] The Arias administration refused to consider the necessity for diplomatic recognition and rejected the overtures of governments that offered it.[167] Minister Davis was instructed on January 15 to attend the inauguration of Alfaro and to continue normal relations with his government.[168] On the following afternoon Alfaro took the oath of office in the old bullet-scarred French canal building with all the diplomatic corps present.[169] The first revolution, a palace insurrection, of the Republic of Panama had passed. Perhaps it would have occurred sooner if the United States had not stood ready to protect the government in power; perhaps it would not have been necessary but for the menace of American intervention. Opinions differ as to whether the Washington government was following a principle of nonintervention or merely desired to remove an administration that was unfriendly.[170]

Thus the United States appears to have veered away from the anti-revolutionary policy laid down by Root and Taft and followed by State Department officials in intervening years. It is to be hoped that the United States will cease its interference and permit the Isthmians to have a taste of independence in working out their own destiny—at least until the Canal is actually endangered. From the point of view of the Panamanians, however, there is no assurance that the Washington government will not return to its traditional ideals. They can have none so long as the State Department continues to apply a bilateral contract—the treaty of November 18, 1903—at its own discretion and with little regard for the views of the other party.

NOTES

1. *Sen. Doc.*, No. 208, 58 Cong., 2 Sess. (Ser. 4591), pp. 22-23.

2. Charles C. Magoon, U. S. minister to Panama, to Elihu Root, U. S. secretary of state, No. 27, Dec. 30, 1905, Despatches, Panama, IV.

3. Loomis to Buchanan, Jan. 6, 1904, Instructions, Panama, I; Buchanan to Hay, No. 46, Jan. 30, 1904, Despatches, Panama, I.

4. Gudger to Loomis, No. 492, Feb. 6, 1904, Consular Letters, Panama, XXV.

5. *Sen. Doc.*, No. 208, 58 Cong., 2 Sess. (Ser. 4591), pp. 22-23.

6. *Panama Morning Journal*, Sept. 27, 1905, enclosed with Magoon to Root, Sept. 28, 1905, Despatches, Panama, IV.

7. *Idem* to *idem*, No. 9, Oct. 3, 1905, *loc. cit.*

8. *Idem* to *idem*, Nov. 10, 1905, *For. Rel.* (1905), p. 716.

9. Root to Magoon, Dec. 4, 1905, *loc. cit.*, p. 720.

10. Magoon to Root, No. 27, Dec. 30, 1905, Despatches, Panama, IV.

11. *Idem* to *idem*, No. 24, Dec. 18, 1905, *loc. cit.*

12. *Idem* to *idem*, No. 25, Dec. 23, 1905, *loc. cit.*

13. *Idem* to *idem*, No. 27, Dec. 30, 1905, *loc. cit.*

14. *Ibid.*

15. Root to Taft, Feb. 21, 1906, *For. Rel.* (1906), pp. 1203-1206.

16. Sands to Root, No. 49, Feb. 4, 1906, Despatches, Panama, IV.

17. *Idem* to *idem*, No. 50, Feb. 7, 1906, *loc. cit.*

18. *Idem* to *idem*, No. 83, Mar. 28, 1906, *loc. cit.*, V.

19. *Idem* to *idem*, No. 84, Mar. 31, 1906, *loc. cit.*

20. Taft to Magoon, Apr. 26, 1906, *For. Rel.* (1906), pp. 1206-1207.

21. Magoon to Ricardo Arias, Panamanian foreign secretary, May 9, 1906, *loc. cit.*, p. 1206.

22. Magoon to Root, May 11, 1906, Despatches, Panama, V.

23. Obaldía to Root, May 12, 1906, *For. Rel.* (1906), p. 1207.

24. Belisario Porras, *A Lesson in Civics Which Should Remain Eternally Present in the Minds of All Panamanians* (Panama, 1924), p. 8.

25. *Ibid.*, p. 9.

26. Magoon to Root, No. 121, June 25, 1906, and enclosures, Despatches, Panama, V; Arnold Shanklin, U. S. consul, No. 116, June 26, 1906, Consular Letters, Panama, XXVII.

27. Magoon to Root, No. 138, July 25, 1906, and enclosures, Despatches, Panama, V.

28. Ricardo Arias, Panamanian minister at Washington, to Huntington Wilson, acting secretary of state, May 6, 1912, *For. Rel.* (1912), p. 1140.

29. Arias to H. G. Squiers, U. S. minister at Panama, May 15, 1908, Panama, Sec. R. E., *Memoria*, 1908, pp. 191-192.

30. Squiers to Arias, May 15, 1908, *loc. cit.*, p. 193.

31. See República de Panamá, Comisión Investigadora Electoral, *Informe de la comisión investigadora electoral de la Provincia de Bocas del Toro* (Panama, 1908). Similiar reports were issued for the other provinces.

32. República de Panamá, Secretario de Gobierno y Justicia, *Memoria*, 1908, p. xi. Hereafter cited as Panama, Sec. G. y J., *Memoria*, 1908.

33. George T. Weitzel, U. S. chargé, to Root, Oct. 2, 1908, *For. Rel.* (1908), p. 666.

34. Dodge to Knox, Apr. 25, 1912, *loc. cit.*, (1912), p. 1136.

35. *Idem* to *idem*, May 8, 1912; Arias to Wilson, May 6, 1912, *loc. cit.*, pp. 1136-1137, 1140; Eduardo Chiari, Panamanian foreign secretary, May 9, 1912, Panama, Sec. R. E., *Memoria*, 1912, pp. 115-116.

36. Dodge to Chiari, May 14, 1912, *loc. cit.*, p. 117; President William H. Taft to Wilson, May 10, 1912, *For. Rel.* (1912), p. 1141.

37. Panama, Sec. R. E., *Memoria*, 1912, pp. 117-123.

38. Dodge to P. C. Knox, U. S. secretary of state, May 20, 1912; June 9, 1912, *For. Rel.* (1912), pp. 1144, 1146.

39. *Idem* to *idem*, June 8, 1912, *loc. cit.*, pp. 1145-1146; Panama, Sec. R. E., *Memoria*, 1912, pp. 27-28, 167, 191-192, 202.

40. Dodge to Knox, June 14, 1912, *For. Rel.* (1912), p. 1148.

41. *Idem* to *idem*, June 30, 1912, *loc. cit.*, p. 1154.

42. *Idem* to *idem*, July 1, 1912; Knox to Dodge, July 3, 1912, *loc. cit.*, pp. 1154-1155.

43. Dodge to Knox, July 1, 1912, *loc. cit.*, pp. 1154-1155.

44. *Idem* to *idem*, July 20, 1912, *loc. cit.*, p. 1162.

45. *Idem* to *idem*, July 16, 1912, *loc. cit.*, p. 1159.

46. *Idem* to *idem*, July 20, 1912, *loc. cit.*, p. 1163.

47. Price to E. T. Lefevre, Panamanian foreign secretary, May 6, 1916, Panama, Sec. R. E., *Memoria*, 1916, p. 221.

48. Lefevre to Price, May 7, 1916, *loc. cit.*, pp. 222-223.

49. *The Canal Record* (Ancón, C. Z.), IX (1916), 381.

50. Panama, Sec. G. y J., *Memoria*, 1916, p. xviii.

51. *Star and Herald* (Weekly), June 10, 1918.

52. *Ibid.*, June 24, 1918; *The New York Times*, June 29, 1918, 3:4.

53. Raymond Leslie Buell, "Panama and the United States," in *Foreign Policy Reports*, VII (1932), 416; *Star and Herald* (Weekly), July 1, 1918.

54. *Star and Herald* (Weekly) June 10, 1918.

55. *Ibid.*, June 24, 1918.

56. *Ibid.*, July 8, 1918.

57. Urriola to Wilson, June 28, 1918, *N. Y. Times*, June 30, 1918, 8:5.

58. *Star and Herald* (Weekly), July 8, 1918.

59. Buell, "Panama and the United States," *loc. cit.*, p. 416.

60. *N. Y. Times*, July 6, 1918, 4:5; *Star and Herald* (Weekly), July 15, 1918.

61. *N. Y. Times*, July 8, 1918; *Star and Herald* (Weekly), Sept. 9, 1918; Panama, Sec. G. y J., *Memoria*, 1918, pp. 307-308.

62. *Star and Herald* (Weekly), Oct. 7 and 14, 1918.

63. *La Estrella de Panamá*, Jan. 30; Jan. 31; Oct. 1; Oct. 2, 1920.

64. *Ibid.*, July 31; Aug. 1; Aug. 2; Sept. 2, 1920.

65. Reprinted in *The Nation*, CXVI (1923), 503-504.

66. *Estrella*, May 24, 1924.

67. *Ibid.*, Aug. 4, 1924; *Star and Herald*, Aug. 3, 1924.

68. *Estrella*, Aug. 5, 1928; *N. Y. Times*, Dec. 17, 1927, 9:4; Alfaro to Kellogg, Dec. 15, 1927, U. S. Department of State, *Press Releases*, Jan. 4, 1928.

69. Kellogg to Alfaro, Dec. 23, 1927, *loc. cit.*

70. *Estrella*, June 17, 1928; *N. Y. Times*, June 18, 1928, 21:4.

71. *Estrella*, July 28, 1928; *N. Y. Times*, July 28, 1928, 12:8.

72. *Estrella*, July 30, 1928; *N. Y. Times*, July 28, 1928, 12:8.

73. *Estrella*, July 24, 27, 31, 1928; *N. Y. Times*, July 24, 33:1; July 26, 8:5; July 27, 34:3; July 28, 1928, 21:3.

74. *Estrella*, Aug. 3, 1928; *N. Y. Times*, Aug. 4, 1928, 5:7.

75. *Estrella*, Aug. 5, 1928; *N. Y. Times*, Aug. 6, 1928, 2:5.

76. *N. Y. Times*, June 6, 1932, 6:1.

77. *For. Rel.* (1905), 713-714.

78. Gudger to Loomis, No. 508, Apr. 4, 1904, Consular Letters, Panama, XXV.

79. Barrett to Hay, Apr. 28, 1905; Barrett to Guardia, May 8, 1905, *For. Rel.* (1905), pp. 709-710.

80. Lee to Loomis, No. 77, Oct. 9, 1905, and enclosures, Consular Letters, Panama, XXVI.

81. Lee to Loomis, No. 22, May 29, 1905, Consular Letters, Panama, XXVI.

82. Sands to Root, No. 49, Feb. 4, 1906, Despatches, Panama, IV.

83. *Idem* to *idem*, No. 74, Mar. 15, 1906, *loc. cit.*

84. The conduct of soldiers and sailors on leave has been taken into consideration.

85. Magoon to Root, No. 103, June 5, 1906, and enclosures; No. 132, July 18, 1906, and enclosures, Despatches, Panama, V; James C. Kellogg, U. S. consul at Colón, to the assistant secretary of state, No. 40, June 6, 1906, and enclosures, Consular Letters, Colón, XIX.

86. Magoon to Root, No. 103, June 5, 1906, Despatches, Panama, V.

87. Root to Magoon, June 15, 1906, Instructions, Panama, I.

88. Magoon to Root, No. 116, June 15, 1906, Despatches, Panama, V.

89. *Idem* to *idem*, June 19, 1906, *loc. cit.*

90. *Idem* to *idem*, No. 103, June 5, 1906; No. 116, June 15, 1906, *loc. cit.*

91. Weitzel to Root, Oct. 1, 1908, *For. Rel.* (1909), pp. 472-473.

92. Bacon to Squiers, Dec. 10, 1908, *loc. cit.*, p. 479.

93. Narciso Garay, *Panamá y las guerras de los Estados Unidos* (Panama, 1930), pp. 58, 83.

94. Samuel Lewis, Panamanian foreign secretary, to Squiers, July 31, 1909, *For. Rel.* (1909), pp. 493-494; *The Canal Record*, III (1909), 18; Panama, Sec. R. E., *Memoria*, 1910, pp. 32-33.

95. Dodge to Knox, July 4, 1912; July 9, 1912; Adee to Dodge, Aug. 22, 1912, *For. Rel.* (1912), pp. 1250-1251.

96. Dodge to Chiari, Aug. 31, 1912, *loc. cit.*, p. 1255.

97. Dodge to Knox, July 9, 1912, *loc. cit.*, p. 1251.

98. E. T. Lefevre to W. W. Andrews, U. S. chargé, Nov. 9, 1912, Panama, Sec. R. E., *Memoria*, 1914, p. 241.

99. Price to E. T. Lefevre, Apr. 30, 1914, *loc. cit.*, pp. 244-247.

100. E. T. Lefevre to Price, May 12, 1914, *loc. cit.*, pp. 249-255.

101. Price to E. T. Lefevre, May 14, 1914; May 19, 1914, *loc. cit.*, pp. 255-257.

102. Price to Robert Lansing, U. S. secretary of state, Apr. 17, 1915, *For. Rel.* (1915), p. 1170.

103. *Idem* to *idem*, Apr. 26, 1915, *loc. cit.*, p. 1171.

104. *Sen. Doc.*, No. 348, 67 Cong., 4 Sess. (Ser. 8167), III, 2778-2779.

105. Panama, Sec. R. E., *Memoria*, 1918, pp. 96-102.

106. Narciso Garay, Panamanian foreign secretary, to Price, Dec. 9, 1916, *loc. cit.*, p. 103.

107. E. T. Lefevre to Dodge, Feb. 19, 1913; E. T. Lefevre to Cyrus T. Wicker, U. S. chargé, Sept. 25, 1913, *loc. cit.*, 1914, pp. 228-237.

108. E. T. Lefevre to Price, July 18, 1914, *loc. cit.*, pp. 237-238.

109. Price to E. T. Lefevre, July 23, 1914, *loc. cit.*, pp. 238-240.

110. Price to W. J. Bryan, U. S. secretary of state, Feb. 14, 1915; Feb. 19, 1915, *For. Rel.* (1915), pp. 1186-1189.

111. *Idem* to *idem*, Apr. 2, 1915; H. D. Mitchell, chief of the Canal Zone police, to Goethals, Apr. 5, 1915; Wm. H. Gale, U. S. consul, to Price, May 3, 1915, *loc. cit.*, p. 1194, 1197-1198, 1200-1201.

112. Lansing to Price, Sept. 11, 1915, *loc. cit.*, p. 1213.

113. Price to Lansing, Sept. 8, 1915, *loc. cit.*, p. 1212.

114. Price to Garay, Aug. 20, 1917, Panama, Sec. R. E., *Memoria*, 1918, pp. 105-109.

115. Garay to Price, Sept. 28, 1917, *loc. cit.*, pp. 109-122.

116. Price to Lefevre, Oct. 8, 1918, *loc. cit.*, 1920, pp. 119-122.

117. Evenor Hazera, Panamanian foreign sub-secretary, to Clarence B. Hewes, U. S. chargé, June 30, 1920, *loc. cit.*, pp. 128-129.

118. Bert L. Hunt, *American and Panamanian General Claims Arbitration under the Conventions between the United States and Panama of July 28, 1926, and December 17, 1932* (Washington, 1934), pp. 273, 339; *Press Releases*, Aug. 23, 1926; *Gaceta oficial*, Jan. 13, 1931.

119. Lansing to Price, Aug. 25, 1915, *For. Rel.* (1915), pp. 1227-1228.

120. Goethals to Price, Oct. 15, 1915, *loc. cit.*, p. 1232.

121. E. T. Lefevre to Price, Nov. 12, 1915, *loc. cit.*, pp. 1233-1234.

122. Price to Bryan, Nov. 17, 1915, *loc. cit.*, p. 1233.

123. *Idem* to *idem*, Dec. 1, 1915, *loc. cit.*, pp. 1235-1236.

124. Willing Spencer, U. S. chargé, to Lansing, Jan. 14, 1916, *loc. cit.* (1916), pp. 938-939.

125. Frank L. Polk, for the secretary of state, to Price, Apr. 15, 1916, *loc. cit.*, p. 940.

126. Lansing to Price, May 12, 1916, *loc. cit.*, p. 942.

127. Price to Lansing, May 13, 1916, *loc. cit.*, p. 942.

128. *Idem* to *idem*, May 20, 1916, *loc. cit.*, p. 943; Panama, Sec. R. E., *Memoria*, 1916, pp. 174-210.

129. Garay to Price, May 29, 1917, Panama, Sec. R. E., *Memoria*, 1918, p. 237.

130. *Idem* to *idem*, Oct. 8, 1917, *loc. cit.*, pp. 239-240.

131. Price to Garay, Feb. 20, 1918, *loc. cit.*, pp. 240-241.

132. Panama, Sec. R. E., *Memoria*, 1918, pp. xxxviii-xxxix; *ibid.*, 1920, p. xxiii.

133. E. T. Lefevre to J. E. Lefevre, Panamanian chargé, Jan. 28, 1919; J. E. Lefevre to Polk, Jan. 29, 1919, *loc. cit.*, pp. 38-40.

134. Knox to J. E. Lefevre, Feb. 18, 1919, *loc. cit.*, p. 41.

135. J. E. Lefevre to Lansing, Aug. 29, 1919, *loc. cit.*, pp. 42-43.

136. William Phillips, U. S. assistant secretary of state, to J. E. Lefevre, Sept. 27, 1919, *loc. cit.*, p. 44.

137. J. E. Lefevre to Lansing, Sept. 30, 1919, *loc. cit.*, pp. 44-45.

138. *Idem* to *idem*, Oct. 14, 1919, *loc. cit.*, pp. 45-46.

139. Lansing to J. E. Lefevre, Nov. 12, 1919, *loc. cit.*, pp. 46-47.

140. J. E. Lefevre to Polk, Mar. 3, 1920; Mar. 22, 1920, *loc. cit.*, pp. 48-49, 51-52.

141. J. E. Lefevre to Bainbridge Colby, U. S. secretary of state, Mar. 23, 1920; Mar. 24, 1920, *loc. cit.*, pp. 52-54.

142. Angel D. Rodríguez, "American Powers in Panama," in *Current History,* XIV (1921), 302.

143. Johnson, *op. cit.*, p. 257.

144. Panama, Sec. R. E., *Memoria,* 1920, p. xxiii; *Estrella,* Sept. 1, 1920.

145. *N. Y. Times,* Mar. 1, 1921, 1:1; *Estrella,* Mar. 1, 1921.

146. *N. Y. Times,* Mar. 1, 3:3; Mar. 2, 1921, 5:2-3; *Estrella,* Mar. 1, 1921.

147. *N. Y. Times,* Mar. 13, 1921, 14:1.

148. Garay to J. E. Lefevre, Sept. 27, 1921, Panama, Sec. R. E., *Memoria,* 1922, II, 101.

149. Hughes to J. E. Lefevre, Mar. 9, 1922, *loc. cit.*, p. 163.

150. Susie Pearl Core, *Trails of Progress of the Story of Panama and Its Canal* (New York, 1925), pp. 181-182.

151. *Press Releases,* Feb. 28, 1925.

152. Panama, Sec. G. y J., *Memoria,* 1926, pp. xii-xiii.

153. *Press Releases,* Mar. 6, 1925.

154. Panama, Sec. G. y J., *Memoria,* 1926, p. xiii.

155. Great Britain, Department of Overseas Trade, *Report on the Economic, Financial and Commercial Conditions in the Republics of Costa Rica . . . and Panama . . .* (London, 1926), p. 26.

156. H. F. Alfaro to Dana G. Munro, U. S. Chargé, Oct. 12, 1925, Panama, Sec. R. E., *Memoria,* 1926, pp. 253-254; Panama, Sec. G. y J., *Memoria,* 1926, pp. vii-ix.

157. *Current History,* XXIII (1925), 412-413; *N. Y. Times,* Jan. 3, 1931, 3:2.

158. *Current History,* XXXIII (1930), 276-277; *Revue de L'Amerique Latine,* XXI (1931), 84-85.

159. *Press Releases,* Jan. 3, 1931; "Panama Follows Suit," in *Outlook and Independent,* CLVII (1931), 48-49.

160. "Unrest in Panama," in *The New Republic,* LXV (1930), 33-34.

161. *Estrella,* Jan. 3, 4, 5, 1928; *N. Y. Times,* Jan. 3, 3:3; Jan. 4, 19:1-2; Jan. 5, 7:2; Jan. 8, 1931, 8:1-2; *Press Releases,* Jan. 10, 1931; *Current History,* XXXIII (1931), 756.

162. Buell, "New Latin-American Revolts Test Our Recognition Policy," in *N. Y. Times,* Jan. 11, 1931, IX, 5:1-3; *Memorandum on the Change of Government in the Republic of Panama—January 2, 1931* (n. p., 1931), pp. 1-10; *BPAU,* LXV (1931), 109-111; *N. Y. Times,* Jan. 3, 1931, 1:1, 3:1-3; *Press Releases,* Jan. 3, 1931; *Estrella,* Jan. 3, 1931.

163. *N. Y. Times,* Jan. 3, 1931, 3:2-3.

164. *Press Releases,* Jan. 3, 1931; *Estrella,* Jan. 3, 1931.

165. *Star and Herald,* Jan. 3, 1931.

166. *N. Y. Times,* Jan. 6, 1931, 28:3.

167. *Ibid.,* Jan. 9, 1931, 48:8; *Current History,* XXXIII (1931), 756.

168. *Press Releases,* Jan. 17, 1931.

169. *N. Y. Times,* Jan. 17, 1931, 9:6.

170. "Revising Our Caribbean Policy," in *The New Republic,* LXV (1931), 286.

CHAPTER V

AMERICAN MILLIONS

THE ACTIVITIES of American financiers in the Republic of Panama must be viewed in the light of the gigantic investment of the government of the United States on the Isthmus. Over five hundred millions have been spent on the Canal enterprise. The Panama Railroad, luxurious hotels, thousands of dwellings, spacious warehouses, expensive public buildings, extensive commissaries, and numerous other developments in the Canal Zone belong to the American government, which has established a régime sometimes called "complete socialism" in the heart of the Isthmian republic.[1] The salaries of thousands of employees of the Canal and the vast business of the Canal Zone commissaries are factors of decided influence on Panamanian economics.

PRIVATE ENTERPRISES

Long before Panama broke away from Colombia and formed an independent republic American gold was being invested on the Isthmus. The construction by Americans of the Panama Railroad, the first transcontinental railway in the world, between 1850 and 1855, its transfer to the French, and its ultimate purchase by the American government, is a familiar story. In 1881 American investments in Colombia totaled $14,000,000 and a large part of them was in Panama.[2] As early as 1903 the United Fruit Company owned 73.3 miles of railway and 23,263 acres of land, 21,006 of which were in bananas, in Panama valued at $2,021,627.06.[3] The Central and South American Telegraph Company had offices on the Isthmus;[4] the American Trade Developing Company of New Jersey was in business there;[5] C. E. Pratt, Syracuse, New York, was concerned with concessions for games of chance in the province of Panama;[6] Isaac Brandon and Brothers of New York City held the tobacco monopoly;[7] and the Caribbean Manganese Company was attempting to exploit deposits near Nombre de Dios.[8]

In order to visualize the influence of American expansion in Panama, the undeveloped state of the country must be taken into consideration. In 1906 only 76,450 of the total estimated area of 20,781,000 acres were in cultivation. Of this, 37,000 acres of bananas and 13,630 acres of cocoanuts comprised more than two-thirds. Less than 1 per cent of the total acreage was in cultivation and almost one-third of that belonged to the United Fruit Company. The live stock of the republic consisted of 65,000 cattle, 28,000 hogs, 17,000 horses, 3,000 goats, and 1,500 mules.[9]

American investors flocked to Panama in increasing numbers after 1903, and many Canal Zone employees aided in the development of the country. Land grants for agriculture, lumbering, and mining were acquired in large numbers. In 1905 the Chiriquí Improvement Company of California had offices in David for its developments in the province of Chiriquí.[10] In 1906 Americans were reported interested in the bankrupt Darién Gold Mining Company,[11] and the Panama Company was organized by residents of Orange, New Jersey, and St. Louis, Missouri, for starting an agricultural colony in the San Blas Peninsula.[12] Panama City and Colón had at least thirty-two American establishments in 1908; nine of them were saloons.[13]

The interest of Americans, especially in the provinces of Panama and Chiriquí, became more evident in 1910.[14] Americans and Panamanians organized the *Ingenio de las Minas* for large-scale sugar production and secured several thousand acres of land near Colón.[15] California capitalists acquired 100,000 acres on the Bayano River for a saw mill and rum distillery in connection with agricultural developments.[16] In the following year the Panama Developing and Manufacturing Company contracted to establish a sugar refinery on public lands in the province of Colón; and Albert Voigh, an American citizen, was granted 25,000 acres of land in the province of Chiriquí.[17] American residents in Panama became interested in the coffee lands around Boquete in Chiriquí during 1912.[18] The Panama Development and Manufacturing Company, owned principally by Canal Zone employees, was incorporated in Panama and received from the government 2,500 acres and an option on 15,000 more.[19] The Panama Timber Company, owned by American and British interests, was engaged in the export of mahogany and other valuable woods from Panama,[20] and A. E. P. Schade, an American citizen, acquired 10,000 hectares in the province of Bocas del Toro for an agricultural colony.[21]

Few foreign laborers remained in Panama after the completion of the Canal, but many of the better-class Americans bought land in Chiriquí around David and Boquete. A number settled on their properties and established small colonies about the two towns. They were primarily interested in coffee culture and stock-raising, but expected to grow sugar cane, cacao, rubber, and cocoanuts.[22] The Central American Land and Improvement Company was reported to have received six titles to gold mines in the province of Colón in 1914; B. F. Ellinger, an American, secured 1,000 hectares in Chiriquí for an agricultural settlement; and former Canal Zone residents established Nueva Gorgoña on the Pacific Coast about forty miles from Panama City.[23]

The Río Indio Company was organized partly by Americans in May, 1918, for the development of 120,000 acres on Río Indio thirty miles west of Colón.[24] In the following year the Panama Sugar Company was reported to have six hundred of its 11,456 hectares in Chiriquí planted in sugar cane,[25] and A. Hyatt Verrill, an American, signed a contract for mining rights on about 3,000 hectares.[26] In 1920 the United Fruit Company had 251.76 miles of railway, 26,245 acres of bananas, 19,941 of cacao, 1,178 of cocoanuts, and 80,600 acres of unimproved lands in Panama valued at $7,811,353.18.[27] Three years later the American Lumber Company was reported to have taken over 80,000 acres in the province of Panama and was expected to ship 18,000,000 feet of mahogany logs to Norfolk, Virginia, in 1924; and a group of Californians had bought 25,000 hectares in the El Volcán region of Chiriquí.[28] Besides the Di Giorgio Fruit Company which owned 65,000 acres in Panama, other American enterprises active on the Isthmus in 1925 were the Gatún Lake Banana Company, the Pacific Fruit Company, the Panama Products Company, the Panama Sugar Company, the Pan-American Sugar and Fruit Company, the All America Cables, Inc., Albert Wilcox and associates, the Panama Lumber and Development Company, the Panama Pacific Mail Steamship Company, and the Tropical Fruit Company.[29] In 1927 the Tonosi Fruit Company and the Chiriquí Land Company, subsidiaries of the United Fruit Company, announced plans for extensive developments in Chiriquí and Los Santos. Plans called for several thousand hectares of bananas and the construction of railways, irrigation systems, hospitals, laboratories, and ports to take the place of declining properties in Bocas del Toro. The proposed expenditures were estimated at from nine to twelve millions, but the stage of projection had not been passed by 1929.[30]

British investments in Panama were estimated at $7,500,000 in 1929.[31] Important among them were the holdings of the Panama Corporation which had attracted the attention of the United States. That concern obtained a mining concession in 1924 covering 1,150 square miles seventy miles west of the Canal Zone and another in 1925 of 3,400 square miles along the Colombian frontier.[32] These large tracts, lavish entertainment of Panamanian officials, and no evident return on the investment caused some apprehension. Senator William E. Borah introduced a resolution in the American Senate on June 5, 1926, requesting all available information. After an investigation the State Department apparently was satisfied that the company held ordinary mining concessions and refused to treat the matter diplomatically with Panama.[33] Between four and five thousand square miles of land west of the original grant and including about thirty miles of the Caribbean Coast were acquired in 1929, and another thousand square miles were added in 1930 on the west side of and contiguous to the Canal Zone for about twenty miles.[34] The British have been charged with attempting to block American production of rubber on the Isthmus and of trying to get a monopoly of Panamanian oil fields. The press has declared that the operation of the company has been inimical to Canal defense and productive of anti-American feeling in Panama.[35]

Americans have played an important part in the banking business of the Isthmus. The Panamanian government early established the *Banco Hipotecario y Prendario*, a mortgage bank,[36] which later became the *Banco Nacional*, but carried on no regular banking operations. No bank in the ordinary sense of the word existed in Panama in 1906,[37] but the International Banking Corporation of Connecticut, Brandon Brothers, Ehrman and Company, the American Trade Developing Company, and the Panama Banking Company of West Virginia were engaged in banking activities on the Isthmus.[38] The International Banking Corporation had branches in Panama, Colón, and Empire; and the Panama Banking Corporation was in business in Panama and Colón in 1910. The total deposits in all banks were estimated at $3,000,000; loans at $2,000,000; and monthly exchange at $2,000,000.[39] The Continental Banking and Trust Company was established on the Isthmus in 1913, and two years later the Commercial National Bank of Washington, D. C., had branches in Panama City and Cristóbal, and the Canal Zone Bank had been opened in Colón.[40] In 1916 the Provident Life and Trust Corporation of Panama, partly owned by Americans, was established in Panama City.[41] Toward the end of that year the Continental Banking and Trust Company failed and closed its branches in Panama, Colón, David, and Bocas del Toro.[42] In 1918 the Isthmian interests of the Commercial National Bank were transferred to the American Foreign Banking Corporation of New York,[43] in 1925 the Chase National Bank of New York took over the Panama and Colón branches of the American Foreign Banking Corporation, and in 1926 the branches of the International Banking Corporation passed into the hands of the National City Bank of New York.[44] The business of the National City had so increased by 1928 that it could afford a quarter of a million dollar building in Panama City.[45] In 1929 the Royal Bank of Canada opened branches in Panama City and Colón to give the Americans competition.[46]

Aside from highway and railway construction,[47] Americans have been prominent in the development of various public utilities projects on the Isthmus. On October 29, 1906, Henry T. Cook secured a fifty-year franchise from Panama for a street railway in its capital.[48] In 1910 the Panama Public Utilities Corporation of Connecticut was organized to take over Cook's contract, but was liquidated and replaced in 1912 by the Panama Tramways Company, organized by Minor C. Keith under the laws of New Jersey. On January 23, 1912, R. W. Hebard was engaged to build the system.[49] In 1913 the Central American Construction Company, an American concern, was building a laundry for the Consumer's Electric Light and Manufacturing Company of Colón, another American enterprise.[50] Hebard completed a power plant in Panama City in 1915; he also constructed the *Ferrocarril Nacional de Chiriquí* and various Panamanian highways and government buildings.[51] The Panama Electric Corporation, an American firm, took over the street railway franchise of the Panama Tramways Company in 1916; the Panama-American Corporation, which was founded in 1904 and which in 1916 supplied Panama City with telephone service, ice, and electricity, was acquired by the Electric Bond and Share Company of New York; and Starr and Reed of Philadelphia controlled the Panama Gas Company and the Colón Gas Company. In 1921 the General Electric Company controlled, through the Electric Bond and Share Company, the Panama Power and Light Corporation, which furnished the cities of Panama and Colón with telephone and electric service.[52]

Manufacturing in the sense of converting raw materials into finished products was non-existent in Panama in 1915,[53] and has virtually remained so until the present. Americans have had little influence industrially outside of the Canal Zone except in sugar, lumber, and power developments. They have been concerned mostly with the manufacture of ice and beverages, but have been interested in a vegetable ivory button factory, a plant for manufacturing dairy products, and in the La Perla Cigar Company.[54]

Most of the oil companies arrived late on the Isthmus. The

Sinclair Panama Oil Corporation was granted a concession by the Panamanian government in 1917;[55] and by 1924 the Gulf Oil Company through the Panama Gulf Oil Company, the Texas Oil Company through the Chorcha Petroleum Company, the Standard Oil Company of California, and the Carib Syndicate of Maine had contracts for prospecting in Panama. Only the first three had attempted any extensive drilling operations; Sinclair and Gulf withdrew in 1928 and 1929 without apparent success.[56]

American investments in the Republic of Panama in 1913 were estimated to total $5,000,000,[57] but the United Fruit Company valued its Panamanian properties at more than five millions in 1910 and above eight millions in 1915.[58] The significance of American developments may be determined to some extent by the fact that all Panamanian lands, buildings, and livestock in private hands in 1913 were valued at only $33,-175,501.[59] Roger W. Babson, however, reported in 1915 that American business establishments were scarce on the Isthmus. Belisario Porras complained to him that capital from the United States flowed very slowly into Panama and stated that Americans would profit more by spending money on Panamanian interior development than on Canal Zone fortifications. After describing the great opportunities that his nation offered the Americans he concluded: "All we now need is affection and capital, to make the rose blossom where the cactus now flourishes."[60]

The investments of citizens of the United States in Panama were estimated to total $12,000,000 in 1926.[61] This might be accepted as correct if the Panamanian loans floated in New York were excluded. The national debt on June 30, 1926, was $13,248,973, practically all of which was advanced by Americans, and the United Fruit holdings were worth $8,026,-052.10 in 1925.[62] The total American investment in Panama was placed at $36,381,000 in 1929,[63] and in 1930 the Department of Commerce reported that citizens of the United States had a direct investment of $28,709,000 in Panama and held approximately $18,000,000 in Panamanian bond issues, or a total of $46,709,000.[64]　Then came the depression to draw the American purse strings.

Public Finance

The Republic of Panama came into existence with practically no debt.　No long struggle for freedom depleted its scanty resources.　Philippe Bunau-Varilla advanced the necessary funds for initiating the revolution,[65] and a small sum borrowed from J. P. Morgan was shortly repaid from funds derived from the sale of the Canal Zone.[66]　As soon as the treaty was signed, Panama became the recipient of $10,000,000 in gold and of a $250,000 perpetual annuity to begin nine years after its ratification.[67]　The Panamanians were not eager to take the whole of the initial payment.　Minister Bunau-Varilla informed the State Department that the United States might retain $8,000,-000 at 3 per cent interest.[68]　Minister Buchanan was approached with the view of converting that sum into a "perpetual rental against the Federal Treasury of the United States,"[69] but the proposal did not meet with favor in Washington.　In May, 1904, the entire amount was paid to J. P. Morgan, the Panamanian fiscal representative in the United States.　The State Department, however, informed the Isthmians that they were expected to invest $8,000,000 in the United States for the stabilization of their finances.[70]　The decision of Panama to place $6,000,000 in first mortgages on American real estate as a "constitutional fund" was embodied in its constitution.[71]　Ricardo Arias and Eusebio A. Morales were sent to the United States in 1904 to invest permanently that sum and to loan temporarily an additional $3,000,000 as advantageously as possible.[72]　William Nelson Cromwell was shortly appointed fiscal agent in the United States to keep a watchful eye on these investments.[73]

Arias and Morales signed a monetary agreement with Secretary Taft on June 20, 1904, establishing the gold *balboa*, equal in value to the American gold dollar, as the basic unit of currency for Panama.　The Panamanians agreed to issue enough silver to redeem all Colombian money on the Isthmus and to emit when the United States desired three million silver one-half *balboa* pieces called *pesos*. Panama was bound further to maintain a gold deposit in a reliable American bank equivalent to 15 per cent of its silver coin. The gold dollar was to be accepted in Panama, and the Panamanian gold and silver currency was to be used in the Canal Zone. The Isthmian Canal Commission was obligated to help maintain the parity of Panamanian and American money and to use that of Panama in the Canal Zone when convenient.[74] Panama validated the agreement by Law 84 of June 28, 1904, and by a decree of December 6, 1904, promising to issue three million *pesos* for the redemption of Colombian silver and a like amount for Canal Zone convenience when requested by the United States.[75] The first set of coins minted was presented to President Roosevelt.[76] With the aid of William Nelson Cromwell and the Philadelphia mint Panama had issued four million *pesos* by 1905 and had deposited $300,000 with the Banker's Trust Company of New York to insure the stability of its currency.[77]

The Republic of Panama incurred its first obligation of any consequence on September 20, 1907, when a contract was signed with the United States for waterworks and paving in the cities of Panama and Colón. The Washington government agreed to build and administer the water system for fifty years and to pave and maintain the streets for ten years. Panama promised to pay $65,525 for Panama City and $69,850 for Colón annually for fifty years. The total debt was $6,768,750, but the yearly payments were to be taken from the water rents of the cities.[78]

The Panamanians were able to resist the temptation to increase the national debt until 1914, when the government sought and eventually obtained the permission of the United States for a $3,000,000 issue of thirty-year bonds to be used in building the *Ferrocarril Nacional de Chiriquí*. The American government agreed to hypothecate a sufficient amount of the Canal annuity to cover interest and amortization.[79] Accordingly, $2,250,000 worth of 5 per cent bonds were issued through J. P. Morgan and the National City Bank, and $190,258.61

were assigned from the annuity to cover the interest and sinking fund.[80] Panama realized $2,194,187.76 from the loan.[81] A second bond issue of $1,200,000 was made in 1915 for the purpose of paying all debts of the national treasury and for constructing public works. These securities were handled by Lawrence Turnure and Company of New York and were sold at 100.5. They were secured by the income of the constitutional fund, and payment was to be made in yearly installments terminating on December 1, 1925.[82]

In 1916 the Panamanian government asked the State Department for permission to issue between $400,000 and $450,000 in bonds for an extension of the *Ferrocarril Nacional de Chiriquí* and inquired if the United States was disposed to make further assignment from the annuity for interest and amortization.[83] The State Department assented after an unreasonable delay, but stipulated that the bonds were not to be sold at less than 97, that one-half might be delivered at once, and that the remainder might be issued when the Washington government deemed it necessary.[84] Panama replied that the proposed issue was a part of the $3,000,000 authorized in 1914, and accepted the terms,[85] but war conditions prevented the completion of the railway plans.

The United States advised Panama in 1916 to select an American to act as fiscal agent. The proposal was greeted with considerable protest, but was renewed by the State Department in 1918. One prominent Panamanian complained that the acceptance of American fiscal control meant the approval of the most absolute dictatorship and an admittance of the death of the republic, but notwithstanding all opposition a law was passed on December 30, 1918, authorizing the appointment of a fiscal agent.[86] On the recommendation of the State Department Addison T. Ruan was appointed to that position at a salary of $10,000 per year.[87] Shortly thereafter Dr. Clarence J. Owens was engaged for an economic survey of Panama.[88] Ruan recommended a loan for debt consolidation, a 15 per cent reduction in government salaries, a new system of accounting, government collection of alcohol taxes, a central purchasing and storage department, and the selection of a local bank to act as agent and depository for government funds.[89] Some of these reforms were instituted successfully, and on June 20, 1921, the surplus was $3,520,460.[90] Ruan was also prominent during his terms from 1919 to 1923 in the development of the Panamanian highway system.[91] He was succeeded by W. W. Warwick, and in 1925 Floyd H. Baldwin was appointed. His contract was reported renewed in 1928 and again in 1930.[92] These men have served Panama well and have had no direct connection with the Washington government, but they have brought American methods into the Panamanian system of administration.

In 1923 Panama secured the permission of the State Department to issue $4,500,000 worth of thirty-year bonds bearing 5 per cent interest. These were sold at 97.5 through W. A. Harriman and the Guaranty Trust Company of New York. The interest and sinking fund were guaranteed by the net income from the constitutional fund, which was averaging $229,-910 annually, $59,741 of the Canal annuity for twenty-one and one-half years, and the entire $250,000 thereafter. At a discount of 7 per cent the issue produced $4,185,000, of which $3,714,100.66 were expended on highways.[93]

After more than ten years of discussion the Panamanian government finally decided to extend the *Ferrocarril Nacional de Chiriquí* from Concepción to Puerto Armuelles. In June, 1926, a $2,600,000 issue of thirty-five-year bonds bearing 6.5 per cent interest was offered at 103 in the United States by Kissel, Kinnicutt and Company and Bauer, Pond and Vivian. The interest and amortization were secured by the revenues of the extension, the wharf at Puerto Armuelles, the export tariff, and the stamp tax.[94] A few months later a loan of $2,200,000 to mature in thirty years was negotiated under similar conditions, but for bond retirement and public works.[95]

The *Banco Nacional* began to extend its operations in 1925. In December it floated a million dollar issue of twenty-year gold sinking fund bonds bearing 6.5 per cent interest. These securities were offered by Morgan, Livermore and Company at

100.75 and were secured by Panamanian real estate mortgages of not less than 140 per cent of their face value. Another issue was made in May, 1927, through Otis and Company of New York.[96] The Republic of Panama went outside the United States for a small loan in 1927, when $147,000 were borrowed in Canada. However, the bulging purses of Americans supplied Panama City with $500,000 for public improvements in 1927. The *Banco Nacional* turned to Canada in 1928 and 1929 for financial aid. Two issues of $1,000,000 each in 6.5 per cent twenty-year gold bonds were offered through the Royal Financial Corporation at 99 and 99.5 respectively. These were secured by not less than 110 per cent of their value in Panamanian real estate mortgages. All four issues of the *Banco Nacional* were guaranteed by the Panamanian government.[97]

The Panamanian national debt was $6,755,443 in 1916, $11,048,970.34 in 1926, and $13,248,973 in 1927.[98] The burden became increasingly heavy, but on March 23, 1928, the National Assembly provided for a $16,000,000 loan for debt consolidation and highway construction.[99] The *Porrista* party opposed the measure warmly and, sending a telegram to Secretary of State Kellogg, urged him not to countenance the loan in any way. The followers of Porras claimed that the contraction of further obligations in the United States would endanger the liberty of the republic.[100] The amount was reduced to $12,-000,000 to be used for retiring the $6,218,912.77 outstanding of the loans of 1914 and 1926 and for highway building.[101] The securities were thirty-five-year sinking fund gold bonds bearing 5 per cent interest and were secured by the export duties, the stamp and retail liquor tax, the net income from the *Ferrocarril Nacional de Chiriquí* and the Puerto Armuelles wharf, the Canal annuity, and the constitutional fund revenue, subject to a charge for the loan of 1923, which was not redeemable until 1933.[102] The entire issue was offered at 96.75 in the United States in June, 1928, by the National City Company; Kissel, Kinnicutt and Company; the Illinois Merchants Trust Company; and the Continental National Company. Subsequently the sum of $1,200,000 was withdrawn for offering in The Netherlands.[103]

The national debt of Panama reached $18,686,055.01 by September, 1926.[104] As the burden became increasingly great, the National Assembly authorized the appointment of a commission of American financial experts for a survey of the republic.[105] President Arosemena selected a group, headed by a vice-president of the National City Bank of New York, which was facetiously referred to as the proprietor of Panama and which was probably an influential factor in initiating the project.[106] The committee visited the Isthmus early in 1929 and submitted a report to the president on September 20.[107] One American writer sarcastically commented:

Soon the government will be told by a National City commission of experts how to conduct its financial affairs and a special session of the National Assembly, to convene, so it is humorously stated, at the call of the National City, will give weighty consideration to the report submitted by the financial geniuses after a comprehensive study of the republic and its resources and expenditures.[108]

The Panamanian government refused to make the findings of the commission public until the National Assembly met in 1930. Then various charges were made that it either misrepresented or falsified the facts reported. Arosemena made some effort at reform, but his changes were insufficient to prevent the downfall of his political faction and his removal from office by a revolution on January 2, 1931.

The fact might be noted that the Republic of Panama early coined four million silver *pesos*, most of which were melted and exported during the World War.[109] Approximately two million dollars of American currency were in circulation on the Isthmus in 1915 and that had increased to $5,000,000 in 1924.[110] The parity deposit of Panama in New York had decreased from $300,000 to $150,000 by 1927, but only 125,000 *balboas* of Panamanian currency were in use. Since the monetary agreement of 1904 required no more than a 15 per cent backing, the government authorized the withdrawal of $131,250 on

November 9, 1927.[111] Panama has never issued any gold or paper currency, and the silver *balboa* was coined for the first time in 1931.[112]

The depression was late in reaching Panama, but the government began early to have trouble in meeting obligations. The external debt in 1932 was $15,549,000, and the internal incumbrance was $3,708,968, or a total of $19,257,968. In addition, the government guaranteed $3,282,154 outstanding of the four *Banco Nacional* issues. Three of these went into default in 1932, and the fourth followed on January 1, 1933.[113] Notwithstanding the campaign promises of President Ricardo Arias in 1932 that Panama would continue to meet its debts, the interest payments on the $12,000,000 loan of 1928 were suspended on May 15, 1933.[114] On September 1 the national debt was $18,720,000, and practically all of it was owed to Americans. For the support of its obligations Panama had a total estimated taxable property of $87,500,000, of which $49,-731,153 was in the city and province of Panama.[115]

On November 22, 1933, the Panamanian government announced a plan by which the holders of the 1928 bonds were to receive a minimum of one-third of their interest for 1933, 1934, and 1935. These payments were to be met with the excess from the constitutional fund and the Canal annuity after the 1923 loan was serviced. The sinking fund was suspended; all assenting bondholders were given their share of the interest and certificates for their arrears; the investors who refused to agree to the arrangement were to take a chance on any surplus.[116]

TRADE

Not only has the Republic of Panama purchased the greater part of its imports from the United States every year since 1903, but the Americans have been the best and almost the only customers of Panama for the past thirty years. During the fiscal year ending June 30, 1904, the United States exported $979,724 to and imported $440,747 worth of goods from the Isthmus, thus establishing a balance of trade unfavorable to the Panamanian republic that has existed each year

since that time.[117]   In 1905 the United States shipped to
Panama and the Canal Zone goods valued at $4,745,562 and
received in return raw materials worth $813,154.[118]   These
totals had mounted to $20,596,371 and $2,229,189 in 1910.[119]
In the same year the republic proper had an exportation of
$1,769,330.15, of which $1,508,421.94 went to the United
States.   The Americans supplied $5,627,642.58 of its $10,-
043,395.11 of imports.   A peak was reached in 1913, when
Panama exported products to the United States valued at $4,-
801,608.48 out of a total of $5,383,027.54 and imported from
the United States $6,065,128.43 out of a total of $11,182,-
674.96.[120]

Exports to the Canal Zone and Panama had declined in
1915 to $19,209,053, the lowest mark of the decade, and the
imports were $4,388,136.[121]   In that year Americans pur-
chased from Panama proper $3,118,453.63 or 93.1 per cent
of its total of $3,422,455.10 of exports and supplied the Pana-
manians with $6,822,236.48 or 75.5 per cent of their total
imports of $9,032,977.17.[122]   Both imports and exports in-
creased during the World War, and American exportations to
Panama and the Canal Zone reached a new peak in 1920.
Goods shipped to the Isthmus amounted to $33,333,155 and the
imports into the United States were $8,272,586.[123]   The United
States supplied Panama with $13,012,608.73 of its total of $17,-
561,995.02 and received $3,197,049.27 of Panama's total ship-
ments of $3,552,165.52.[124]   Post-war conditions caused exports
from the United States to Panama and the Canal Zone to fall
in 1922 to $14,517,059, the lowest figure since 1906, but im-
ports to the United States were $3,607,014.[125]   By 1925 the
Canal Zone and Panama were able to take $28,237,000 worth
of American products and to supply the United States with
$6,431,000.[126]   Panama imported $10,903,124.74 or 67.6 per
cent of its total of $16,129,013.96 from the United States and
exported $3,286,675.49 or 88 per cent of its total of $4,-
029,739.67 to the United States.[127]

Panamanian foreign commerce reached its greatest volume
in 1929.   Good business and importations for highway and rail-

way construction raised the total imports of the Isthmus to $41,133,000. Exports were fair, but the total of $5,351,000 showed a decline.[128] The republic imported $19,278,000, of which the United States furnished 68.2 per cent or $13,134,000. The exports of Panama were $4,144,000 and the United States took $3,902,000 or 94.2 per cent of them.[129] In 1930 Panama and the Canal Zone imported from the United States goods valued at $35,900,000 and exported $4,735,000 to it. The imports of Panama proper were $18,337,000, of which Americans supplied $10,878,918, and its exports were down to $3,-302,000, of which $3,120,847 went to the United States.[130]

After 1930 the decline was sharp and Panamanian suffering became acute. In 1931 the United States furnished $8,159,000 of Panama's imports of $13,492,000 and received $2,364,000 of its $2,608,000 worth of exports.[131] In 1932 Panama and the Canal Zone absorbed American goods to the value of $15,609,-000, and the total exports to the United States were $3,530,-000.[132] Panamanian imports in 1932 were only $8,853,000, and its exports were $2,006,000.[133] The imports of Panama and the Canal Zone rose to $15,887,000 in 1933, but their exports declined to $3,376,000.[134]

The chief competitor of the United States in Panama has been Great Britain, but the British have seldom been able to command more than two million dollars of Panamanian trade. Their best years were 1910 with $2,166,642.99; 1911 with $2,273,386.39; 1912 with $2,421,637.14; and 1913 with $2,505,842.50.[135] Germany surpassed the British in 1929, when a shipment of machinery for a brewery raised its total to $1,865,-514. Besides the United States, these are the only countries that have been able to do as much as a million dollars worth of business on the Isthmus in one year, but the Japanese have made considerable progress in recent months.

The question arises as to the manner by which Panama has been able to weather a continual unfavorable balance of trade. The answer seems clear. The figures quoted do not tell the entire story of Panamanian commercial life. A large volume of Panamanian exports go to the Canal Zone and, consequently, is not recorded. According to estimates, tourists and Canal Zone employees account for almost one-half the imports of Panama.[136] American soldiers and sailors spend their money freely in Panama. For example, the United States fleet remained in Panamanian waters for six weeks in 1923 and left between three and four million dollars on the Isthmus. Tourists, Canal Zone employees, and American service men were reported to have expended $11,500,000 with Panamanians during 1930.[137] The income from the constitutional fund, the Canal annuity, and services rendered Canal Zone employees also help to destroy the unfavorable balance of trade.

The United States furnishes Panama with manufactured articles and food products. Although Panama is predominantly agricultural, approximately one-sixth of its imports as late as 1932 was composed of meats, lard, dairy products, wheat flour, and vegetables.[138] The chief export of Panama has been bananas, which comprise from 50 to 75 per cent of the annual total. Other exports are cacao, cocoanuts, ivory nuts, hides, cabinet woods, and mother-of-pearl shell.[139]

The Washington government has had little trouble with the Panamanian government concerning the investments of American citizens. Perhaps the outstanding instance was the controversy over the rights of the Central and South American Telegraph Company during the early years of the republic when the State Department exerted pressure.[140] Steps have been taken also in regard to banana developments. Railway and radio projects have likewise been interfered with at various times, but for the protection of the Canal. Panama is naturally somewhat dominated by the Americans, but actual interference and exploitation has been gradual and guarded. The vast holdings of the United Fruit Company have made it a factor in Panamanian politics.[141] The Isthmians have borrowed too much money for public improvements, and these loans have provided openings for further domination. The cupidity of native politicians has always been a favorite avenue in the game of imperialism. Bankers seek extraordinary rights when they make loans. The burden becomes too great for the people. The banker then calls on his government for protection of the "modern sacred cow," private property. Americans, however, seem able to deal directly with the Panamanian government and with more satisfaction than is usually derived from indirect means.

Numerous charges of American financial and political *dominación* in Panama have been made, and predictions of its increase in the future are not lacking. *Norteamericanos*, undoubtedly, will continue their preponderant influence on the Isthmus, but the danger probably has been overdrawn. The following statement has been made by a Central American: "We are bound to be swallowed in the end, whatever happens; nothing remains for us but to try to make the process of deglutition as slow and difficult as possible. And let us keep the hope that our bones may stick in Uncle Sam's throat."[142] It may be doubted whether such a statement would apply to the actual facts or to the sentiment of Panama.

NOTES

1. M. E. Dimrock, *Government-Operated Enterprises in the Panama Canal Zone* (Chicago, 1934), pp. 6, 30.

2. Rippy, *The Capitalists and Colombia*, p. 37.

3. United Fruit Company, *Annual Report* (1903), pp. 15-19.

4. Sands to Root, No. 82, Mar. 26, 1906, Despatches, Panama, V.

5. Gudger to Hill, No. 293, May 16, 1902, and enclosure, Consular Letters, Panama, XXIV.

6. *Idem* to *idem*, No. 238, Jan. 6, 1902, *loc. cit.*

7. Ehrman to Hill, No. 332, Aug. 30, 1902, *loc. cit.*

8. Malmros to Hill, No. 47, Jan. 21, 1902, Consular Letters, Colón, XVIII.

9. International Bureau of American Republics, *Monthly Bulletin*, XXIII (1906), 469; XXV (1907), 108-109. Hereafter cited as IBAR, *Monthly Bulletin*.

10. Lee to Loomis, No. 16, May 20, 1905, Consular Letters, Panama, XXVI.

11. Shanklin to Hill, No. 135, July 14, 1906, *loc. cit.*, XXVII.

12. Sands to Root, No. 81, Mar. 26, 1906, Despatches, Panama, V.

13. República de Panamá, Secretaría de Agricultura y Obras Públicas, *Boletín de estadística*, No. 8, Mar., 1908.

14. U. S. Department of Commerce, *Daily Consular and Trade Reports*, Oct. 31, 1910, p. 401.

15. IBAR, *Monthly Bulletin*, XXXI (1910), 547-548.

16. IBAR, *Monthly Bulletin*, XXX (1910), 1060.

17. *Daily Consular and Trade Reports*, June 7, 1911, p. 1043; BPAU, XXXII (1911), 802.

18. *BPAU*, XXXV (1912), 1324.

19. *Ibid.*, XXXV (1912), 1090; XXXVI (1913), 472; *Daily Consular and Trade Reports*, May 14, 1912, pp. 597-598.

20. *BPAU*, XXXIV (1912), 565.

21. República de Panamá, Secretaría de Agricultura y Obras Públicas, *Memoria*, 1912, II, 341-342. Hereafter cited as Panama, Sec. A. y O. P., *Memoria*, 1912.

22. Garrard Harris, *Central America as an Export Field* (Washington, 1916), pp. 198, 202.

23. *BPAU*, XXXVIII (1914), 149, 304.

24. *Ibid.*, XLVII (1918), 883.

25. *Ibid.*, XLIX (1919), 211.

26. R. W. Dunn, *American Foreign Investments* (New York, 1926), p. 116.

27. United Fruit Company, *Annual Report*, 1920, pp. 11-15.

28. *BPAU*, LVII (1923), 614; LVIII (1924), 725.

29. Max Winkler, "America, the World's Banker," in F. P. A., *Information Service*, III (1927), special supplement 3, p. 13; *Gaceta oficial*, Aug. 11, 1922; Dunn, *op. cit.*, pp. 115-117.

30. *BPAU*, LXI (1927), 395, 1032; LXIII (1929), 1058-1059; U. S. Department of Commerce, *Commerce Reports*, Aug. 5, 1929, p. 332; Winkler, "Prosperity and Foreign Investments; a Summary of U. S. Foreign Investments in 1929," in *Foreign Policy Reports*, VI (1930-1931), 13-15; *Star and Herald*, Jan. 16, 1927.

31. Winkler, *Investments of United States Capital in Latin America* (Boston, 1929), p. 283.

32. H. K. Norton, "Why Britishers in Panama," in *The World's Work*, LIX (1930), 31.

33. *Current History*, XXIV (1926), 786-787.

34. Norton, *op. et loc. cit.*, p. 31.

35. "British Rubber Ghost in Panama," in *The Literary Digest*, LXXXIX (June 26, 1926), 13; *N. Y. Times*, Feb. 22, 1930, 4:2.

36. Lee to Hay, No. 107, July 5, 1904, Despatches, Panama, II.

37. *Sen. Doc.*, No. 401, 59 Cong., 2 Sess. (Ser. 5098), II, 1177.

38. Sands to Root, No. 49, Feb. 4, 1906, Despatches, Panama, IV; Magoon to Root, No. 123, July 1, 1906, *loc. cit.*, V; *BPAU*, XLV (1917), 835.

39. *Daily Consular and Trade Reports*, Oct. 28, 1910, p. 379; Haskins, *op. cit.*, p. 504.

40. *Daily Consular and Trade Reports*, Sept. 5, 1913, p. 1323; U. S. Department of Commerce, *Trade Directory of Central America and the West Indies* (Washington, 1915), pp. 87, 93; *Commerce Reports*, May 15, 1915, p. 754; Panama, *Compendio estadistico, 1909 a 1916*, p. 36.

41. *BPAU*, XLII (1916), 585-586.

42. Harris, *op. cit.*, p. 209; Panama, Sec. R. E., *Memoria*, 1918, p. 165.

43. *BPAU*, XLVII (1918), 320.

44. *Ibid.*, LX (1926), 718; Panama, Sec. G. y J., *Memoria*, 1926, pp. 157-158; Great Britain, Dept. Overseas Trade, *op. cit.*, 1925, p. 18.

45. *BPAU*, LXII (1928), 301, 1285; "Expansion of Banking in Panama," in *The Pan American Magazine*, XLI (1928), 246-247.

46. Great Britain, Dept. Overseas Trade, *op. cit.*, 1929, p. 9.

47. See chap. viii.

48. *The Canal Record*, IV (1911), 157; V (1912), 305.

49. *Ibid.*; *Daily Consular and Trade Reports*, June 22, 1912, p. 1273.

50. *Daily Consular and Trade Reports*, Aug. 4, 1913, p. 679.

51. *BPAU*, XXXVII (1913), 460, 623; XLI (1915), 289; Panama, Sec. A. y O. P., *Memoria*, 1914, pp. x-xi, xix, 493-498; *Gaceta oficial*, Jan. 31, 1914; F. B. Curran, *Motor Roads in Latin America* (Washington, 1925), p. 33.

52. *BPAU*, XLII (1916), 864; F. M. Hasley, *Investments in Latin America and the British West Indies* (Washington, 1918), p. 440; A. W. Kimber, ed., *Kimber's Record of Government Debts and Other Foreign Securities, 1923* (New York, 1923), p. 795. Hereafter cited as *Kimber's Government Debts*, 1923.

53. Harris, *op. cit.*, pp. 206-213.

54. *Daily Consular and Trade Reports*, May 14, 1912, pp. 597-598; *BPAU*, XLV (1917), 554; XLIX (1919), 333.

55. Price to Lansing, Apr. 21, 1917, *For. Rel.* (1919), II, 694.

56. Great Britain, Dept. Overseas Trade, *op. cit.*, 1924, p. 24; *Kimber's Government Debts*, 1930, p. 913.

57. Winkler, *Investments of United States Capital in Latin America*, p. 284.

58. United Fruit Company, *Annual Report*, 1910, p. 13; 1915, p. 11.

59. Harris, *op. cit.*, p. 200.

60. R. W. Babson, *The Future of South America* (Boston, 1915), p. 89.

61. "American Investments in the Western Hemisphere," in F. P. A., *Information Service*, III (1928), appendix, p. 375.

62. Great Britain, Dept. Overseas Trade, *op. cit.*, 1927, p. 7; United Fruit Company, *Annual Report*, 1925, p. 13.

63. Winkler, *Investments of United States Capital in Latin America*, p. 284.

64. U. S. Department of Commerce, *Trade Information Bulletin*, No. 767 (1931), p. 16; *BPAU*, LXV (1931), 1074.

65. Bunau-Varilla, *Panama*, pp. 324-326, 345, 361.

66. Buchanan to Hay, Dec. 28, 1903; No. 11, Jan. 1, 1904, Despatches, Panama, I.

67. *Sen. Doc.*, No. 32, 58 Cong., 2 Sess. (Ser. 4587), p. 8.

68. Bunau-Varilla to Hay, December 31, 1903, Notes from the Panamanian Legation, I.

69. Buchanan to Hay, No. 40, Jan. 22, 1904, Despatches, Panama, I.

70. Hay to Russell, Apr. 30, 1904; Loomis to Russell, May 19, 1904, *For. Rel.* (1904), pp. 653, 655.

71. *Sen. Doc.*, No. 208, 58 Cong., 2 Sess. (Ser. 4591), p. 23.

72. Tomás Arias to Hay, No. 355, May 17, 1904, Notes from the Panamanian Legation, I.

73. Obaldía to Hay, No. 6, Feb. 18, 1905, *loc. cit.*

74. Panama, Sec. R. E., *Memoria*, 1906, pp. 252-255.

75. *Gaceta oficial*, July 5, 1904.

76. Barrett to Hay, No. 30, Sept. 5, 1905, and enclosures, Despatches, Panama, III.

77. Sands to Loomis, June 12, 1905, *loc. cit.*, IV; Obaldía to Hay, No. 20, June 24, 1905, Notes from the Panamanian Legation, I; IBAR, *Monthly Bulletin*, XXI (1905), 1132, 1717.

78. Panama, Sec. R. E., *Memoria*, 1908, pp. 261-266.

79. Bryan to Price, June 29, 1914; Bryan to Morales, Nov. 7, 1914, *For. Rel.* (1914), pp. 1032, 1035-1036.

80. Morales to Lansing, July 28, 1916, *loc. cit.* (1917), pp. 1179-1180; *The Fitch Record of Government Debts, 1918* (New York, 1918), p. 314. Hereafter cited as *Fitch Government Debts*, 1918.

81. República de Panamá, Secretaría de Hacienda y Tesoro, *Memoria*, 1916, p. xi. Hereafter cited as Panama, Sec. H. y T., *Memoria*, 1916.

82. *Ibid.*, 1926, p. 16; *BPAU*, XLI (1915), 749.

83. Morales to Lansing, July 28, 1916, *For. Rel.* (1917), pp. 1179-1180.

84. Lansing to Porras, Dec. 22, 1916, *loc. cit.*, pp. 1180-1181.

85. Porras to Lansing, Dec. 26, 1916, *loc. cit.*, pp. 1181-1182.

86. Garay, *op. cit.*, pp. 54-55; Guardia, *op. cit.*, pp. 3-9; *BPAU*, XLVII (1918), 883; XLVIII (1919), 708-709; *For. Rel.* (1919), II, 679-688.

87. *BPAU*, XLIX (1919), 96; Price to Lansing, Nov. 10, 1918; Price to the acting secretary of state, Feb. 6, 1919, *For. Rel.* (1919), II, 684, 688; *Estrella*, Feb. 25, 1921.

88. *For. Rel.* (1919), II, 689-693; *BPAU*, XLIX (1919), 96.

89. C. H. Calhoun, "How Panama Paid off Its Debts," in *Current History*, XIV (1921), 298-299.

90. U. S. Department of Commerce, *Trade Information Bulletin*, No. 281 (1921), p. 66.

91. Wm. S. Howell, U. S. chargé, "Roads and Road Construction in the Republic of Panama," MS., p. 2, Columbus Memorial Library, Pan American Union, Washington, D. C.; *Gaceta oficial*, Feb. 26, 1920.

92. *BPAU*, LIX (1925), 950; LXII (1928), 1068; *N. Y. Times*, Mar. 8, 1930, 10:1.

93. Panama, Sec. H. y T., *Report Submitted by the Secretary of State of the Department of Finance and Treasury to the National Assembly of 1924* (Panama, 1924), pp. 24-26; Sec. A. y O. P., *Memoria*, 1924, pp. 1-3; *Kimber's Government Debts*, 1931, p. 942.

94. *Kimber's Government Debts*, 1926, p. 754; Great Britain, Dept. of Overseas Trade, *op. cit.*, 1927, p. 7.

95. U. S. Department of Commerce, *Trade Information Bulletin*, No. 503 (1927), p. 28; *Gaceta oficial*, Oct. 23, 1926.

96. *Kimber's Government Debts*, 1930, pp. 917-919; J. S. Porter, ed., *Moody's Manual of Investments; American and Foreign; Government Securities*, 1934 (New York, 1934), p. 2660. Hereafter cited as *Moody's Government Securities*, 1934.

97. *Kimber's Government Debts*, 1930, pp. 916-920.

98. Panama, Sec. H. y T., *Memoria*, 1926, p. xx; Great Britain, Dept. of Overseas Trade, *op. cit.*, 1927, p. 7.

99. *Gaceta oficial*, Apr. 2, 1928.

100. J. Fred Rippy, "Political Issues in Panama Today," in *Current History*, XXVIII (1928), 226-227.

101. Panama, Sec. H. y T., *Memoria*, 1928, p. xxxi.

102. *Kimber's Government Debts*, 1930, p. 916.

103. *Ibid.*, p. 917.

104. Panama, Sec. H. y T., *Memoria*, 1928, p. xxviii.

105. *Ibid.*, 1930, p. lxiv.

106. "Panama Awaits the Ax," in *The Nation*, CXXIX (1929), 133.

107. Panama, Sec. H. y T., *Memoria*, 1930, p. lxiv; U. S. Department of Commerce, *Trade Information Bulletin*, No. 657 (1929), p. 20; No. 707 (1930), p. 19. See George E. Roberts, *Investigación economica de la República de Panamá* (Panama, 1933).

108. L. C. Fox, "High Financing in Panama," in *The Nation*, CXXVIII (1929), 684.

109. Calhoun, *op. et loc. cit.*, p. 299.

110. Panama, *Compendio estadístico, 1909 a 1916*, p. 95; Great Britain, Dept. of Overseas Trade, *op. cit.*, 1924, p. 5.

111. Panama, Sec. H. y T., *Memoria*, 1916, pp. xvi-xvii; 1928, p. xxxiv.

112. U. S. Department of Commerce, *Commerce Yearbook*, 1928 (Washington, 1929), II, 497; *BPAU*, LXV (1931), 646, 1276.

113. U. S. Department of Commerce, *Foreign Commerce Yearbook*, 1933 (Washington, 1934), p. 225; *Moody's Government Securities*, 1934, pp. 2660-2661.

114. *Current History*, XXXVIII (1933), 471; *N. Y. Times*, May 12, 25:1; May 13, 1933, 23:7.

115. *Moody's Government Securities*, 1934, p. 2658.

116. *Ibid.*; *N. Y. Times*, Nov. 23, 1933, 31:2-3.

117. U. S. Department of Commerce, *The Foreign Commerce and Navigation of the United States for the Year Ending June 30, 1904* (Washington, 1904), I, 140-141. Hereafter cited as *Foreign Commerce and Navigation*, 1904.

118. *Ibid.*, 1905, pp. 44-45.

119. *Ibid.*, 1910, pp. 50-51.

120. Panama, *Compendio estadístico, 1909 a 1916*, pp. 12-25.

121. *Foreign Commerce and Navigation*, 1915, p. xiv.

122. Panama, *Compendio estadístico, 1909 a 1916*, pp. 12-25.

123. *Foreign Commerce and Navigation*, 1920, p. xii.

124. Panama, *Boletín de estadística*, No. 44, pp. 38-43; No. 46, pp. 88-93.

125. *Foreign Commerce and Navigation*, 1922, p. xii.

126. *Ibid.*, 1925, II, viii.

127. Panama, *Boletín de estadística*, No. 57, pp. 71-79; No. 59, pp. 72-78.

128. *Foreign Commerce and Navigation*, 1929, I, xi.

129. *Moody's Government Securities*, 1934, p. 2657.

130. *Ibid.*; *Foreign Commerce and Navigation*, 1932, p. 82.

131. *Foreign Commerce Yearbook*, 1933, p. 224.

132. *Foreign Commerce and Navigation*, 1932, p. 82.

133. *Foreign Commerce Yearbook*, 1933, p. 223.

134. *BPAU*, LXVIII (1934), 259.

135. Panama, *Compendio estadístico, 1909 a 1916*, pp. 12-25.

136. *Commerce Yearbook*, 1928, II, 495; *Foreign Commerce Yearbook*, 1933, p. 223.

137. Great Britain, Dept. of Overseas Trade, *op. cit.*, 1924, p. 13; *Commerce Reports*, May 2, 1932, p. 263.

138. *Foreign Commerce Yearbook*, 1933, p. 224.

139. *Commerce Yearbook*, 1930, II, 443.

140. Sands to Root, No. 82, Mar. 26, 1906, and 128 pages of enclosures, Despatches, Panama, V; Panama, Sec. R. E., *Memoria*, 1908, p. xxxv.

141. See C. D. Kepner, Jr., and J. H. Soothill, *The Banana Empire; A Case Study of Economic Imperialism* (New York, 1935).

142. "Panama Awaits the Ax," in *The Nation*, CXXIX (1929), 134.

CHAPTER VI

THE PANAMANIAN-COSTA RICAN BOUNDARY DISPUTE (1825-1915)

SOON AFTER Great Colombia and the United Provinces of Central America had seceded from Spain and established themselves as independent nations, the question of determining their common boundary arose. Direct negotiations terminated in the Gual-Molina Treaty of 1825,[1] the Herrán-Calvo Treaty of 1856, the Valenzuela-Castro Treaty of 1865,[2] and the Correso-Montúfar Treaty of 1876, but the desired end was attained by none of these.[3]

Eventually the republics of Colombia and Costa Rica became convinced of the futility of attempting to reach a practical result by means of direct negotiations and resolved in 1876 to use the system of arbitration to end, "forever and irrevocably," the controversy that had existed since they had ceased to be Spanish dependencies. With this view they concluded their first arbitration treaty at San José, Costa Rica, on December 25, 1880.[4] This convention, known as the Quijano Otero-Castro Treaty, named King Alfonso XII of Spain as arbitrator, but he died before anything could be accomplished.[5]

In 1886 a second arbitration convention was negotiated in Paris for the purpose of submitting the controversy to the successor of Alfonso XII. This *convención* provided that the arbitral judgment was to be confined to the territory within the extreme limits described as follows:

The territorial limit which the Republic of Costa Rica claims, on the Atlantic side, extends as far as the island of Escudo de Veraguas and the River Chiriquí (Calobebora) inclusive; and on the Pacific side as far as the River Chiriquí Viejo, inclusive, to the east of Punta Burica.

The territorial limit which the United States of Colombia claims extends on the Atlantic side as far as Cape Gracias a Dios inclusive;

and on the Pacific side as far as the mouth of the River Golfito in Gulf Dulce.[6]

Nothing came of this agreement, and finally on November 4, 1896, Jorge Holguín of Colombia and Ascención Esquivel of Costa Rica signed at Bogotá a third arbitration treaty designed to carry out the San José convention of 1880 and the Paris accord of 1886. The president of France was appointed arbitrator, and his judgment was to be accepted as follows: "The arbitral decision, whatever it be, shall be held as a perfect and binding Treaty between the High Contracting Parties, and shall not admit any appeal. Both parties engage themselves to its faithful fulfilment, and waive all claims against the decision, pledging in this the national honor."[7] Under this agreement the controversy was submitted to President Émile Loubet, who, after a study of the mass of documents and inadequate maps supplied by the contending parties, finally handed down an indefinite decision on September 11, 1900, which vaguely indicated a settlement as follows:

The boundary between the Republics of Colombia and Costa Rica shall be formed by the spur of the mountain range which starts from Point Mona on the Atlantic Ocean and closes to the North the valley of the River Tarire or River Sixaola, and the next by the range of division of the waters between the Atlantic and the Pacific, up to approximately 9° of latitude; it shall then follow the line of division of the waters of Chiriquí Viejo and the affluents of Gulf Dulce, terminating at the Point of Burica on the Pacific Ocean.[8]

Costa Rica was not satisfied with the Loubet decision, and on September 29, 1900, Minister Manuel María Peralta requested an interpretation of its meaning. The French foreign minister, Theophile Delcassé, replied on November 23, 1900:

. . . on account of the lack of exact geographic data, the Arbitrator was not able to fix the boundary except by means of general indications; I think, therefore, that there would be no difficulty in fixing them on the map. But there is no doubt, as you observe, that, in conformity with the terms of articles 2 and 3 of the Convention of Paris of January 20, 1886, this boundary line must be drawn within the confines of the territory in dispute, as they are determined by the text of said articles.[9]

Owing to internal disturbances in Colombia and the objection of Costa Rica, the award was never placed in effect.[10] However, the Republic of Panama recognized the award on November 16, 1903, thirteen days after its declaration of independence, when the boundary between the new republic and its northern neighbor was indicated in the formation of the province of Bocas del Toro as follows: "On the northwest the dividing line between this Republic and Costa Rica, according to the arbitral award of the President of the French Republic."[11] This was ratified soon after in Article 3 of the Panamanian constitution, which stated:

The territory of the Republic is composed of all the territory from which the State of Panama was formed by the amendment to the Granada constitution of 1853, on February 27, 1855, and which was transformed in 1886 into the Department of Panama, together with its islands, and of the continental and insular territory which was adjudged to the Republic of Colombia in the award made by the President of the French Republic on September 11, 1900.[12]

The Republic of Panama continued to hold jurisdiction over the disputed territory on the Pacific side, while Costa Rica administered that on the Atlantic side in accordance with the provisions of the treaty of December 25, 1880.[13] However, neither country agreed with the other as to the location of the provisional or *status quo* boundary.[14]

As early as February 18, 1904, Secretary of State Hay ordered Chargé W. W. Russell to inform the Panamanian government that Costa Rica was disposed to begin negotiations for a settlement in regard to the boundary and that the United States would be pleased if an amicable arrangement could be reached.[15] This was especially true since the United Fruit Company and H. L. McConnell of the American Banana Company were having some difficulty over the land about the mouth of the Sixaola River. The United Fruit Company was attempting to develop the area under Costa Rican jurisdiction, while McConnell claimed that he had a concession from Panama.[16]

The *status quo* arrangement being unsatisfactory and the pressure of the United States having some effect, Costa Rica began negotiations on April 6, 1904, with Panama for determining their true frontier.[17] Early in July Leonidas Pacheco arrived in Panama City as special minister from Costa Rica for the purpose of modifying the Loubet Award on the Atlantic side in favor of his country and for finally settling the entire controversy.[18] Because the Costa Ricans were unfavorable to McConnell, he threw his weight against the modification of the award. After several weeks of amicable negotiations Pacheco left for San José on September 28 for further instructions. He was expected to return to Panama late in October for a final solution.[19]

When Pacheco returned about the middle of December the Panamanian government had changed its attitude. Secretary Guardia was disposed to an adjustment, but President Amador refused any change in the Loubet line other than a slight alteration suggested by Tomás Arias before his resignation as foreign secretary. Minister Barrett thought that powerful private interests were blocking adjudication, and warned Hay to watch Minister Obaldía in Washington. He explained that Arias was fighting any concession in order to protect his prestige and that Federico Boyd had informed him that a recession from the Arias line would mean the overthrow of the government. The minister reported that the electric light company of Panama City, in which William Nelson Cromwell was interested, hoped to gain by opposing the settlement of the dispute. Pacheco wanted to reach an agreement whereby his government would acquire a large area on the Caribbean, but was willing to concede almost as much on the Pacific. Barrett believed the time had arrived for action and informed Hay that he would bring pressure to bear on Amador. Pacheco had proposed a *modus vivendi* line to be named by the American minister, but Amador bluntly refused arbitration by the United

States, even though subject to the ratification of the National Assembly of 1906. He claimed that this would be equal to a final award, for Panama could neither object nor maintain an objection to a judgment of the United States. Barrett thought this indicated a weakness in the Panamanian position,[20] but the president was probably displaying wisdom.

In order to break the deadlock, Barrett prevailed upon Amador to promise to accept the good offices of the United States for a final settlement. Because of the political situation, the Panamanian president asked that Hay make the offer through Minister Obaldía and apparently on the initiative of the State Department.[21] Shortly thereafter the United States informed the Costa Rican and Panamanian ministers in Washington that it was prepared to tender its good offices for an amicable adjustment.[22] Barrett continued to work for what he considered a fair settlement. By January 30, 1905, Amador had decided on a compromise between the Arias and Pacheco lines. Since the American minister had suggested the new boundary, the proposal was made that it be called the Barrett line. On his refusal the line was named for Amador.[23] Barrett then urged the president and his cabinet to make every effort to reach an agreement in order that they might receive all credit and honor.[24] Amador conferred with sixteen prominent citizens on February 8 and laid before them some unsigned memoranda by the American minister favoring the Amador line. After this group failed to reach a decision, the president informed Barrett that failure was inevitable unless Tomás Arias and Pablo Arosemena withdrew their objections. The minister then persuaded Arias to remain away from the final conference, which was set for February 15, and convinced Arosemena that he should support the compromise line. The settlement was accepted on February 15, and Barrett advised the State Department that the offer of the mediation of the United States had provided the leverage that terminated the controversy.[25] He also stated that Amador and Guardia wanted a telegram of congratulations from the American president. Roosevelt was asked to intimate that the United States regarded the settlement final in order to remove the danger of its rejection by the National Assembly.[26]   When no response was made, the minister requested that the felicitation be sent after the treaty was concluded, explaining that Amador and Guardia were insistent.[27]

On March 6, 1905, three conventions concerning the final settlement of the boundary dispute were signed.   In order to appease Panamanian pride and to avoid offending French honor, one *convención* accepted the Loubet Award, while another modified it by giving Panama more territory on the Pacific and Costa Rica more on the Atlantic Coast than had been adjudged to them.[28] On the following day Roosevelt sent the desired telegram of congratulations to President Amador.[29]   Guardia and Pacheco profusely thanked the American minister for his untiring efforts.[30]

Rivalry between the United Fruit Company and the American Banana Company continued in a part of the area on the Atlantic littoral.   Costa Rica refused to permit McConnell to continue his developments, and since the Guardia-Pacheco Treaty would transfer that section to the permanent jurisdiction of Panama, the Washington government asked the Panamanian government to take up with Costa Rica the matter of the protection of American interests there.   Guardia refused, explaining that he considered the territory under the complete jurisdiction of Costa Rica until the ratification of the treaty. After the treaty went into effect Panama would give the required protection.   Guardia informed Minister Magoon that he believed the United Fruit Company, the American Banana Company, and others were trying to draw the three governments into a dispute, and that he intended to keep Panama neutral.   The United States, in his opinion, should treat directly with Costa Rica.   Magoon explained to the State Department that Guardia objected to being entangled in the banana dispute in the Sixaola region because Panama was administering a large section on the Pacific Coast that belonged to Costa Rica and interference on the Sixaola might bring retaliation from Costa Rica on the Pacific.   The minister indicated to the State Department the untenableness of its stand in asking Panama to interfere.

Permit me [he wrote] to call attention to the possibility that, if the United States insists that Panama shall attempt to control the exercise of sovereign powers by Costa Rica in the Sixaola country upon the ground that Panama is the permanent sovereign and Costa Rica the administrator, the rule so established may be appealed to by Panama and attempt made to control the exercise of sovereign powers by the United States in the Canal Zone, the excuse for such interference being that Panama is the titular sovereign of the Zone territory and the United States the administrator; the only difference being that the term, in one instance, is temporary and in the other perpetual.[31]

Opposition to the modification of the Loubet Award continued in Panama, but the Guardia-Pacheco Treaty might have been ratified but for the interference of McConnell. He attempted to persuade the National Assembly that the Loubet Award had gone into effect and that Panama rightfully owned the territory that was being ceded to Costa Rica. He proposed that the legislature pass a resolution authorizing the president to take over the area. On November 13, 1906, while Amador and influential members of the government were absent from Panama City, McConnell prevailed upon a committee to report favorably upon his proposal, and a resolution was passed directing the president to assume jurisdiction over the territory. This created a sensation which aroused the government, and the National Assembly shortly revoked its action. The furor also created some interest in Costa Rica and probably was one of the reasons for Costa Rica's rejection of the treaty.[32] The cause given, however, was that the following stipulation made by the Panamanian National Assembly when it approved the agreement on January 26, 1907, was unacceptable: "If the Republic of Costa Rica does not approve this treaty at the latest during the next regular session of its legislature, the executive is authorized to suspend the action of this law and require the execution of the Loubet award."[33]

Costa Rica kept the United States informed of the progress of the negotiations and late in 1907 sent Luis Anderson to Washington to enlist the aid of the American government in ending the discord with Panama.[34] Joaquín Bernardo Calvo, the Costa Rican minister at Washington, had already ascertained that the chief justice of the United States Supreme Court might act as arbitrator. On December 4 Anderson conferred with Secretary of State Root and five days later requested the good offices of the American government. He explained that his government was confident that, through the wise and disinterested co-operation of the United States, Costa Rica would be able "to carry to a happy ending the fixing of the dividing line with her sister Republic of Panama, thus making closer still, if possible, the friendly relations which happily unite[d] those two countries."[35] The State Department soon consented,[36] and on December 24 the Costa Rican request and the American answer were sent to Minister H. G. Squiers with instructions to urge Panama to submit the controversy to the chief justice or some high judicial officer of the United States.[37] However, the opening of the presidential campaign in Panama shortly thereafter forestalled negotiations,[38] and no progress was made for almost a year.[39]

Anderson resumed his discussions with the United States on November 21, 1908, saying that the condition created by the dispute was a constant cause of unrest in both countries "to the impairment of their reciprocal interests and the feeling of good will and amity which . . . [had] always united the Costa Ricans and the Panamans." Considering the time propitious, he solicited anew the impartial mediation of the Washington government.[40] Ten days later the State Department instructed Squiers to renew negotiations with Panama, stating that the United States would "be very happy to extend its impartial good offices and mediation" in the hope that the long-standing boundary dispute might be settled to the satisfaction of both parties.[41] At the same time Anderson was informed that the American government would "cheerfully extend its impartial good offices."[42] Squiers reported on December 24 that Panama accepted in principle the submission of the dispute to the judgment of the chief justice of the United States, but wished to know the questions that were to be treated. The Panamanian government was not inclined to surrender the boundary line fixed by the Loubet Award and by its constitution.[43]

The Panamanian query was given immediately to Anderson,[44] who replied that his government wished to discard the Loubet Award because of the indefiniteness of its terms and to submit the whole boundary question to a new decision. He explained that the award had been interpreted variously and that Colombia had claimed a line that went beyond the limits of the disputed territory. Panama apparently advanced the same contention, thus raising the defect of *ultra petita*, which invalidated the legality of the decision. Since Panama held tenaciously to the provisions of the Loubet Award and its constitution, Anderson suggested the following points for mediation: "Whether the Loubet award is free from defects that, according to the principles of international law, impair its legal force. If, considering that the award is not thus defective, to determine what its meaning is, and through which points the frontier line shall be drawn."[45]

Before Panama could be informed of the proposed questions, J. A. Arango, the Panamanian foreign secretary, stated that Panama appreciated the offer of the United States, but had resolved to establish a legation at San José for the settlement of the controversy. He wanted to know the points for consideration before his government rejected the mediation proposal.[46] On January 9, 1909, the Panamanian government definitely declined to submit the controversy to arbitration, but promised that, if after exhausting all proper methods no solution was reached, all points of disagreement in determining the boundary line in accordance with the Loubet Award would be submitted with pleasure to an opinion of the chief justice of the United States.[47] The Panamanian special minister arrived in San José on April 19, 1909, and on June 15 he was informed that Costa Rica considered the Guardia-Pacheco Treaty to have expired.[48]

Following Panama's rejection of the mediation of the United States, Root wrote to Squires that, owing to the rival claims of Americans in the disputed area along the Sixaola River, the

situation had become "embarrassing and vexatious" to the Washington government. The settlement of these claims was dependent upon the "issue of the question of sovereign title to the
territory and sovereign jurisdiction over the controversies arising therein," and this condition would exist as long as "the
determination of sovereign title" remained in suspense. Since
Panama left the jurisdiction of the area to Costa Rica, the
United States would look to that government for the alleviation
of the annoyances caused "by the absence of responsible jurisdiction in that quarter."⁴⁹   At the same time Root expressed disappointment at the refusal of the Panamanian government to
accept immediate arbitration and indicated that he believed the
mission to San José would be as ineffectual as previous efforts.
He recalled the fact that for "three years and more" the United
States had "repeatedly and urgently shown its earnest desire
and expectation" of a termination of the conflict, and also clearly
indicated that his government's chief interest in the disputed
sector was its citizens and their property. Squiers was instructed
to read these declarations to the foreign secretary and to give
him a copy of the despatch.⁵⁰

On January 30 the State Department referred Squiers to
the instructions sent Minister Magoon on April 16, 1906,⁵¹
which held that Costa Rica could do no more than preserve the
property over which it exercised temporary jurisdiction and
which advised Panama to reach an agreement with that government for the protection of existing rights and titles to lands in
the territory.⁵²   The earlier note was to be presented to the
foreign secretary "in order to show not only the constant attitude of the United States, but the necessity of such attitude for
the protection of the property interests of American citizens in
the disputed territory."⁵³

On February 16 the State Department expressed to Anderson the hope that the controversy might be settled in San José,
but stated that in the event of failure the United States would
look to Costa Rica to relieve the "annoying and embarrassing
situation" caused by the lack of responsible jurisdiction in the
disputed region.⁵⁴   Anderson immediately accepted the position

of the United States and promised American citizens "the ample and most efficient protection" possible under Costa Rican law.[55]

On July 30, 1909, Carlos C. Arosemena, the Panamanian minister at Washington, informed Secretary of State P. C. Knox that his government considered that all means of terminating the controversy had been exhausted and requested the *buenos oficios* of the Washington government.[56] At the same time he presented a memorandum prepared by Samuel Lewis which gave a brief survey of the boundary dispute, proposed the execution of the Loubet Award, and asked that the chief justice of the Supreme Court determine which of two lines decided upon by Panama was the correct border between the two countries. If Costa Rica accepted this basis for arbitration, Panama wanted that government to agree formally with the United States that the decision of the American jurist should be final.[57]

While the Panamanian proposal was passing through the sluggish channels of diplomacy, excitement arose concerning the disputed sector. On August 31 the Panamanian minister protested to the State Department that Costa Rica continued granting land on the left bank of the Sixaola in violation of the *status quo* and the sovereignty of Panama. Because this was not in accord with the Magoon note of April 16, 1906, Arosemena requested the United States to express its disapproval to Costa Rica,[58] but the State Department declined.[59]

On October 14, 1909, Minister Calvo informed Knox that the Panamanian mission to San José had accomplished nothing and again solicited the aid of the United States.[60] Two days later Anderson wrote Knox that he had been instructed to resume negotiations for the "so much desired settlement."[61] The State Department immediately informed Anderson that Panama was willing to submit to the chief justice the question of which of the two lines evolved from the Loubet Award was the correct one, provided Costa Rica formally agreed with the United States to accept the decision of the arbiter as final.[62] Anderson replied that he welcomed with "real satisfaction" the attitude of the Panamanian government, and apparently accepted its basis for arbitration, but countered with the following points for submission: "Which of the two interpretations given by the interested parties to the Loubet award should prevail as the correct one according to law. Whether the Loubet award, understood in the way of Colombia, now Panama, interprets it, would or would not be obligatory."[63]

On October 20 the State Department, finally replying to the Arosemena note of July 30, indicated in a general way that Costa Rica was prepared to submit the matter to the decision of the chief justice according to the terms of Panama.[64] The Panamanian answered that he was empowered to do no more than inform his government of developments and, noting the generalities of the State Department note, called attention to the Lewis memorandum in order to remove all doubt as to the questions for submission to an arbitral decision.[65] Knox explained on November 2 that the purpose of the Washington government was to bring the contending parties "together in the path of arbitration" and that the State Department did not consider it necessary "to take any part in the formulation of the terms of submission." He further clarified his stand:

This Government has assumed that the two parties were in discord as to a part of the Loubet award, and that all that is wanted is for each to submit its interpretation as to that part of the line in disagreement and invite the arbitrator to determine which of these two interpretations is the correct one under the Loubet award.[66]

The Panamanian minister objected to this statement because it indicated that each was to submit an interpretation of the Loubet Award. Foreign Secretary Lewis pointed out that a discrepancy existed between the views expressed by the State Department in the note of October 20 and in that of November 2. The earlier communication had intimated that the Washington government would guarantee the execution of the decision of the chief justice, while the latter disavowed "any intention on the part of the United States to guarantee that the arbitration decree when rendered . . . [would] be acquiesced in by the parties signatory."[67]

Knox invited Arosemena and Anderson to a conference at the State Department on January 15, 1910, for drawing up a "protocol agreement formulating the questions at issue" to be submitted to Chief Justice Melville W. Fuller as sole arbiter.[68] The Panamanian replied that his presence would mean nothing because he had no instructions from his government for reaching an agreement.[69] Anderson accepted and reminded Knox that his government wanted a convention ample enough to include any questions in dispute.[70] The Costa Rican attitude was natural because Panama recognized its gains on the Pacific side and it had nothing to lose on the Atlantic Coast, for the Isthmian republic had profited there by the Loubet Award.

By December 16 the State Department had begun to urge Panama to include all points in dispute in the agreement.[71] On December 18 the American chargé at Panama City was instructed to inform the Panamanian government that the United States would leave the formulation of the questions for arbitration to the contestants and that the United States would not guarantee the acceptance of the decision, but hoped that the agreement would be "so ample as to include" all disputed points.[72]

Until February 2, 1910, the State Department acted as a friendly mediator. At that time Knox apparently became impatient and overbearing and stated that his government had no intention of limiting the boundary issue to a mere interpretation of the Loubet Award. He emphatically specified "that the crucial matter to be submitted" to an arbitral decision was the "respective contentions of the two Republics as to the true boundary line" between them. He expressed surprise that Belisario Porras, the Panamanian special minister at Washington, had not been granted full powers for negotiating a protocol of agreement, but had been instructed to demand an exact acceptance of the Loubet Award. Knox, however, claimed that he was indicating the friendly opinion of his government and disavowed any intention of influencing the "free agreement" of the two nations. He indicated that the controversy could not be settled by a simple interpretation of the Loubet decision, and advised Porras that Punta Burica and Punta Mona be accepted as the terminals of the boundary, which was then to be drawn between them without restriction in the light of the award and all other circumstances. His government felt the importance of urging an amicable settlement because of the large property interests of its citizens in the disputed area and the guaranty under the Canal treaty of the independence of Panama, which gave it the right to know the exact extent of the territory whose independence had been guaranteed.[73]

Secretary Lewis thanked the Washington government for its assurance that it was only expressing a friendly opinion and not attempting to exercise influence on the republics and for its statement that the responsibility for the outcome of the negotiations rested solely with the contending powers. He explained that Porras was invested with the "most ample powers" possible to grant in accordance with the constitution, the Loubet Award, the national laws, and the permanent interests of the nation. Further, he stated that neither the validity nor the obligatory force of the Loubet decision had ever been discussed between Panama and Costa Rica. Its correct interpretation only had been considered, and it had been recognized by the United States as valid. However, his government, in its "vehement and sincere desire to put an end to the boundary controversy," was disposed to amplify the powers of Porras if necessary, "having always as a prior and unalterable basis the recognition of the Loubet award; the sole circumstance" which would make a solution adjustable to its fundamental charter.[74]

On the ground that nothing could be added to the affair except the name of the arbitrator, Porras refused on February 20 to consent to an annulment of the Loubet decision and the re-submission of the controversy to arbitration. He suggested the appointment by the three governments of a commission of engineers for laying out the boundary in accordance with the Loubet Award and the Delcassé letter of November 23, 1900. Should the commission be unable to agree on any part of the line or should either republic become dissatisfied, the chief justice of the United States would be asked to decide as to the part in dispute in accordance with the Loubet Award and with the aid of maps prepared by the engineers.[75]

During a conference at the State Department on March 1, 1910, Knox rejected the proposal for a joint surveying commission, but conceded that the arbiter might use engineers to assemble data for his study. He asked that "valid titles to land and other valid rights of property" in the region, granted at any time by Colombia, Panama, or Costa Rica, be recognized and protected if the arbitration resulted in any transfer of sovereignty. Taking the contentions of the two governments into consideration, he proposed the following indefinite and ambiguous question for submission to the chief justice:

What is the boundary between the Republics of Costa Rica and Panama under and most in accordance with the true interpretation and correct intention of the Loubet award in the light of all the historical, geographical, topographical, and other facts and circumstances surrounding it as well as under the established principles of international law?[76]

Porras was willing to agree that no doubt existed as to the interpretation of the Loubet Award on the Pacific side from Punta Burica to the central *cordillera;* but, fearing that the Knox question might lead to an unwitting modification of the award, he suggested: "What is the boundary between the Republics of Panama and Costa Rica under and in accordance with the correct interpretation and true intention of the Loubet award." He accepted the request for the protection of property rights, but wanted the phrase "other valid rights of property" clarified so as to "exclude any collateral privileges, exemptions, or concessions running with the land or expressed in any grants." Porras still held to the commission of engineers, but would defer to Knox, provided surveys might be made at the call of either party.[77]

By March 12 a protocol had been drawn which recognized the Loubet Award as being clear and indisputable on the Pacific Coast and accepted the Porras question for the decision of the chief justice. However, "all the facts, circumstances and considerations which . . . [might] have a bearing on the case," as well as the limitation of the Delcassé letter, were to be taken into account. Porras wanted to add the statement:

And if at any point the boundary line, as specifically described in said award, would otherwise go beyond the confines of said disputed territory, the line of said disputed territory shall constitute the boundary line from such point to the point where next it intersects the line specifically described as the boundary in said award.[78]

Knox contended that this limitation was immaterial and unnecessary, and it appeared to be superfluous. The State Department practically issued an ultimatum to the Panamanian government that the United States would discontinue its good offices if the Porras suggestion was not withdrawn. The Panamanian foreign secretary was told that the last meeting of the plenipotentiaries would be held on March 16 for the sole purpose of ascertaining what Panama had done. He was warned that failure to withdraw the amendment would "surely involve the rejection of the convention by Costa Rica and responsibility for the utter failure of these negotiations" would rest upon Panama.[79] Strange indeed that an unimportant addition should meet such determined resistance by Knox and the Costa Ricans!

The little Panamanian republic surrendered to the inevitable, and Lewis cabled Knox on March 14 that Porras had been instructed to sign the convention as originally drawn.[80] Thus the six thousand hectares of the United Fruit Company in the Sixaola territory[81] were protected fully by American dollar diplomacy. The arbitration agreement, signed on March 17, 1910, provided for the acceptance of the Loubet Award on the Pacific and for the submission of the following question to the chief justice of the United States Supreme Court: "What is the boundary between Panama and Costa Rica under and most in accordance with the correct interpretation and true intention of the award of the President of the French Republic made the 11th of September, 1900?" This was to be determined in the light of all the facts, circumstances, and considerations, including the Delcassé letter, that might have a bearing upon the case. In the event that the arbiter or either republic deemed it advisable, a surveying commission of four engineers might be chosen to aid the chief justice in reaching a decision. One was to be appointed by Costa Rica, one by Panama, and the other two by the arbitrator. The two governments promised to recognize and protect all "titles to lands and other real property rights" in the disputed region. The protocol provided for a boundary delimiting and marking commission to be appointed in the same manner as the surveying committee. The republics further agreed:

The award, whatever it be, shall be held as a perfect and compulsory treaty between the high contracting parties. Both high contracting parties bind themselves to the faithful execution of the award and waive all claims against it.

The boundary line between the two Republics as finally fixed by the arbitrator shall be deemed the true line, and his determination of the same shall be final, conclusive, and without appeal.[82]

Ratifications were exchanged in Washington on May 17, 1911. Almost a month later Calvo and Porras addressed a joint note to Knox inclosing a request to the chief justice for his services as arbiter.[83] Chief Justice Edward D. White accepted on July 25, 1911, on the condition that all documents submitted to him should be translated into English and that the contending governments accept the responsibility for the "sufficiency and accuracy of the translations."[84] On July 31 Calvo and Porras acquiesced in White's conditions,[85] and he became the agent for further estranging the relations of the two republics.

Little was heard of the controversy for more than two years. The disputants prepared documents to substantiate their respective claims. Panama was placed at a disadvantage, for many of the sources of information were locked in the Colombian archives and thus inaccessible. Perhaps a search for the available documents in Spain was not feasible, or the Panamanians may have trusted the chief justice to render a decision in conformity with the arbitration convention. At any rate, the documents presented by the Panamanian government appear pitifully inadequate when compared with the elaborate briefs of the Costa Rican government. White spent several months in digesting the detailed proof of the Costa Ricans and the impassioned pleas of the Panamanians and eventually handed down on September 12, 1914, a decision favorable to Costa Rica. The Panamanians have not yet understood how a man of his reputed intelligence and legal sagacity could have arrived at his conclusion. Possibly he became lost in the maze of conflicting testimony that began with a letter written by Christopher Columbus to the Spanish sovereigns on July 7, 1503,[86] and covered practically every phase of the case thereafter. More than fifty volumes in English and Spanish fail to produce any definite conviction, but White saw more justice in the argument of Costa Rica.

After reviewing the history of the controversy the chief justice held that Loubet had exceeded his jurisdiction in terminating the boundary on the Atlantic Coast at Punta Mona. This decision was reached notwithstanding the fact that the Paris convention of 1886, which was accepted by the agreement of 1896 under which Loubet had rendered his judgment, expressly stated that Costa Rica's claims extended down to the Island of Escudo de Veraguas and the Chiriquí River and that Colombia claimed territory up to Cape Gracias a Dios. White apparently based his award upon the fact that Colombia had not seriously claimed jurisdiction above the Sixaola River. Anyway the mountain range described by Loubet as extending to Punta Mona actually terminated more than twenty miles from the coast, and the terrain gradually descended into a small swamp. President Loubet, according to White, must have been thinking more of natural boundaries than of justice when he rendered his judgment, and to the mind of the American this was not correct arbitration. Moreover, the maps that showed the mountain range to be a natural boundary were incorrect.

After reaching the conclusion that President Loubet had exceeded his jurisdiction, the American declared the purported line from Punta Mona, along the counterfort or spur of mountains described by Loubet, to the central *cordillera* to be nonexistent, and set the extremity of the line back to the mouth of the Sixaola River as follows:

And it is now adjudged that the boundary between the two countries "most in accordance with the correct interpretation and true intention" of the former award is a line which, starting from the mouth of the Sixaola River in the Atlantic, follows the thalweg of that river, upstream, until it reaches the Yorquin, or Zhorquin River; thence along the thalweg of the Yorquin River to that one of its headwaters which is the nearest to the divide which is the north limit of the drainage area of the Changuinola, or Tilorio River; thence up the thalweg which contains said headwater to said divide; thence along said divide to the divide which separates waters running to the Atlantic from those running to the Pacific; thence along said Atlantic-Pacific divide to the point near the ninth degree of north latitude "beyond Cerro Pando", referred to in Article I of the treaty of March 17, 1910; and that line is hereby decreed and established as the proper boundary.[87]

As early as September 19, 1914, rumors were spreading that the Panamanians were aroused over the White Award.[88] The press reported that the Panamanian National Assembly held a secret session on the night of October 5 and voted to reject the decision and to advise Foreign Secretary Ernesto T. Lefevre to reopen negotiations with Costa Rica for a more favorable boundary. The government organ, *El Diario,* charged that the American jurist went beyond the powers conferred upon him by the arbitration convention.[89] On October 17 Lefevre regretfully informed the Costa Rican government that Panama considered the White Award "null in the light of international law" because the chief justice had exceeded his authority in revising rather than interpreting the decision of Loubet.[90] The Costa Rican foreign secretary, Manuel Castro Quesada, replied that his government accepted the decision, expressed surprise at the Panamanian attitude, and denied that White had exceeded his powers.[91]

By November 25 the State Department had heard that hostilities were impending between the two republics, and Secretary of State William Jennings Bryan instructed the American legations at San José and Panama City to use their good offices that no violent action might be taken "until an amicable adjustment of the differences" could be reached. He displayed his lack of understanding of the problem by saying: "It would seem impossible that the possession of so small an area of land should become a cause of friction between the countries."[92] The American chargé at Panama City immediately replied that he had been assured that no change of *status quo* had occurred or was contemplated by the Panamanians. The only move made was a change of *corregidores* (mayors) in two towns on the Pacific side, but strict orders had been issued that authority was to be asserted only in territory previously occupied by Panama.[93] Quesada informed Minister E. J. Hale at San José on December 12 that an outbreak between Costa Rica and Panama was "a danger in the highest degree remote."[94]

In the meantime Eusebio A. Morales, the Panamanian minister at Washington, presented the State Department with a memorandum in defense of his government's position. Panama definitely refused to accept the White Award and intended to maintain the *status quo*.[95] This left Costa Rica possession of the territory adjudged it on the Atlantic side by White, and Panama jurisdiction over the area given on the Pacific Coast to Costa Rica by Loubet. The State Department replied that the memorandum was assumed to be only for its information because nothing was indicated as requiring immediate attention.[96]

On January 14, 1915, Quesada informed Hale that Costa Rica had been preparing to use force against the location by Panama of "various administrative authorities" in Costa Rican territory when the United States offered its mediation.[97] He also gave the American a copy of his protest against the placing of officials by Panama in the area north of Punta Burica.[98] Secretary E. T. Lefevre stated on January 30 that Panama would never accept the White Award and explained that the regular Panamanian officers north of Punta Burica only had been changed according to custom.   He pointed out that these authorities were maintained for the same reason that Costa Rica had officials on the left bank of the Sixaola.   Panama had decided to retain the *status quo* line because neither the Loubet nor the White Award had been accepted by both countries and the Porras-Anderson Treaty had provided only for an interpretation of the former decision.[99]   Quesada gave Hale this note and his reply six days later.   The Costa Rican ended a voluminous defense of the White Award with the statement that he doubted not that the justice and equity which inspired the acts of Panama would lead to the retirement of the officers located, in October, 1914, north of Punta Burica.[100]

On March 9 R. Brenes Mesén, the Costa Rican minister at Washington, wrote Bryan, urging that the United States should use its good offices for an early execution of the White Award. He advanced seven reasons that should impel the American government to that task: the magnitude of its interests on the Isthmus and its guarantee of Panamanian independence; the recognition of the *de facto* line on the Atlantic littoral by a State Department note of February 16, 1909; a statement by Root on March 12, 1910, that the United States would recognize the *de facto* or *status quo* line as the permanent boundary unless Panama signed the proposed arbitration protocol; the binding character of Article VII of the Porras-Anderson Treaty; the fact that White had awarded Costa Rica no territory that was under Panamanian jurisdiction; the previous recognition of the new boundary as the *status quo* line by Colombia, Panama, and the United States; and finally the support of the White decision would add moral value to the arbitration treaties that Bryan had placed before a cynical world.[101]

Bryan informed Minister Price on April 28 that no defect could be found in the award of the chief justice, that the United States could be a party to nothing that would discredit the arbiter nor could it "view with indifference the baneful influence which a rejection of this award" would have on arbitration in general, and that "it would be a matter of deep regret" if Panama indicated a lack of respect for the principle of arbitration or the United States Supreme Court. Although Panama was awarded no territory over which Costa Rica exercised jurisdiction, Bryan suggested that each country buy real estate of the nationals of the other in areas that would change hands by the execution of the White Award. Price was instructed to ask Panama to acquiesce promptly and completely in the decision and to offer the aid of the United States for a final and satisfactory settlement.[102]

On May 5 Mesén inquired as to the action that was to be taken on his request of March 9.[103] Bryan replied that the Washington government would lend such influence as it might properly exert and that a communication to that effect had been made to Panama.[104] On June 24 the State Department was notified that Santiago de la Guardia had arrived in San José in the hope of modifying the White Award, but that the Costa Rican government had refused to treat with him.[105]

Lefevre replied on July 28 to Bryan's request for the execution of the White decision with an interesting argument. He claimed that Panama had refused to agree to the award because of its desire "not to impair the principle of arbitration." The Porras-Anderson Treaty had provided for an interpretation of the Loubet Award; Chief Justice White had annulled and modified the decision of the French president; therefore, Panama could not accept the new adjudication which violated the Loubet Award and thus the principle of arbitration. Lefevre carefully explained that Panama was showing no disrespect toward the arbiter, for an appeal from a tribunal did not indicate a lack of reverence.[106]

After the Costa Rican government complained on September 27, 1915, of the Panamanian officials north of Punta Burica and requested the United States to urge Panama to accept the White Award as "a final effort to arrive at a solution of that question without having recourse to the lamentable excesses of violence,"[107] the affair was left suspended. The World War had absorbed all attention. Almost a century of negotiation and bickering had produced no final result. Probably more money had been expended in efforts to reach a settlement than the area in dispute was worth. A permanent adjustment might have been reached, but the world was plunged into the chaos of the great war, and the small matter of a Central American boundary dispute was relegated to the background in the chivalrous but chimerical effort of the United States to make the world safe for democracy.

NOTES

1. Ricardo J. Alfaro, *Límites entre Panamá y Costa Rica* (Panama, 1913), pp. 1-2.

2. B. W. Palmer, *The American Banana Company* . . . (Boston, 1907), p. xii.

3. *For. Rel.* (1910), pp. 784-791.

4. Luis Anderson, *El Laudo Loubet* . . . (San José, 1911), pp. 77-80.

5. *For. Rel.* (1910), p. 785.

6. República de Costa Rica, Sec. R. E., *Documentos relativos al conflicto de jurisdicción territorial con la República de Panamá y sus antecedentes* (San José, 1921), pp. 10. Hereafter cited as Costa Rica, *Documentos.*

7. Alfaro, *Límites entre Panamá y Costa Rica,* p. 5.

8. Costa Rica, *Documentos,* p. 17; República de Panamá, Sec. R. E., *Controversia de límites entre Panamá y Costa Rica* (Panama, 1914), p. 10. Hereafter cited as Panama, *Controversia,* 1914.

9. Delcassé to Peralta, Nov. 23, 1900, Costa Rica, *Documentos,* p. 18; Luis Anderson, *op. cit.,* p. 14.

10. Chandler P. Anderson, "The Costa Rica-Panama Boundary Dispute," in *The American Journal of International Law,* XV (1921), p. 236.

11. *For. Rel.* (1910), p. 787.

12. *Sen. Doc.,* No. 208, 58 Cong., 2 Sess. (Ser. 4591), p. 2.

13. Costa Rica, *Documentos,* p. 7; Lewis to Weitzel, Feb. 5, 1910; Bacon to Anderson, Costa Rican special minister at Washington, Feb. 16, 1909; Anderson to Root, Feb. 23, 1909, *For. Rel.* (1910), pp. 782-784, 806-809.

14. Fernández Guardia, Costa Rican foreign secretary, to Porras, Panamanian foreign secretary, Aug. 13, 1909, *loc. cit.* (1915), p. 1141; Anderson to Root, Feb. 23, 1909, *loc. cit.* (1910), p. 784.

15. Hay to Russell, No. 17, Feb. 18, 1904, Instructions, Panama, I.

16. Barrett to Hay, No. 32, Sept. 6, 1904, Despatches, Panama, III; *Congressional Record,* 60 Cong., 1 Sess., XLII, 5149-5152; 160 *Federal Reporter,* 184; Palmer, *op. cit.,* pp.

17. *For. Rel.* (1910), p. 788.

18. Lee to Hay, July 12, 1904, Despatches, Panama, II.

19. *Idem* to *idem,* Oct. 3, 1904, *loc. cit.,* III.

20. Barrett to Hay, Dec. 20, 1904; Dec. 27, 1904, *loc. cit.*

21. *Idem* to *idem,* Dec. 29, 1904, *loc. cit.*

22. Loomis to Barrett, Jan. 16, 1905, Instructions, Panama, I.

23. Barrett to Hay, No. 96, Jan. 30, 1905, Despatches, Panama, III.

24. *Idem* to *idem,* No. 106, Feb. 14, 1905, *loc. cit.*

25. *Idem* to *idem,* Feb. 21, 1905, *loc. cit.*

26. *Idem* to *idem,* No. 108, Feb. 21, 1905, *loc. cit.*

27. *Idem* to *idem,* No. 110, Feb. 28, 1905, *loc. cit.*

28. Treaty enclosed with *idem* to *idem,* No. 113, Mar. 7, 1905, *loc. cit.*

29. *Idem* to *idem*, No. 110, Feb. 28, 1905, *loc. cit.*
30. *Idem* to *idem*, No. 113, Mar. 7, 1905, *loc. cit.*
31. Magoon to Root, No. 91, May 1, 1906, *loc. cit.*, V.
32. Palmer, *op. cit.*, pp. xxvi, 226-263.
33. *For. Rel.* (1910), p. 788; Panamá, *Controversia*, 1914, p. 38.
34. Alfaro, *Límites entre Panamá y Costa Rica*, p. 18.
35. Anderson to Root, Dec. 9, 1907, *For. Rel.* (1910), pp. 772-773.
36. Bacon to Anderson, Dec. 19, 1907, *loc. cit.*, pp. 773-774.
37. Bacon to Squiers, Dec. 24, 1907, *loc. cit.*, p. 774.
38. Anderson to Root, Nov. 21, 1908, *loc. cit.*, pp. 774-775.
39. Adee to Squiers, Dec. 1, 1908, *loc. cit.*, p. 775.
40. Anderson to Root, Nov. 21, 1908, *loc. cit.*, pp. 774-775.
41. Adee to Squiers, Dec. 1, 1908, *loc. cit.*, p. 775.
42. Adee to Anderson, Dec. 1, 1908, *loc. cit.*, pp. 775-776.
43. Squiers to Root, Dec. 24, 1908, *loc. cit.*, p. 776.
44. Bacon to Anderson, Dec. 26, 1908, *loc. cit.*, p. 776.
45. Anderson to Root, Dec. 28, 1908, *loc. cit.*, p. 777.
46. Arango to Squiers, Dec. 28, 1908, *loc. cit.*, p. 779.
47. J. M. Fernández, Panamanian foreign secretary, to Squiers, Jan. 9, 1909, *loc. cit.*, p. 780.
48. *For. Rel.* (1910), p. 789.
49. Root to Squiers, Jan. 23, 1909, *loc. cit.*, pp. 781-782.
50. *Ibid.*
51. Bacon to Squiers, Jan. 30, 1909, *loc. cit.*, p. 782.
52. Root to Magoon, Apr. 16, 1906, *loc. cit.* (1906), p. 1201.
53. Bacon to Squiers, Jan. 30, 1909, *loc. cit.* (1910), p. 782.
54. Bacon to Anderson, Feb. 16, 1909, *loc. cit.*, pp. 782-783.
55. Anderson to Root, Feb. 23, 1909, *loc. cit.*, pp. 783-784.
56. Arosemena to Knox, July 30, 1909, *loc. cit.*, pp. 784-785.
57. *For. Rel.* (1910), pp. 785-791.
58. Arosemena to Wilson, Aug. 31, 1909, *loc. cit.*, pp. 791-792.
59. Wilson to Arosemena, Oct. 11, 1909, *loc. cit.*, p. 793.
60. Calvo to Knox, Oct. 14, 1909, *loc. cit.*, p. 793.
61. Anderson to Knox, Oct. 16, 1909, *loc. cit.*, pp. 793-794.
62. Adee to Anderson, Oct. 18, 1909, *loc. cit.*, p. 794.
63. Anderson to Knox, Oct. 18, 1909, *loc. cit.*, p. 795.
64. Wilson to Arosemena, Oct. 20, 1909, *loc. cit.*, pp. 796-797.
65. Arosemena to Knox, Oct. 23, 1909, *loc. cit.*, pp. 797-798.
66. Knox to Arosemena, Nov. 2, 1909, *loc. cit.*, p. 798.
67. Weitzel to Knox, Dec. 2, 1909, *loc. cit.*, pp. 799-800.
68. Knox to Arosemena, Dec. 4, 1909, *loc. cit.*, p. 800.
69. Arosemena to Knox, Dec. 6, 1909, *loc. cit.*, pp. 800-801.
70. Anderson to Knox, Dec. 6, 1909, *loc. cit.*, pp. 801-802.
71. Wilson to Arosemena, Dec. 16, 1909, *loc. cit.*, pp. 802-803.
72. Adee to Weitzel, Dec. 18, 1909, *loc. cit.*, pp. 803-804.
73. Knox to Porras, Feb. 2, 1910, *loc. cit.*, pp. 804-805.
74. Lewis to Weitzel, Feb. 5, 1910, *loc. cit.*, pp. 806-808.
75. Porras to Knox, Feb. 20, 1910, *loc. cit.*, pp. 808-810.
76. Knox to Porras and Anderson, Mar. 1, 1910, República de Panamá, *Arbitration before . . . Edward D. White . . . of the Differences between the Republic of Panama and the Republic of Costa Rica; Additional Documents . . . May 18, 1914* (n. p., n. d.), p. 37.

77. Porras to Knox, Mar. 10, 1910, *For. Rel.* (1910), pp. 812-814.
78. Knox to Weitzel, Mar. 12, 1910, *loc. cit.*, pp. 814-815.
79. *Ibid.*
80. Lewis to Knox, Mar. 14, 1910, *loc. cit.*, p. 815.
81. Porras to Lewis, May 16, 1909, Panama, *Controversia*, 1914, p. 65.
82. *For. Rel.* (1910), pp. 820-822; Panamá, *Controversia*, 1914, pp. 193-195; Costa Rica, *Documentos*, pp. 19-23.
83. Calvo and Porras to Knox, June 10, 1911, *For. Rel.* (1911), p. 674.
84. White to Knox, July 26, 1911, *loc. cit.*, pp. 675-676.
85. Calvo and Porras to Knox, July 31, 1911, *loc. cit.*, pp. 676-677.
86. Costa Rica, *Documents Annexed to the Argument of Costa Rica*, I, 3-7.
87. Opinion and decision of Edward D. White, Sept. 12, 1914, *For. Rel.* (1914), pp. 1000-1015; Costa Rica, *Documentos*, pp. 27-63; Panamá, *Controversia*, 1914, pp. 351-372; *Fallo arbitral del Chief Justice de los Estados Unidos de América* . . . (San José, 1914).
88. *N. Y. Times*, Sept. 20, 1914, II, 9:1; Jan. 7, 1915, 10:3.
89. *Ibid.*, Oct. 7, 1914, 8:8.
90. Lefevre to Quesada, Oct. 17, 1914, *For. Rel.* (1914), pp. 1016-1017; Costa Rica, *Documentos*, pp. 64-66; Panamá, *Controversia*, 1914, pp. 373-374.
91. Quesada to Lefevre, Oct. 30, 1914, *For. Rel.* (1914), pp. 1017-1021.
92. Bryan to Wm. P. Cresson, U. S. Chargé, Nov. 25, 1914, *loc. cit.*, p. 1022.
93. Cresson to Bryan, Nov. 27, 1914, *loc. cit.*, pp. 1022-1023.
94. Quesada to Hale, Dec. 12, 1914, *loc. cit.*, pp. 1027-1028.
95. Morales to Bryan, Dec. 8, 1914, *loc. cit.*, pp. 1025-1026.
96. Lansing to Morales, Dec. 19, 1914, *loc. cit.*, p. 1028.
97. Quesada to Hale, Jan. 14, 1915, *loc. cit.* (1915), pp. 1131-1132.
98. Quesada to E. T. Lefevre, Jan. 14, 1915, *loc. cit.*, pp. 1133-1134.
99. E. T. Lefevre to Quesada, Jan. 30, 1915, *loc. cit.*, pp. 1139-1142.
100. Quesada to E. T. Lefevre, Mar. 1, 1915, *loc. cit.*, pp. 1142-1146.
101. Mesén to Bryan, Mar. 9, 1915, *loc. cit.*, pp. 1134-1138.
102. Bryan to Price, Apr. 28, 1915, *loc. cit.*, p. 1147.
103. Mesén to Bryan, May 5, 1915, *loc. cit.*, p. 1148.
104. Bryan to Mesén, May 8, 1915, *loc. cit.*, p. 1148.
105. Endicott, U. S. chargé at San José, to Bryan, June 24, 1915, *loc. cit.*, p. 1150.
106. E. T. Lefevre to Price, July 28, 1915, *loc. cit.*, pp. 1151-1152.
107. Quesada to Bryan, Sept. 28, 1915, *loc. cit.*, pp. 1152-1154.

CHAPTER VII

TERRITORIAL EXPROPRIATION

BY MEANS of the Hay-Bunau-Varilla Treaty the Republic of Panama granted to the United States "in perpetuity
the use, occupation and control of a zone of land and land
under water for the construction, maintenance, operation, sanitation and protection" of the proposed Panama Canal. The
Zone was "of the width of ten miles extending to the distance
of five miles on each side of the center line of the route of the
Canal to be constructed." This strip, which traversed the heart
of the territory of the Isthmian republic, began three marine
miles from mean low watermark in the Caribbean Sea on the
north and extended three marine miles from mean low watermark into the Pacific Ocean on the south. In addition, Panama
conceded under the same conditions the islands of Perico, Naos,
Culebra, and Flamenco in the Bay of Panama. However, the
cities of Panama and Colón, which lay within the boundaries
thus described, were excluded from the transfer. The joker
in the treaty, so far as Panama was concerned, was the following provision:

The Republic of Panama further grants to the United States in
perpetuity the use, occupation and control of any other lands and
waters outside of the zone above described which may be necessary
and convenient for the construction, maintenance, operation, sanitation and protection of the said Canal or of any auxiliary canals or
other works necessary for the construction, maintenance, operation,
sanitation and protection of the said enterprise.[1]

The United States agreed to make an initial payment of
$10,000,000 and an annual payment during the existence of the
treaty of $250,000, beginning nine years after the exchange of
its ratifications. In the numerous controversies that have arisen
since 1903 the United States has held steadfast to its interpretation that the above sums covered all concessions of the treaty,

while Panama has contended with even greater if less effective tenacity that the payments applied only to the originally defined area of land and not to further territory taken within Panamanian borders for Canal use.

On May 19, 1904, as already noted, the United States took formal control of the Canal Zone and issued regulations for its administration.[2] The Panamanian government protested at the summary manner in which Governor George W. Davis assumed jurisdiction without a previous delimitation of the lands of the Zone.[3] Thereupon, a provisional boundary convention was signed on June 15, 1904.[4]

One of the first instances of the United States' demanding land outside of the Canal Zone occurred in 1908, when on June 8 the Canal Zone authorities informed Panama that in order to get materials for Gatún lock construction it was necessary to buy a quarry in Portobelo from the Rodríguez family. Foreign Secretary Ricardo Arias replied that foreign governments could not acquire land in Panama except under special treaty. The United States had that right by the terms of the Canal treaty, and only had to prove that the land was needed for the Canal. He suggested, however, that in order to avoid delay the Panama Railroad Company should buy the area for the Isthmian Canal Commission. Arias believed this would be a satisfactory solution of the problem because the United States wanted the stone and not title to the property.[5] The suggestion was not pleasing to the American government, for it affected the interpretation of a part of the Hay-Bunau-Varilla Treaty. Panama asked that the matter be treated through the State Department,[6] but the United States obtained the quarry without much further ceremony. Later, Foreign Secretary Samuel Lewis complained to the National Assembly that the Washington government contended that the acquisition of territory for Canal use was a question for determination solely by the honest judgment of its own officials. In concession to that contention the Panamanian government had granted the Canal authorities permission to take over and exploit the quarry of the Rodríguez family in Portobelo.

On December 14, 1908, the Canal Commission applied to Panama for permission to extract sand from the beaches of Punta de Chamé for Canal use, promising to indemnify the owners of any lands damaged by the excavations. Panama assented without argument, and was subsequently informed by Canal authorities that the sand was being taken and that more land might be needed in that vicinity.[7]

The concession covering the greatest area of land acquired since 1903 was made in 1912, when the United States was given the territory covered by Lake Gatún and all the land on its shores up to one hundred feet above sea-level. That body of water, as increased by dams for Canal purposes, extends across the Canal strip into Panamanian territory on both sides, covering approximately 167 square miles outside of the Canal Zone. The government of Panama acquiesced without delay in the request for the land, surrendering it to the United States on May 17, 1912. In conformity with Articles II and III of the treaty and the permission of Panama, the Canal Zone government assumed control of the lake, its shores, islands, and peninsulas from which there was no access except from the lake or the Canal Zone.[8]

On May 9, 1914, C. A. McIlvaine, the executive secretary of the Canal Zone, informed Panama that the defense of the Canal required the construction of roads from Empire to Chorrera, from Balboa to Chorrera, and from Juan Díaz to the mouth of Juan Díaz River. Panama was asked to assist in obtaining the necessary right of way and in arranging for damages.[9] On July 11 permission was granted for the construction of the highways.[10]

The boundaries between the Canal Zone and the Republic of Panama were definitely determined by the convention of September 2, 1914, which replaced the provisional delimitation of June 15, 1904. The United States was given final title to the Lake Gatún area and gained minor concessions, such as two small islands in the Pacific and a battery site on the Colón water front. The Sabanas on the Pacific side were transferred to Panama, thus placing Panama City within contiguous Panamanian territory for the first time since the ratification of the treaty of 1903. The Isthmian capital was no longer severed from Panamanian territory and entirely surrounded by land under the jurisdiction of the United States.[11]

On May 27, 1915, the Canal Zone government bluntly informed Panama that certain uncultivated public lands about the mouth of the Chagres River were being taken over under Article II of the Canal treaty for the defense of the Canal Zone. Panama was asked to notify the native population.[12] On June 8 Secretary Lefevre asked for a map showing the location and extent of the lands required.[13] Six days later he protested that the territory had been taken over on June 6 and that it was partly cultivated. Provisional Governor Chester Harding was reminded that this was a violation of his statement of May 27, and the hope was expressed that the tract would not be occupied until Panama had issued a decree ceding it to the United States.[14]

On June 25 Harding acknowledged making a mistake in that two renters were on the land required, but stated that they had not been molested and that he had arranged to send commissioners to placate them for any damages they might incur. Lefevre was informed that Panama did not need to emit a decree before the United States occupied the territory, but should advise the inhabitants affected that the land had been taken for Canal use.[15]

Before the end of the year the Canal authorities decided to take over a larger area at the mouth of the Chagres River. On December 8, 1915, Governor Goethals advised the Panamanian government in a much more diplomatic tone that a triangular space bounded by the Chagres, the Caribbean Sea, and the Canal Zone was necessary for Canal defense and asked that it be abandoned. The land had been needed for some time, but had not been taken because many of its inhabitants were sufferers of the Colón fire in 1915. The time was not considered propitious for their removal, but Canal defense made action imperative. The proprietors would be moved to some suitable location and would be compensated for their losses. Goethals graciously inquired if Panama had any desires or suggestions to offer.[16]

Lefevre stated on December 21 that Panama was always disposed to comply with the obligations imposed by the Canal treaty, even though a real sacrifice was often involved. He considered the necessity for defenses at the mouth of the Chagres evident, but prayed to God that the military authorities might work out a plan that would not require the occupation of the village of Chagres. He contended that the Panamanian government should be compensated for land expropriated by the United States because the payments made under Article XIV of the Canal treaty covered only that territory within the limits fixed by the convention of September 2, 1914. The matter of remuneration, he stated, would be taken up by the Panamanian minister in Washington.[17]

On December 28 Goethals answered that the solatium granted in Article XIV of the treaty did not pertain exclusively to the Canal strip, but to whatever other lands and waters that were necessary and convenient for the construction, maintenance, operation, sanitation, and protection of the Canal and auxiliary works. The convention of 1914 had fixed the limits of the lands taken before that time and contained nothing contrary to the provisions of the Hay-Bunau-Varilla Treaty. The land over which the United States was on the point of assuming sovereignty was necessary and convenient for Canal use and would be taken under Articles II and III of the treaty. The proprietors, he promised, would be compensated and moved to any place named by Panama, but the United States was not obligated to make any compensation to the Panamanian government.[18]

Lefevre responded that the matter of reimbursement for his government would be discussed in Washington, but that would not hinder the occupation of the land by the military authorities.[19] Later he stated that the inhabitants should be moved to the north side of the Lagarto River.[20] Considerable discussion then ensued concerning a road from the new village of Chagres to Colón. Panama asked that a highway be built from the mouth of the Lagarto River to Lake Gatún, but the Canal authorities suggested that the trail from the mouth of the Lagarto to the Chagres and the military road on the expropriated territory be used. The removal and re-erection of two public buildings occasioned some controversy, but these matters were settled satisfactorily, if Panama could be satisfied with an uncompensated loss of territory.[21]

On May 22, 1918, Foreign Secretary Narciso Garay protested that American troops were stationed on Punta Paitilla and had driven Panamanian fishermen away from that point with rifles. He wanted to know under what conditions the United States had established this military reservation within the jurisdiction of the Republic of Panama. Neither the Washington government nor the Canal authorities had solicited or obtained the permission of his government for the establishment of a military post on Panamanian territory.[22] On July 12 Governor Harding replied that the United States had taken 2.63 hectares on Punta Paitilla for the defense of the Canal.[23] On August 21 Garay notified Harding that Panama did not find it inconvenient to concede the United States the use, occupation, and control of the land on Punta Paitilla in accordance with Article II of the Canal treaty.[24]

On July 3, 1918, Harding asked for approximately 3,168 acres of land that lay between the Chagres River, the Majagual River, the Atlantic Coast, and the Canal Zone. Panama was requested to arrange for the immediate abandonment of the land.[25] Seven weeks later the Panamanian government indicated that the cabinet had seen fit to concede the use, occupation, and control of the territory to the United States under the provisions of Article II of the Hay-Bunau-Varilla Treaty. However, instructions would be given the Panamanian legation in Washington to seek indemnification for this area along with that on the Chagres granted in 1916.[26]

On August 16 the United States requested permission for establishing coaling stations along the Atlantic and Pacific coasts, explaining that they were necessary for the defense of the Canal and the Republic of Panama against German submarines.[27] Five days later the required permission was given for the duration of the war, and Panama expressed pleasure at being able to co-operate for the defense of the Canal and its own territory.[28]

Three days after the termination of the World War came the worst blow of all to Panama in respect to its territory. In the midst of its celebration of the armistice of the "war to end war" Panama was rudely shocked by a demand for prac-tically the whole of beautiful Taboga Island. For the defense of the Canal, after the war was over, the military authorities of the United States wanted only 1,160 acres of the total of 1,410 acres of the health resort and garden spot of Panama City. The United States would gladly indemnify the owners for this desecration.[29]

If the Canal Zone authorities thought they had heard the Panamanians protest before, something new was in store for them. President Porras had recovered sufficiently by November 17 to demand a reconsideration and a delay in taking posses-sion.[30] Governor Harding stated that he was acting on orders from the War Department and could not defer action.[31] On the same day that Porras protested to Harding, the Panamanian legation in Washington was instructed to appeal to the State Department to stop this "immensely prejudicial" trangression against Panama.[32] Minister Price was also entreated to aid in saving Taboga.[33]

On November 19 Chargé José E. Lefevre reported that Secretary of State Robert Lansing knew nothing of the projected expropriation of Taboga Island, but had promised to confer with the War Department.[34] On November 21 he sent Lansing a long despatch asking that Taboga be spared and pointing to the sad condition of the inhabitants of its two villages, Taboga and Restinga. The people were attached sentimentally to their homes on the salubrious little island, and were about to be removed forcibly from their lands and possessions. Panama could not understand in this solemn hour the attitude of the United States when its president was the spokesman for and apostle of the self-determination of nationalities. Now was an opportunity to give proof of this historical tradition by turning away from despoiling the Tabogans of their homeland. Why not take Taboguilla, Urabá, or Cerro de Chamé? They were just as useful for Canal defense and their loss would not be such a sad blow.[35]

Complaints poured in from all sides. Chargé Lefevre protested that an American official had been among the Tabogans and had caused them great alarm. Strange indeed was it that the United States should trespass on Panamanian territory. This had been tolerated before because it had been for the progress of the world, but such was not the case with Taboga Island. Lefevre could not understand why fortifications should be built on Taboga in time of peace. Neither fear nor danger of aggression against the United States, much less against Panama, existed. Why should Panama, the first among the Latin American nations to proclaim, without fear and without vacillation, its solidarity with the United States in the great war, be obliged to sacrifice a dear and valuable portion of its soil to be dedicated to military objects? Was it indispensable that fortifications be erected on Taboga Island? Would some other site not afford the same protection? Could the area demanded not be reduced? What would be done for the unfortunate Tabogans? What would be Panama's compensation for the beautiful island? Finally the Panamanian appealed in the name of the honorable relations of his government since 1903 with America, the cradle of Washington, Lincoln, and Wilson, that the hand of the despoiler might be stayed.[36]

On December 11 the State Department acknowledged Lefevre's note of November 21, stating that the War Department deemed 1,160 acres of Taboga essential and that no other place would serve. The military authorities would trouble the inhabitants as little as possible and would give them sufficient time to move.[37] A week later Lefevre again protested that Taboga was as much an integral part of Panama City as Arlington was of Washington and asked for an answer to his previous complaints.[38] The State Department stated that its note of December 11 was a sufficient reply to his supplication.[39]

The vehement protests of the Panamanians began to pierce

the consciences of War and State Department officials. On January 4, 1919, Chargé Lefevre was informed that the War Department had decided not to take possession immediately of Taboga Island.[40] There the disagreeable affair remained until January 19, 1920, when the demand was renewed. The United States did not plan to begin large-scale construction of fortifications and was "anxious to adopt a liberal policy" in regard to the inhabitants.[41] The Panamanian government made no reply, apparently hoping that the seizure might be delayed as long as possible. On April 6 Minister Price called attention to the demand of January 19, and Panama answered that the expropriation of Taboga Island could not come under the provisions of Article II of the Canal treaty. Price was asked how much land the United States wanted and how much Panama would be paid for it.[42]

After reminding the State Department of the acquisition of Largo Remo in Las Minas Bay the year before, and asking that a *modus operandi* be reached concerning such matters, Chargé Lefevre resumed his protests in Washington on April 30.[43] Eventually the area was reduced to 14.95 hectares,[44] but Panama continued its claim for compensation. Expropriation of territory, it believed, should be the subject of a special convention. However, in order not to delay the work of the Canal authorities, the small tract was granted provisionally.[45] The area was ceded to the American government on June 12, 1920,[46] and the Panamanian government continued negotiations for payment. The loss received attention in the New Year message of President Porras in 1921, when he stated that his government had saved almost the whole island, but was well aware that the victory was indefinite.[47]

On September 18, 1919, Governor Harding informed the Panamanian government that Droque Island, a part of the island of Largo Remo, and two other small islands in the *Bahía de las Minas* had been taken for Canal defense and that the owners of the property on them would be indemnified.[48] Secretary E. T. Lefevre observed that the occupation of the land before obtaining the permission of Panama had caused some surprise, but stated that the cabinet had seen fit to grant the use, occupation, and control of the areas in accordance with Article II of the treaty. The Panamanian legation in Washington would seek compensation for the public lands on the islands.[49] On February 17, 1920, Chargé Lefevre protested to the State Department against the occupation of Panamanian territory without previous communication with his government. He stated that the expropriation of Panamanian lands was not a one-sided affair and that he wished to reach some arrangement for future guidance that would be equitable and satisfactory to the interests of both countries.[50] However, Lefevre and Secretary of War Newton D. Baker were able to agree on a settlement of the claim for compensation by February 24; a debt owed by Panama would be cancelled by the acquisition of the islands.[51]

By 1920 the Republic of Panama had begun to formulate definite ideas about a new treaty with the United States to take the place of the Taft convention of 1904 and to secure some measure of protection against alleged misinterpretations of the Hay-Bunau-Varilla Treaty. Every memorandum submitted to the United States contained some reference to its expropriation of Panamanian territory. Panama wanted the American government to declare that it had taken all lands necessary for the Canal and that it had no right to ask for more.[52] While Panama would not object to granting the United States lands for defense by special agreement made before the areas were occupied, its typical protest was:

> Some Canal authorities insist on the theory that the demand for lands can be continued indefinitely but Panama cannot accept such a theory, for this would be as much as to admit the possibility that under the pretext of needing all the Isthmus for the construction, operation, maintenance and protection of the Canal the Republic of Panama would at any time cease to exist as an independent and sovereign state.[53]

On December 20, 1920, the Canal officials informed Panama that a tract of 125 hectares known as *El Cerro de Docientos*

Pies, east of Colón in the region of *Bahía de las Minas,* was needed and would be taken over shortly.[54] Panama demurred, protesting that the assumption of jurisdiction over its territory should be treated diplomatically. The occupation of the hill, which was accomplished before December 30, was characterized as an act of force, and Panama feared that a dangerous precedent had been established.[55] The United States finally decided that the land was not needed, and informed the Panamanian government on July 29, 1921, that the notification of December 20, 1920, was annulled.[56]

Before the demand for *El Cerro de Docientos Pies* was relinquished, the Panamanian government instructed Ricardo J. Alfaro, who was to attend Warren G. Harding's inauguration, to take up the matter of compensation for lands expropriated by the United States and to attempt to make some arrangement regarding future acquisitions. Panama complained that the United States had taken without the slightest indemnification the following parcels of its territory: 167 square miles in connection with the formation of Gatún Lake, a large area about the mouth of Chagres River, approximately 50 hectares about Punta Paitilla near Colón, approximately 220 hectares on the islands in the *Bahía de las Minas,* 14.95 hectares on Taboga Island, and 125 hectares on *El Cerro de Docientos Pies.*[57] However, hostilities broke out in February, 1921, between Panama and Costa Rica over their boundary dispute, and Alfaro was forced to give all his attention to the protection of his country from its enemy and its guardian.

On October 18, 1923, the Canal authorities informed the Panamanians that approximately twenty-two square miles of land on the Chagres River were being taken for a water reservoir. The acquisition was being made under the terms of the treaty of 1903, and the owners of the land would be compensated.[58] Panama expressed great surprise at the assumption of jurisdiction over the area by the United States. Secretary Garay stated that the treaty was not unilateral but a pact between two sovereign and independent nations; therefore, the previous acquiescence of Panama was necessary. The expropriation of Panamanian territory could be accomplished only by proceedings established by the laws of the republic and by international rights and practices.[59] Ricardo J. Alfaro, then Panamanian minister at Washington, protested to the State Department that his government had made numerous demands that its land not be seized but acquired through diplomatic channels. He stated that Panama had asked in 1921 that arrangements be made by which territorial questions might be settled and hinted that nothing had been done because of the negligence of the State Department. Panama was especially opposed to the contention that the United States could assume jurisdiction over Panamanian territory with no more formality than a notice to the Isthmian government.[60] Secretary of State Hughes replied that there could be no question of the right of the United States to acquire land in Panama for Canal use, but that the Canal authorities had signified their readiness to comply with any reasonable requests in regard to the occupation of such areas. He concluded:

On March 7, 1921, the Executive Secretary of the Panama Canal requested suggestions from the Government of Panama with respect to the *modus operandi* to be observed in such cases. No reply has yet been received to that letter. If no satisfactory arrangement has yet been arrived at, the fault cannot be attributed to the American authorities.[61]

Minister John G. South notified Panama on January 12, 1924, that the United States would assume formal jurisdiction over the Alhajuela territory on February 1.[62] On January 18 Garay wrote South that commissioners had been appointed to act with a commission named by the Canal Zone governor to inspect the lands and take note of any important circumstances.[63] South replied immediately that inspection by the joint commission would in no way destroy or modify the right of the United States to acquire Panamanian territory under the provisions of the treaty of 1903. He stated that his government did not admit the selection of the commission to be necessary, that it must in no way provide obstacles toward the acquisition, and that its appointment must not be taken as a precedent for altering the practices used in previous expropriations of territory. However, the Canal Zone government would be pleased to cooperate if the commission was instructed to visit the territory and notify the inhabitants of the change of jurisdiction.[64]

Garay answered the same day: "Your Excellency is undoubtedly under the erroneous impression that my Government desires to impede or obstruct the exercise of the rights that Article II of the Hay-Bunau-Varilla Treaty confers on the United States." He stated that the acquisition of land should occur only after diplomatic negotiations and that areas expropriated should be delivered solely by executive decree. Informing the inhabitants of the change of jurisdiction was beneath the dignity of an engineering commission; this would be done by decree. If more land was needed later, Panama would gladly co-operate.[65] The commission made its tour of inspection, and on January 30 President Porras issued a decree transferring the Alhajuela territory to the United States and notifying the inhabitants.[66]

In reference to a highway, about six miles of which would lie within Panamanian jurisdiction, from Summit in the Canal Zone to the projected dam at Alhajuela, the American officials assumed a more diplomatic tone. The highway, which would be a link of the proposed trans-Isthmian thoroughfare, was necessary and convenient for Canal use. McIlvaine explained: "Our government desires to avoid, if possible, the necessity of exercising to any further extent the acquisition of additional lands under the jurisdiction of the Republic of Panama." He proposed that the United States be granted the right to build and maintain the highway, but that Panama retain political jurisdiction over the right of way.[67] Panama readily agreed and expressed satisfaction that the United States had declared that no further acquisitions of territory were desired.[68]

In spite of the agitation concerning the right of the United States to take Panamanian territory, the treaty of July 28, 1926, was silent, strangely silent, on that right. The United States did agree to notify Panama diplomatically when it needed territory. No other restrictions were placed on the American government, and the land was to be considered as having passed into its possession when the notice was given. The value of private property was to be set by an appraisal commission composed of a member of the Panamanian supreme court and the district judge of the Canal Zone. Negotiations were broken off or delayed several times partly due to the demand of the United States for a part of Colón, but Panama finally gave in and ceded a portion of Manzanillo Island known as New Cristóbal. In return, the United States agreed to slight modifications in the Canal Zone boundaries.[69]

On July 18, 1927, McIlvaine notified Foreign Secretary Horacio F. Alfaro that five small parcels of land on Taboga and Taboguilla Islands were needed for Canal defense. He explained that a careful study had been made in order to limit the required area to a minimum, for the military officials wished to take only the land that was indispensable and to consider the sentiments of the Panamanians. The secretary of war had conferred with the State Department as to the correct procedure for notifying Panama that the property was necessary, and the Canal Zone government had been instructed to ask the Panamanian president to issue a decree transferring the five areas of about thirty-three hectares to the United States on August 1.[70] Alfaro replied that the method, since the expropriation of land was a diplomatic matter relating to the execution of a treaty between two governments, would have been a notification from the American minister to the foreign secretary or from the State Department to the Panamanian legation in Washington. Panama wanted one of these means used in the future. Alfaro had given the request careful consideration and did not wish to appear to be hindering the United States, but the description furnished of the lands was inadequate. He suggested that a specified highway be built and maintained the same way as the road from Summit to Alhajuela.[71] Alfaro immediately notified Minister South of the manner in which Panama wished to be informed when land was needed, and asked that an agreement toward that end be adopted.[72] The minister acknowledged the Alfaro note, but ignored the question of proper notification.[73]

After all the correspondence concerning procedure in taking Panamanian territory, the United States only slightly changed its practice. When the military authorities decided in 1928 that 3.19 hectares of *El Cerro de Docientos Pies* were needed for Canal defense, Minister South merely notified the Panamanian government that the land had been taken.[74] Foreign Secretary J. D. Arosemena reported to the National Assembly that such sacrifices were painful, but that Panama was unable to withdraw its pledged word. He stated, however, that if demands were made for any land not necessary for the defense of the great interoceanic way the patriotism and honor of the country would impose the duty of rejecting them, whatever the real or apparent compensation.[75]

On July 22, 1930, Panama accorded the United States jurisdiction over twenty-five hectares on Jicarita Island and sixty on *Punta de Morro de Puercos* for the construction of lighthouses in connection with Canal navigation.[76] On November 10, 1930, Minister Roy T. Davis asked for additional areas for the Madden Dam at Alhajuela.[77] Panama complied on December 3 and the United States assumed jurisdiction on April 15, 1931.[78]

In the light of experience it appears that Philippe Bunau-Varilla deliberately granted the United States the privilege of expropriating Panamanian territory wherever and whenever it pleased. One Isthmian writer has advanced the contention that this right is limited by the first article of the Canal treaty, whereby the United States guarantees the independence of the Republic of Panama. He pointed to the indisputable fact that a state cannot exist without territory and stated that if the United States should assume jurisdiction over all the land of the republic, Panamanian sovereignty and independence would be destroyed in violation of Article I of the Hay-Bunau-Varilla Treaty. Therefore, the acceptance of the principle that the American government might take over whatever territory of Panama it desired would make the existence of the Republic of

Panama conditional, a state of affairs inconceivable to the Panamanians.[79]

The fact remains that the United States, in accordance with Article II of the Hay-Bunau-Varilla Treaty, has expropriated Panamanian territory practically at will and without compensation to the government of Panama. The Colossus of the North eventually may become more considerate in its treatment of the proud Panamanians in reference to territorial despoilment, but probably will never renounce completely the right to carve out areas here and there on which to erect fortifications for the protection of the Panama Canal.

NOTES

1. *For. Rel.* (1904), pp. 544.
2. *Ibid.*, pp. 582-583.
3. Tomás Arias to Davis, May 25, 1904, *loc. cit.*, p. 584; Russell to Hay, May 25, 1904, Despatches, Panama, II.
4. *Sen. Doc.*, No. 348, 67 Cong., 4 Sess. (Ser. 8167), III, 2752-2756.
5. R. Arias, to Blackburn, June 17, 1908, Panama, Sec. R. E., *Documentos, Memoria*, 1908, II, 122.
6. H. F. Alfaro to Blackburn, July 25, 1908, *loc. cit.*, p. 123.
7. Panama, Sec. R. E., *Memoria*, 1910, pp. lii-liii.
8. *Sen. Doc.*, No. 348, 67 Cong., 4 Sess. (Ser. 8167), III, 2771; Ricardo J. Alfaro, Panamanian minister at Washington, to Hughes, Nov. 6, 1923, Panama, Sec. R. E., *Memoria*, 1924, p. 301.
9. McIlvaine to E. T. Lefevre, May 9, 1914, *loc. cit.*, 1914, pp. 319-320.
10. E. T. Lefevre to McIlvaine, July 11, 1914, *loc. cit.*, p. 321.
11. *Sen. Doc.*, No. 348, 67 Cong., 4 Sess. (Ser. 8167), III, 2770-2777; *Gaceta oficial*, Sept. 30, 1914; Panama, Sec. R. E., *Memoria*, 1914, pp. 301-308.
12. Harding to E. T. Lefevre, May 27, 1915, *loc. cit.*, 1916, pp. 318-319.
13. E. T. Lefevre to Harding, June 8, 1915, *loc. cit.*, p. 319.
14. *Idem* to *idem*, June 14, 1915, *loc. cit.*, pp. 319-320.
15. Harding to E. T. Lefevre, June 25, 1915, *loc. cit.*, pp. 321-322.
16. Goethals to Porras, Dec. 8, 1915, *loc. cit.*, pp. 322-323.
17. E. T. Lefevre to Goethals, Dec. 21, 1915, *loc. cit.*, pp. 323-324.
18. Goethals to E. T. Lefevre, Dec. 28, 1915, *loc. cit.*, pp. 324-325.
19. E. T. Lefevre to Goethals, Jan. 18, 1916, *loc. cit.*, pp. 325-326.
20. E. T. Lefevre to McIlvaine, Feb. 23, 1916, *loc. cit.*, p. 331.
21. McIlvaine to E. T. Lefevre, Apr. 10, 1916; June 29, 1916; E. T. Lefevre to McIlvaine, Apr. 14, 1916, *loc. cit.*, pp. 333-339.
22. Garay to E. G. Greene, U. S. chargé, May 22, 1918, *loc. cit.*, 1918, p. 303.
23. Harding to Urriola, July 12, 1918, *loc. cit.*, pp. 303-304.
24. Garay to Harding, Aug. 21, 1918, *loc. cit.*, p. 305.
25. Harding to Urriola, July 3, 1918, *loc. cit.*, p. 307.
26. E. T. Lefevre to Harding, Aug. 21, 1918, *loc. cit.*, p. 308.
27. Greene to E. T. Lefevre, Aug. 16, 1918, *loc. cit.*, p. 311.

28. E. T. Lefevre to Greene, Aug. 21, 1918, *loc. cit.*, p. 312.

29. Harding to Porras, Nov. 14, 1918, *loc. cit.*, 1920, pp. 58-59.

30. Porras to Harding, Nov. 17, 1918, *loc. cit.*, pp. 59-60.

31. Harding to Porras, Nov. 18, 1918, *loc. cit.*, p. 60.

32. Lefevre to Lefevre, Nov. 17, 1918, *loc. cit.*, p. 60.

33. E. T. Lefevre to Price, Nov. 18, 1918, *loc. cit.*, p. 61.

34. Lefevre to Lefevre, Nov. 19, 1918, *loc. cit.*, p. 62.

35. J. E. Lefevre to Lansing, Nov. 21, 1918, *loc. cit.*, pp. 67-69.

36. *Idem* to *idem*, Dec. 18, 1918, *loc. cit.*, pp. 73-75.

37. Polk to J. E. Lefevre, Dec. 11, 1918, *loc. cit.*, p. 79.

38. J. E. Lefevre to Polk, Dec. 18, 1918, *loc. cit.*, pp. 80-81.

39. Polk to J. E. Lefevre, Dec. 27, 1918, *loc. cit.*, p. 81.

40. *Idem* to *idem*, Jan. 4, 1919, *loc. cit.*, p. 82.

41. Lansing to J. E. Lefevre, Jan. 19, 1920, *For. Rel.* (1920), III, 314.

42. Evenor Hazera, Panamanian sub-secretary of foreign relations, to Price, Apr. 13, 1920, Panama, Sec. R. E., *Memoria*, 1920, pp. 85-86.

43. J. E. Lefevre to Colby, Apr. 30, 1920, *loc. cit.*, pp. 89-90; *For. Rel.* (1920), III, 315-319.

44. McIlvaine to Hazera, June 9, 1920, Panama, Sec. R. E. *Memoria*, 1920, p. 93.

45. Hazera to McIlvaine, June 12, 1920, *loc. cit.*, pp. 93-94.

46. J. E. Lefevre to Hughes, Feb. 8, 1921, *loc. cit.*, 1922, II, 164-165.

47. *N. Y. Times*, Jan. 3, 1921, 21:2; *Estrella*, Jan. 1, 1921.

48. Harding to Porras, Sept. 18, 1919, Panama, Sec. R. E., *Memoria*, 1920, p. 100.

49. E. T. Lefevre to Harding, Oct. 7, 1919, *loc. cit.*, p. 101.

50. J. E. Lefevre to Polk, Feb. 17, 1920, *loc. cit.*, pp. 103-104.

51. *Idem* to *idem*, Feb. 24, 1920, *loc. cit.*, pp. 104-105.

52. Panama, Sec. R. E., *Memoria*, 1920, pp. xxiii-xxviii.

53. *Memorandum de diversos asuntos que la República de Panamá desea arreglar con los Estados Unidos* . . . (Panama, 1923), p. 11.

54. McIlvaine to R. J. Alfaro, in charge of Panamanian foreign relations, Dec. 20, 1920, Sec. R. E., *Memoria*, 1922, II, 267.

55. R. J. Alfaro to J. E. Lefevre, Jan. 11, 1921, *loc. cit.*, pp. 268-269.

56. McIlvaine to R. J. Alfaro, July 29, 1921, *loc. cit.*, pp. 281-282.

57. Sec. R. E., *Memoria*, 1922, II, 196-197.

58. McIlvaine to Garay, Oct. 18, 1923, Panama, Sec. R. E., *Memoria*, 1924, pp. 294-296.

59 Garay to J. J. Morrow, Canal Zone governor, Oct. 29, 1923, *loc. cit.*, pp. 297-298.

60. Alfaro to Hughes, Nov. 6, 1923, *loc. cit.*, pp. 300-302.

61. Hughes to Alfaro, Dec. 3, 1923, *loc. cit.*, pp. 302-303.

62. South to Garay, Jan. 12, 1924, *loc. cit.*, p. 304.

63. Garay to South, Jan. 18, 1924, *loc. cit.*, pp. 304-305.

64. South to Garay, Jan. 24, 1924, *loc. cit.*, pp. 305-307.

65. Garay to South, Jan. 24, 1924, *loc. cit.*, pp. 307-310.

66. Decree 8 of 1924, *loc. cit.*, pp. 310-313.

67. McIlvaine to Garay, Jan. 23, 1924, *loc. cit.*, pp. 281-283.

68. Garay to McIlvaine, Feb. 1, 1924, *loc. cit.*, p. 284.

69. *Cong. Rec.*, 69 Cong., 2 Sess., LXVIII, 1848-1849.

70. McIlvaine to H. F. Alfaro, July 18, 1927, Panama, Sec., R. E., *Memoria*, 1928, pp. 166-167.

71. Alfaro to McIlvaine, Aug. 11, 1927, *loc. cit.*, pp. 168-169.
72. Alfaro to South, Aug. 13, 1927, *loc. cit.*, p. 171.
73. South to Alfaro, Aug. 16, 1927, *loc. cit.*, p. 171.
74. *Idem* to *idem*, Sept. 24, 1928, *loc. cit.*, *Anexos*, 1930, II, 159-161.
75. Panama, Sec. R. E., *Memoria, Anexos*, 1930, I, xxii.
76. J. D. Arosemena to Davis, July 22, 1930, *loc. cit.*, II, 162.
77. Davis to Ricardo A. Morales, Panamanian assistant foreign secretary, Nov. 10, 1930, *loc. cit.*, 1932, pp. 176-178.
78. Morales to George R. Merrell, Jr., U. S. chargé, Dec. 3, 1930, *loc. cit.*, p. 179; *ibid.*, p. li.
79. Publio A. Vásquez Hernández, "La personalidad internacional de Panamá," in *Boletín de la Academia Panameña de la Historia*, año I (1933), 587.

CHAPTER VIII

TRANSPORTATION AND COMMUNICATION

THE INTERFERENCE of the United States in the development of means of communication and transportation in the Republic of Panama is an unsavory chapter in the history of American foreign relations. The republic began its existence in 1903 with practically no facilities for conveyance or intercourse. The only railways of any importance were the Panama Railroad and a system of some fifty-five miles of the United Fruit Company in the province of Bocas del Toro.[1] The ancient *Camino Real*, the best highway the Isthmus had ever known, had succumbed to jungle growth decades ago. The use of the telephone and telegraph was almost unknown except in Panama City and Colón.

While American investors have supplied the greater part of the requisite funds, the American government continually has hampered and retarded the development of railways, highways, and wireless communication in Panama. The use of aircraft has been supervised closely, but apparently has been permitted normal growth. The United States has based its interference principally upon the necessities of Canal defense and upon its monopoly of all means of transportation across the Isthmus as given by the original Panama Railroad contract and Article V of the Hay-Bunau-Varilla Treaty. Much of the interference undoubtedly has been prompted by the idea that marching men played the transcendent rôle in warfare. The virgin jungles that stretched for hundreds of miles on each side of the Canal have been retained in order to simplify defense. Some of the interference may have been justified, but it is doubtful whether the lack of a highway across the Isthmus can ever be vindicated. One instance of intermeddling, however, was not prompted by reasons of defense. The Washington government delayed the construction of a street railway in Panama

City for a time in order to prevent damage to the paved thoroughfares it graciously but not gratuitously had provided for the Panamanians. The efforts of Henry T. Cook, Minor C. Keith, and R. W. Hebard finally removed this obstacle and produced an excellent system in 1913.[2]

RAILROADS

Panama eventually made an effort to remedy its lack of railroad facilities when the National Assembly passed a bill on January 5, 1909, providing for the initiation of railway construction. The president was directed to appoint a commission to make a survey of the needs of the country and to construct one or more lines necessary for the development of the interior. He was authorized to borrow funds at not more than 5 per cent interest, but was prohibited from selling at a discount bonds for railway building.[3] On November 18, 1909, the assistance of the Canal Zone government was solicited for the construction of a railroad from Panama City to David, the capital of the province of Chiriquí. The line was to follow the route surveyed in 1893 for the Pan American Railway. Panama desired American engineers for a new survey and suggested buying discarded materials from the Panama Railroad for the project.[4] After definite plans had been made to build the Panama-David road with branches from Santa María to Pedasí, province of Los Santos, and from the foot of the *cordillera* to Antón, province of Coclé, the Panama Railroad signed a contract for the survey. Five parties of American engineers began the work by sections on April 1, 1910, and reported on December 16 that the system of 350 miles might be built for $9,894,-595.90.[5]

Despite the fact that President Pablo Arosemena opposed in his inaugural speech of October 5, 1910, the construction of the railway,[6] the National Assembly authorized him on January 11, 1911, to proceed with plans for the *Ferrocarril de Panamá a David* with branches into Los Santos and Coclé. He was to borrow a maximum of $10,000,000 at not more than 5 per cent. If funds could not be raised in this manner he was to contract for building and operating the line on the terms of a 5 per cent guarantee on the investment.[7] A call for bids brought proposals from one French and three American firms. W. K. Knowlton offered to build the 350 miles for $7,000,000 gold; R. W. Hebard proposed $9,730,000; and L. E. Myers wanted 10 per cent of the cost not to exceed $10,000,000. When the proposals were opened on August 31 the French bid was discarded because of technicalities. On September 12 the American offers were rejected because the law of January 5, 1909, did not permit the sale of government bonds at a discount for railway development.[8] The contractors were satisfied, for they did not wish to accept bonds at par in payment for their work.

Arosemena then called a special session of the National Assembly for the purpose of modifying the law in order that bonds might be sold at less than face value. The Panamanians also were discussing the use of the constitutional fund of $6,000,000 for building the line. The American chargé was of the opinion that the Washington government was able to prevent the application of any part of that sum to railroad construction.[9] The State Department apparently made no objection to the building of the proposed line if it was necessary and was done under its watchful eye.[10] On October 9, 1911, the National Assembly passed two bills providing for the construction of the *Ferrocarril de Panamá a David* without incurring debt. The $6,000,000 and other government funds deemed necessary and proper by the president were to be expended. Article 138 of the constitution which established the investment in 1904 was repealed, and no attention was given to modifying the law of 1909. Arosemena immediately vetoed both bills,[11] and the status of the railway question remained unchanged.[12]

Secretary of Public Works Carlos C. Arosemena later explained to Minister Dodge that the bills had been passed as political measures designed not to facilitate railway development but to prevent the government in power from gaining prestige. The legislation had been formulated to hold the matter over for the next administration which hoped to increase its popularity by carrying out the project.[13] Dodge also was informed of a proposal from August Dziuk, a German subject, for building the railroad. Arosemena considered this the best made, but had resolved to deal only with Americans. Dodge was somewhat irked that the Dziuk proposition, which he believed "onerous" to Panama, had been viewed favorably.[14]

On September 20, 1911, Acting Secretary of State Huntington Wilson sent Chargé W. W. Andrews a detailed account of the activities of the Balboa and Pacific Estates, an English-German corporation, which had been attempting to build a railway east of the Canal Zone. He reviewed the attitude of the United States and instructed Andrews to place the despatch before the Panamanian government for its future guidance in railway policy.[15] According to this note, the American legation at Panama had informed the State Department on October 22, 1910, that the Balboa and Pacific Estates had applied to the Panamanian government for a ninety-nine year concession, apparently monopolistic in nature, for constructing a narrow-gauge railroad in the Darién region from the mouth of river Piñas to a point on the left bank of river Tuira. The company also wished to continue the line to a point more or less adjacent to the headwaters of river Chucunaque. The contract provided for a wholesale grant of public lands along the right of way. The legation believed the corporation, which owned three mines near the mouth of river Piñas, was more interested in getting public land than in railway construction and that the enterprise would fail because the Darién region was beyond doubt the most unhealthful in the world. The legation concluded that a State Department telegram of objections might remove the project from the consideration of the National Assembly. On November 7 the Washington government instructed the legation to suggest to Panama the desirability of granting only alternate sections along the right of way and to intimate in general terms the interest of the United States in the development of Panama. The reply was that the modification of the concession was likely; "both the executive and legislative branches of the Government of Panama evinced every desire to act in conformity with the wishes of the United

States." The Latin American division of the State Department was somewhat aroused over press reports of the matter, but stated that properly safeguarded railway development should be encouraged, even if American exploitation of Panama was preferable. Objection was made to any contract that conferred a monopoly in Darién or the Chucunaque Valley.

On February 4, 1911, the American legation finally received a copy of the concession, which had passed the National Assembly on January 29. The contract enabled the continuance of the railroad across river Tuira and partially across the Chucunaque Valley to a point near the headwaters of river Chucunaque. For each ten kilometers of main line forty square kilometers of land were ceded, and a similar area was retained along the line. The right to establish necessary branches was granted, but each extension required the assent of the Panamanian president.[16] Until the contract was received the State Department did not have sufficient evidence to challenge the intentions of Panama, "even if it had been possible to assume that the Government of Panama could have for the moment considered proceeding beyond the most tentative steps, in a matter involving problems of such obvious joint interest, without officially seeking thorough and deliberate consultation with the Government of the United States."[17]

On April 19, 1911, the legation informed the State Department that the corporation had cabled its representative to get the right to build a line from Chepo to Panama City, which would traverse a portion of the Canal Zone, and had intimated that construction materials would be purchased in the United States. The extension apparently was considered more important than the main line. On May 2 the State Department requested the legation to report on the location and purposes of the branch and suggested that Colonel Goethals be interviewed. The Panamanian president would be expected to defer granting the application pending full consideration by the Washington government. On May 9 the legation replied that the president, "in spite of the syndicate's insistence," had taken the ground that the Panama-Chepo line could not be termed a branch under the provisions of the concession. Goethals stated that if no objection was raised to the construction of the proposed Panama-David railroad by foreign capital the Panama-Chepo line might be built by the same means, "inasmuch as the relations of both roads to the Canal Zone were identical." He also informed the War Department that President Taft, while in Panama in 1910, had discussed the exchange of a part of the Canal Zone for certain water rights in the Colón Harbor, an action which would permit the building of a railroad to the capital wholly on Panamanian territory. He did not wish to express an opinion in regard to the extension because he felt that it should be treated as a matter of policy rather than Canal development. The legation had reached the conclusion that the acquisition of exclusive railway rights in Panama by foreigners would be detrimental to American interests and that the line in Darién would never be built unless access was gained to Panama City.

On June 2 Carlos C. Arosemena informed Dodge that the extension had been refused on the ground that it was not a branch. However, he stated, "with an unconscious indifference to the interests or the attitude of the United States," that Panama was ready to consider a new concession for the railroad to Panama City. He also told Dodge that it was rumored that a branch line from a point near river Chucunaque to the Colombian frontier was projected. The company expected to extend the branch across the Isthmus partly in Panama and partly in Colombia. This would be of great importance to the United States, and Arosemena promised to keep the State Department informed. The Panamanian recognized the concern of the American government, but felt that under the contract Panama would be obliged to give permission for the extension. On July 10 the legation reported that the line was not being considered and that Panama would guard the interests of the United States if the privilege to build such a road should be requested.

During July Secretary of War Henry L. Stimson visited Panama, where he found Dziuk of the Balboa and Pacific Estates pressing for approval of a branch line from the headwaters of river Chucunaque via Chepo to Panama City. When this matter came up during a discussion of the modification of the boundaries between Panama and the Canal Zone, the secretary stated that the railway problem had not existed when Taft broached the change in 1910, and that the power of the United States to prevent its construction would be destroyed if Panama should be joined to the main part of the republic east of the Canal. The United States would consent to boundary adjustments only "upon a distinct understanding that no such concessions for railroads would be granted except under such safeguards as would enable the United States to control absolutely the railroads in case of war or other disturbance." Panama apparently accepted the dictation of the Washington government, for President Arosemena was reported to have "acceded to the reasonableness of this position."

The War Department informed the State Department on July 21 that the original concession for a railway about one hundred miles in length from the mouth of river Piñas to the valley of El Real de Santa María on river Tuira and thence northwest toward the headwaters of river Chucunaque, no point of which would be within a hundred miles of the Canal Zone, would not affect Canal construction or Canal Zone government, but should be studied from the standpoint of policy. A line any nearer, however, would be more or less contrary to the interests of the United States and absolutely contrary if "within striking distance." Attention was called on August 19 to a telegram from Colonel Goethals saying: "Panaman authorities desire [to] extend Dziuk railroad concession from headwaters of Chucunaque via Chepo to Juan Diaz River, stipulating that road shall not be nearer than 10 miles to Caribbean Sea or Colombian frontier, and request consent of the United States." The secretary of war stated that the Juan Díaz River was only ten miles from Panama City and as objectionable from a strategic point of view as a line into the city. The War Department had the American legation instructed that a study was being made of the matter and that Panama should "studiously refrain meanwhile from any further commitments."

After the discussion of the Balboa and Pacific Estates concession Wilson proceeded to outline the policy of the United States. He stated that Panama apparently felt that it might act in disregard of interests essential to both countries and that many Panamanians did not believe the United States would interfere with their endeavors. He wished to emphasize to the Panamanian government that the United States was not to be trifled with and that it would protect its interests in Panama. In regard to Isthmian internal politics, he said:

> Distortion of the policy of the United States, the cry of American aggression, the appeal to national pride in Panama, scheming for this or that private interest, coquetting with foreign enterprises as a barrier against American preponderance, and depending upon American protection and disinterestedness as a cloak for all sorts of irresponsible activities—such, unfortunately, have sometimes been pawns in Panama's domestic politics.[18]

In definitely refusing approval of the extension to the Juan Díaz River, Wilson stated that the United States had a sincere desire for the prosperous development of Panama, but did not wish to see its wealth "frittered away in unsound or ill-considered schemes." If Panama wished to construct railways for "beneficial and economically sound exploitation" of its resources, the United States would be glad to assist. The American government felt, however, that all foreign concessions should be examined in advance, for otherwise it might have to exert its treaty rights after some project had been started and "in a manner which might involve the Republic of Panama in serious financial losses."[19] The reading of this despatch to Foreign Secretary Federico Boyd on October 7 by Andrews caused the Panamanian "considerable concern," but he expressed pleasure at the willingness of the United States to foster the development of his country.[20]

Minister Dodge wrote Secretary of State Knox on November 29 that President Arosemena and Secretary Arosemena had assured him that all proposals for extensions in the direction of Panama City had been refused. Doubt had been expressed as to whether Dziuk would ever begin the construction of the main line.[21]   The matter was settled definitely to the satisfaction of the United States by March 5, 1912, when Dodge reported that the concession of the Balboa and Pacific Estates had been revoked because maps, profiles, and plans required by the contract had not been deposited with the government.   Foreign Secretary Aristides Arjona, however, explained to Dodge that the real reason for cancellation "was his Government's opinion that this would be agreeable to the American Government and would facilitate the resumption of negotiations for the exchange of certain lands in the Sabanas adjoining Panama City and forming part of the Canal Zone, for certain water rights in the harbor of Colon."   The minister stated that this action had been considered for some time and had been mentioned repeatedly to him by members of President Rodolfo Chiari's government, but that he had refrained from showing any interest except to remark casually "that although over a year had elapsed since this contract was approved, the contractor had as yet apparently done nothing, while his financial support seemed not to be clear."[22]

After the two railway bills were vetoed in October, 1911, Panama entered a tentative contract with R. W. Hebard for the construction of a section of the *Ferrocarril de Panamá a David* from Aguadulce to Santiago de Veraguas, but nothing was done.[23]   Three other Americans, J. M. Hyatt, H. G. Prescott, and Robert Wilcox, attempted to get a contract for a part of the system from the port of Aguadulce to the town of Aguadulce, where it was to divide into two branches: one to pass through Natá to Antón and to extend on to Penonomé, the other to reach Santiago de Veraguas.[24]   On March 21, 1912, Panama asked the State Department to approve the part of this line from the port of Aguadulce to Santiago.[25]   Minister Dodge was instructed to form a commission for examining the technical merits of the proposition,[26] and a favorable report was rendered on May 13.[27]   The Panamanian government wished to use the Canal annuity or the interest from the constitutional fund to finance the estimated $1,736,908 cost of approximately

seventy-two miles.[28] By June 5 the United States had agreed
to the hypothecation of the $250,000 for the project.[29] The
Washington government apparently objected to the use of
neither,[30] but Carlos C. Arosemena exclaimed during the negotiations to a colleague that it was inconceivable for a reputedly
independent state to have to ask permission of another power to
spend its own income in legitimate and authorized business of
its own government.[31] The matter was dropped about the end of
August because the incoming president was opposed to the construction of that section of the Panama-David road first.[32]

President Belisario Porras soon started proceedings toward
building the *Ferrocarril Panamá a David*.[33] A bill for beginning the line was brought before the National Assembly on
January 14, 1913.[34] Seven days later Dodge requested the
new foreign secretary, Ernesto T. Lefevre, to delay the measure
until the State Department could consider it, and action was
deferred.[35] The proposed line from Panama City to David
with branches in Los Santos and on the Pacific slope of the
province of Chiriquí found favor with the State Department,
but objections were raised to the pledging of the Canal annuity
or the income from the constitutional fund.[36] This greatly
vexed Porras, who declared that the United States had no right
to control the use of either fund, for both belonged to Panama
to be employed as it deemed fit.[37] Under the provisions of
Law 29 of 1913, the Panamanian government signed a contract
on February 4, 1914, with R. W. Hebard for laying a three-
foot gauge railway in the province of Chiriquí.[38] Panama
apparently wanted to construct a line in Chiriquí twenty-eight
miles in length from the port of Pedregal to Boquete with a
twenty-three mile branch from David to Concepción and another
in Los Santos from the port of Mensabe to Macaracas.[39] The
Washington government eventually gave its permission for a
$3,000,000 issue of thirty-year bonds for the project and indi-
cated that the hypothecation of the income from the constitutional fund for interest and amortization would be approved,
provided the bonds were used only for the construction of a
railway in Chiriquí.[40]

Hebard formally inaugurated the construction of the road on April 5, 1914, when President Porras drove the first spike.[41] The line was to pass through one of the most fertile, salubrious, and promising sections of the country. The government hoped to stimulate cattle raising on the llanos, sugar industry around Potrerillos and in the Caldera River Valley, and coffee culture in the Boquete mountain district.[42] The contractor bore the expense of the development until arrangements were made concerning the $3,000,000 bond issue. The Washington government was asked to set aside $63,-125 from the Canal annuity for interest and sinking fund charges on the first $750,000 issued on November 2, 1914. A total of $2,250,000 was floated through J. P. Morgan and the National City Bank of New York, and the sum of $190,258.61 was assigned to cover interest and amortization.[43] The road, known as the *Ferrocarril Nacional de Chiriquí*, from the port of Pedregal via David to Boquete with branches from David to Concepción and from Dolega to Potrerillos, a total distance of 91.85 kilometers, was completed on schedule in 1916 at a cost for construction and equipment of $2,102,201.96.[44]

In July, 1916, Minister Eusebio A. Morales began negotiations with the Washington government for permission to issue from $400,000 to $450,000 in bonds for extending the railway eighteen miles from Concepción in the direction of Charco Azul. Panama wanted further assignment made from the Canal annuity.[45] American investors in the region were urging the construction of the branch, and the Amalgamated Sugar interests of Utah apparently were interested.[46] On December 22, 1916, the State Department finally handed down its decision, but had forgotten the place where the road was to be built and the funds that were to be used. An issue of $400,000 in 5 per cent bonds to mature within thirty years would be approved on condition that they were for an eighteen-mile extension from David in the direction of Charco Azul. A part of the constitutional fund might be hypothecated for servicing the loan.[47] Minister Porras accepted the terms, but corrected the State Department as to the direction of the branch and the source of the funds.[48]   On January 4, 1917, Lansing agreed to Panama's original proposition.[49]

The Republic of Panama accepted American supervision of its railway development, but not without resentment.   Porras complained to Roger W. Babson in 1915 that the United States seemed interested only in building a naval station and military base in Panama such as England had at Gibraltar.   He charged that American officials looked at everything from a military point of view and only thought of Canal defense when his government considered railroad building or other developments.[50] Distaste for American interference did not prevent the National Assembly from passing a law on December 20, 1916, that provided for obtaining assistance from the United States in railway and highway building.[51]   Under its provisions President Ramón M. Valdés sent a committee to Washington in 1917 to secure the co-operation of the American government, but the mission was a failure.[52]   After this attempt the extension from Concepción was broached again, and the State Department was still favorable.[53]   In accordance with Law 26 of 1917, the president created a technical commission on September 1 for surveying the route of the branch, and the Canal Zone government placed L. L. Lowery at the disposition of Panama for the survey, but the extension was not built because of abnormal conditions created by the war.[54]

On December 30,1912, Basil Burns Duncan, an American, signed a contract with the Panamanian government for the construction within five years of a railroad from the west side of the mouth of Chagres River to extend in a southwesterly direction at least fifty kilometers.   He was given the privilege of building branch lines, provided he gained the consent of the Panamanian president.[55]   On January 8, 1913, Dodge reported that the contract needed only the assent of the National Assembly, but that President Porras had acquiesced gladly in delaying further action pending consultation with the State Department.[56]   At the request of Secretary Knox a commission was formed by Dodge, and disapproval of the contract was recommended on January 27 because the indefiniteness of its provisions rendered the proper consideration of its technical merits impracticable.[57]   Colonel Goethals objected to a stipulation that Duncan might build wharves at the mouth of the Chagres. A port there would have required a change in Canal defense plans, and branch lines might have interfered with the Panama Railroad monopoly.[58]   The contract was withdrawn eventually,[59] but Duncan continued his activities. By December, 1916, he had requested approval for a railway from the mouth of the Chagres to Chiriquí Lagoon with a branch to Penonomé.[60]   The United States approved the main line, but objected to the branch because it might prove detrimental to Canal defense.[61]   On March 5, 1917, the National Assembly enacted a law modifying the Duncan contracts of December 30, 1912, and January 24, 1917, by eliminating the line to Penonomé, but necessary and convenient branch lines were to be constructed with the approval of the president.[62]   The War Department did not like the provision in regard to branches and asked the State Department to make an agreement with Panama whereby no extension would be started without the consent of the Washington government.[63]   Duncan promised Minister Price that he would work in harmony with the interests of the United States,[64] and Foreign Secretary Garay agreed that Duncan would be permitted to build no extension without the acquiescence of the American government.[65]   So far these negotiations have proved useless; Duncan has never been able to construct the main line from which to extend his feared branches.

On February 28, 1919, the National Assembly approved a contract with J. M. Hyatt of the Hyatt Panama Manganese Company for the construction of a railroad from a point on the Atlantic Coast between Portobelo and Colón to the headwaters of river Boquerón. Again the United States objected. Minister Price complained to Secretary Ernesto T. Lefevre that the contract was signed before his government had given an opinion, and referred him to the position the United States always had maintained that Panama should celebrate no contracts for railway construction before submitting them for its consideration.[66]   Lefevre answered on December 26, 1919, that nothing had been done in conflict with the interests of the United States.[67]   After repeated American protests the Panamanian government stated on July 10, 1920, that the Hyatt concession violated neither the treaty of 1903 nor the Panama Railroad contract.   Both applied only to ways of transportation across the Isthmus, and the United States did not have the right to oppose the construction of a line between river Boquerón and the Atlantic Coast.[68]   Hyatt proceeded to build the railway from Nombre de Dios to his company's property near river Boquerón, a distance of 25.5 kilometers, and completed it in 1925.[69]

In 1920 Panama engaged G. V. Barril, an American, to inspect the *Ferrocarril Nacional de Chiriquí* and to make recommendations concerning branches to Dávila or Chiriquí Viejo.[70]   In 1921 the line was placed under the control of the *Junta Central de Caminos* in an effort to make it pay expenses, but the operating deficit that year was $12,289.22, and the expense of reconstruction $98,019.06, producing a total deficit of $110,309.28. The American consul at Panama City reported: "The Chiriqui Railroad has never been satisfactorily operated by native officials, and it has been the policy for some time past to place an experienced official of the Panama Railroad in full charge of operating the road."[71]   On December 30, 1922, the Panamanian government signed a contract with Gregorio Miró for a narrow-gauge railway approximately thirty miles in length from river Tuira to the midpoint of the Colombian frontier. Miró was rumored to have planned to transfer the concession to a subsidiary of the Standard Oil Company for use in developments in northern Colombia, but nothing came of it.[72]

A survey of the railroad facilities of the Republic of Panama in 1925 showed two common carriers: a main line of 47.61 miles and a total trackage of 161.78 miles of the Panama Railroad owned by the United States government and a main line of approximately 57 miles of the *Ferrocarril Nacional de Chiriquí* belonging to the Panamanian government. The United Fruit Company had a total trackage of 282.7 miles of railway and 58.64 miles of tramway over which a limited amount of public business was done. The Hyatt Panama Manganese Company was building a short line from Nombre de Dios to the river Boquerón; the Panama American Lumber Development Company operated a narrow-gauge track three or four miles in length in the Río Congo district of the province of Panama; Del Valle, Henríquez and Company had a seven kilometer narrow-gauge line in connection with its sugar interests in Coclé; and the Panama Sugar Company operated about fourteen miles of narrow-gauge track with its development at Progreso in Chiriquí. The Darién Gold Mining Company was reported to own about 61 kilometers of track in 1916, but was not mentioned in 1925.[73]

The National Assembly authorized by Law 47 of 1924 the extension of the *Ferrocarril Nacional de Chiriquí* from Concepción to Puerto Armuelles.[74] In 1926 a loan of $2,600,000 was floated through a New York banking house for building the branch and for harbor improvements at Puerto Armuelles, and the J. G. White Company contracted for extending the road 34.5 miles from Concepción through Progreso to Puerto Armuelles and for building a concrete dock at the port.[75] The line was completed in 1929 and might have been a factor in the revenue increase of the *Ferrocarril Nacional de Chiriquí*, which failed to show a deficit in 1929 for the first time in its history.[76] Before the extension was completed the Chiriquí Land Company, a subsidiary of United Fruit, had leased the thirteen-mile section between Puerto Armuelles and Progreso and had acquired the right to use jointly with the Panamanian government the thirty-nine miles from Progreso to David. The company got very favorable treatment, including the right of way of both empty and loaded banana cars over all other trains, in this contract and another signed about the same time for private lines in the districts of Alanje and Bugaba.[77] The United States indicated that it did not approve all acts of the United Fruit Company when a protest was made in 1927 concerning a concession granted the Tonosi Fruit Company, which included a railway in Los Santos.[78]

WIRELESS COMMUNICATION

The active interest of the United States in wireless communication in the Republic of Panama was not aroused fully until 1911, when the secretary of the navy asked the State Department for information concerning wireless installations on the Isthmus.[79] The Navy Department had decided that the erection of private wireless stations in Panama should be prevented, and requested the secretary of state to reach such an agreement with the Panamanian government.[80] The Panamanian foreign secretary indicated a willingness to enter an understanding in compliance with the wishes of the Navy, but hoped that the use of wireless necessary for the development of his country would not be prohibited.[81] Later the government stated that it was opposed to any agreement restricting private and commercial wireless on the Isthmus because the development of the republic might be hindered, but would acquiesce for the sake of protecting the Canal. At that time the only wireless equipment in the republic not owned by the United States was a small government apparatus in Panama City and the United Fruit station at Bocas del Toro. Minister Dodge asked that no change be permitted in the wireless situation without the knowledge of the State Department, and Foreign Secretary Federico Boyd agreed to the extent of offering to rescind a United Fruit contract for erecting a station in Colón before December 27, 1911.[82]

On January 23, 1912, the Navy Department requested Knox to get sites for the erection of wireless stations in Bocas del Toro, Portobelo, Armila, Piñas Bay, Cape Mala, and David Bay. The Navy wanted the exclusive right to erect and operate all wireless installations in Panama and would handle free all messages of the Panamanian government, accept all other messages at rates set by the American Congress, and would furnish additional stations pursuant to agreement between the two governments.[83] Dodge reported on February 10, 1912, that the Panamanian government had ordered several months before a wireless set to be placed on the National Theater in Panama

City and that it would interfere with the Navy apparatus in Balboa and near Culebra. He had obtained a delay in the installation of the equipment; Secretary Arjona had said that it was not needed anyway.[84] On April 15 the State Department sent Dodge an opinion that under the terms of the Canal treaty the United States did not have to get the permission of Panama for the erection of wireless stations on the Isthmus and that interfering stations might be disposed of under Article VII.[85] On May 13 the minister was instructed to use his influence to prevent the installation of radio stations in Panama.[86] A month later he reported that Panama wished to sell the wireless equipment bought for the National Theater, and recommended that the United States purchase it. Accordingly, arrangements were made for the Navy Department to pay for it.[87]

The Panama Canal Act of August 24, 1912, authorized the president of the United States to cause to be erected and operated in the Canal Zone and on the coast adjacent to the Canal terminals such wireless telegraphic stations as he might deem "necessary for the operation, maintenance, sanitation and protection of said Canal, and for other purposes." He was further empowered to make agreements with Panama for wireless installations in the republic for the transmission of private, commercial, and official messages, provided communications of the American government were given precedence. Operating contracts might be made with private companies for wireless telegraphic communication.[88]

The War Department complained to the State Department on August 26, 1913, that Panama had signed a new contract with the United Fruit Company for the erection of a wireless station in Colón and that the Marconi Company of America was seeking a franchise for a "wireless outfit" in the republic. Secretary of State Bryan was asked to frustrate the efforts of the Marconi Company, for its activities were considered contrary to the interests of the United States.[89] The Navy Department insisted that the wireless situation be settled.[90] On January 16, 1914, Minister Price advised the State Department that Panama wished to enter an agreement for the exchange of wireless messages with the United States, but wanted its employees in charge of stations on Panamanian territory.[91] The State Department answered that the Joint Army and Navy Board had recommended the cancellation of all wireless concessions not in actual operation and the assumption of all means of radio communication in Panama.[92]   On February 16 Price suggested to Secretary Lefevre that Panama grant the United States a monopoly of radio communication on the Isthmus, in compensation for which the American government would build and operate four stations in Panama in addition to the two at the Canal terminals.[93]

Secretary of State Bryan reached the conclusion that the United States might take over all radio stations on the Isthmus under the terms of the Hay-Bunau-Varilla Treaty, but considered it more feasible to agree with Panama regarding the conduct of radio communication in order to avoid future difficulties.[94]   The Panamanian government continued its dilatory tactics, claiming that more stations were needed than the Navy proposed to erect, but promised to sign no contracts for radio communication.   The United States was urged to put in six installations and to erect at once those projected for the San Blas Coast, Puerto Obaldía, and Darién.[95]   The American terms were finally accepted, but Panama claimed that a grant of monopoly rights required a treaty which could not be ratified until the National Assembly met in September.[96]   The Navy Department continued its pressure, and on August 13, 1914, Bryan cabled Price that war conditions made it "absolutely essential that the United States exercise immediate monopoly of all wireless stations in the Republic of Panama and control the radio equipment of all ships in the territorial waters of Panama."[97] Panama prepared a decree on August 15 giving the United States provisional control for the duration of the European crisis,[98] but Price protested that it was insufficient, and its publication was withheld.[99]   On August 29 the Panamanian government issued a decree transferring to the United States complete and permanent control of all radio telegraphic stations and everything relating to wireless communication in the territory and territorial waters of Panama.[100]

Since 1914 the United States has maintained complete supervision of all radio communication in the Republic of Panama. An attempt was made in the treaty of 1926 to adjust matters by permitting the erection and operation of private stations. These were to have a license from the Panamanian government and were to be subject to the inspection and censorship of the Washington government. Panama agreed to close any objectionable stations and was to retain sovereignty over territory occupied by American government installations, but surrendered jurisdiction over their sites, equipment, and personnel.[101]

The Republic of Panama has not relished interference with its radio development. American interests were ignored in the Tonosi Fruit Company and the Chiriquí Land Company contracts of 1927 and in the Panama Corporation concession of 1929. The Tropical Radio Telegraph Company advised the State Department in June, 1929, that it had taken over the Chiriquí Land Company contract, and in November received the permission of the American government for a radio station near the Canal Zone. Late in 1929 and early in 1930 the Pan American Airways attempted to get permits from the Washington government for two stations on the Isthmus. When the company declined an offer that the Navy construct and operate the stations, the State Department rejected its petition.[102] On December 29, 1930, President Arosemena abrogated the decree of August 29, 1914. Since that time no agreement regulating radio communication in Panama has existed. The naval stations, however, have continued to take official and private messages of the Panamanians.[103]

HIGHWAYS

The Republic of Panama began its existence with practically no highways worthy of the name. The streets of its cities were little more than dust beds or quagmires, according to the season. The United States soon undertook to pave the streets of Panama and Colón and to build modern highways in the

Canal Zone, being careful that no road crossed the Isthmus. President Amador made some effort to increase transportation facilities, but the task of transforming jungle trails and worse into serviceable highways was too great.   In 1912 and again in 1915 Panama was reported devoid of decent roads other than those of the American government in the Canal Zone.   The lack of means of transportation continued to retard the development of the country.   Often the cost of getting products to market more than consumed their value.   Some president always was making plans for improvement, but the loquacious stage was seldom passed.   In fact, the interior was too sparsely settled to make highway construction economically sound.[104]

The Panamanian government attempted to capitalize on the war in 1917 in order to increase its transportation conveniences. A law was passed late in 1916 for getting the co-operation of the United States,[105] and a committee was later sent to Washington. The officials of the American government appeared interested in the highway proposals of the Panamanians, but maintained a "guarded silence" on the subject of a road from Panama City to Portobelo.[106]   The United States finally refused the offers, but stated that it planned to build 110 miles of highways on the Isthmus, and hoped that Panama would help maintain them.[107] Secretary Garay believed that assistance was wanted only on roads outside the Canal Zone.[108]   Nothing was done.   Porras, referring to the emergencies of the war and explaining that he realized it was an American affair, courteously inquired as to the time the work would be started.[109]   Lansing replied that funds would be provided in the 1919 budget.[110]   The Panamanians thought Lansing had made a mistake in the date,[111] but Porras assured Garay that the appropriation would not be considered until 1919.[112]

When the World War ended, the Panamanians could boast of no more than one hundred miles of good highways,[113] but they were soon started toward a good system through the efforts of Addison T. Ruan, the American fiscal adviser to the republic. Among other things he secured legislation allotting three-fourths of the government surplus to road building, and by 1920 that fund had grown to three million.[114]   On February 6, 1920, the National Assembly provided for a *Junta Central de Caminos*, which was organized with Ruan's aid.[115]   Not only did he lend his services, but his successors and various American engineers have been members of the *junta*.[116]   Early in 1921 contracts for approximately 135 kilometers of road building each were let to the Panama Construction Company and to R. W. Hebard.[117]   In 1923 Panama realized $3,714,100.66 for highway developments from a $4,500,000 sale of bonds through W. A. Harriman and the Guaranty Trust Company of New York.   The interest and amortization were secured by the income of the constitutional fund and part of the Canal annuity.[118]

The United States was approached again in 1923 by Panama concerning assistance in highway building.   The result was a study by a joint commission which recommended the construction of various roads, but that each government should build and maintain its own system.   Both might have the free use of all highways, and the United States might have telephone and telegraph lines along the roads of Panama.   The committee suggested that the recommendations be incorporated in a new treaty,[119] and some of them were included in the treaty of July 28, 1926, but its most important highway stipulation provided for a road across the Isthmus from Panama City to Portobelo. The United States agreed to build the remainder of the road and to bear $1,250,000 of the cost.[120]   Various estimates placed the Panamanian share of the expense of the forty-five miles from Alhajuela to Portobelo at $4,500,000.   This was regarded as excessive and was given as one of the reasons for the rejection of the treaty.[121]   While it was being negotiated the American consul at Colón reported the Panamanian feeling on the lack of a trans-Isthmian highway as follows:

The failure to build a motor car road connecting the cities of Colon and Panama has been charged, whether rightly or wrongly, against the government of the Canal Zone.   In other words it is claimed that the preponderant opposition is based on the idea of protecting the earning capacity of the Panama Railroad operated by the United States. So long as it is impossible for motorists to make the through trip in trucks and motor cars the railroad is bound to profit from all passenger and freight traffic, no matter whether the volume is great or small.[122]

In 1924 the *Junta Central de Caminos* had under construction and maintenance 397 kilometers of highway surfaced mostly with concrete, macadam, or gravel. The United States had an additional 86 miles of paved roads in the Canal Zone.[123] Four years later the Panamanian government floated a $12,-000,000 bond issue through American banking firms and devoted approximately $5,000,000 of the proceeds to highway development.[124] In July, 1930, Panama had under construction or finished 1,370 kilometers of roads at a cost of $14,-352,000 and needed $4,800,000 more to complete the system.[125] The next year Panama had 458 kilometers of first-class highway mainly west of the Canal Zone, 277.6 kilometers under construction, 299 kilometers of second-class roads, and 399 kilometers of dry-season trails.[126] On March 31, 1931, the 315 mile highway from Panama City to David was opened officially.[127]

The Panamanians continue to hope for a highway across the Isthmus from Panama City to Colón. In 1928 a member of the Panama Corporation tried to get a contract to build the trans-Isthmian road, but the United States blocked his efforts.[128] After the rejection of the treaty of 1926 the National Assembly passed a bill authorizing the president to grant a concession for the highway, but advances made to the American government in 1930 availed nothing.[129] However, the Panamanians now understand that the United States will not object to the construction of the highway across the Isthmus. Nothing was signed before the recent treaty giving that assurance, but they had been informed that the road would meet no obstacles in the American State Department.[130]

AERONAUTICS

The United States has watched closely the use of aircraft in the Republic of Panama, probably with more justification than its meddling in other communication developments. An attempt was made by the treaty of 1926 to set up a system of joint control over all aircraft and aviation centers in Panama except those owned by the two governments.[131] In 1927 Minister South asked the Panamanian government to inform all aviators seeking permission to fly over or land in its territory of the facilities and regulations of the Canal Zone. All were to be warned that the consent of the United States was necessary for flying over the Canal strip.[132]

The development of commercial aviation began to receive serious attention in 1928. On August 9 South requested a permit from the Panamanian government for a Pan American Airways plane to land, refuel, and make inspections while on a tour of the Caribbean area for a commercial air route.[133] This company inaugurated service between Miami, Florida, and Cristóbal on February 4, 1929, with a plane piloted by Colonel Charles A. Lindbergh.[134] Soon the Pan American planes were making regular landings at David and Panama City on their South American run down the west coast.[135] The *Sociedad Colombo-Alemana de Transportes Aéreos* which operates the *Scadta* lines in Colombia obtained permission from Panama and the United States for air service between Panama and Colombia and on March 27, 1929, the first *Scadta* plane entered the Canal Zone from Barranquilla. Buenaventura and Tumaco, Colombia, were later added, but the service to the Isthmus was discontinued on June 15, 1931.[136] On May 1, 1929, the monopoly of the United States on trans-Isthmian transportation was broken by the establishment of air service by the Isthmian Airways, a local concern, between Panama City and Colón.[137] The 1929 development of air transportation in the "halfway house" of the Americas drew the following comment from the British consul at Panama City:

The last few months have been marked by an extraordinary enthusiasm for aviation, and Panama has suddenly become the centre of a network of lines. So many lines have sprung up and optimism has been such that it would hardly be surprising if there was a reaction before steady and normal development began. The provision of swift air mail lines to South American countries, however, rests on strong American backing. . . .[138]

Negotiations between Panama and the United States resulted in Law 89 of 1929 which created a *Comisión de Aviación* of six members, three to be named by each, for the supervision of all aircraft on the Isthmus except that owned by the two governments. Licenses were to be issued only by the commission, and all private planes and fields were subject to its inspection. Persons wishing to own aircraft in the republic were required to deposit $25,000 with the government until their property holdings in Panama equalled that sum. Planes might land only on designated fields, and flying between sunset and sunrise and the carrying of ammunition were prohibited.[139]

In 1931 the Panamanian government purchased its first air fleet, consisting of an amphibian, the *3 de Noviembre,* and two airplanes, the *Constitución* and the *República,* which was to be used to carry mail from Panama City to the interior. Service was started on November 28, 1931, the anniversary of the independence of the Isthmus from Spain. Two routes were maintained: one on the Pacific side touching important towns up to Puerto Armuelles; the other across from Panama to Colón and to Bocas del Toro.[140]

NOTES

1. United Fruit Company, *Annual Report,* 1903, p. 17.

2. *The Canal Record,* IV (1911), 157; V (1912), 305; VI (1913), 416; VII (1913), 41; *Daily Consular and Trade Reports,* June 22, 1912, p. 1273; *BPAU,* XXXIV (1912), 566; XXXV (1915), 840, 1090.

3. Panama, Sec. A. y O. P., *Memoria,* 1910, p. xviii.

4. Panama, Sec. R. E., *Memoria, Anexos,* 1910, pp. 223-227.

5. Panama, Sec. A. y O. P., *Ferrocarril de Panamá a David* . . . (Panama, 1911), p. 17; Panama, Sec. A. y O. P., *Memoria,* 1912, II, 371.

6. IBAR, *Monthly Bulletin,* XXXI (1910), 889.

7. *Gaceta oficial,* Dec. 6, 1910; Jan. 18, 1911.

8. Panama, Sec. A. y O. P., *Ferrocarril de Panamá a David* . . . , pp. 13-68; Panama, Sec. A. y O. P., *Memoria,* 1912, II, 400-429.

9. Andrews to Knox, Sept. 14, 1911, *For. Rel.* (1912), pp. 1170-1171.

10. Wilson to Andrews, Sept. 20, 1911, *loc. cit.,* p. 1185.

11. *Gaceta oficial,* Oct. 14, 1911; Oct. 19, 1911; Oct. 20, 1911.

12. *Daily Consular and Trade Reports,* Nov. 2, 1911, p. 589.

13. Dodge to Knox, Nov. 28, 1911, *For. Rel.* (1912), pp. 1190.

14. *Ibid.,* p. 1192.

15. Wilson to Andrews, Sept. 20, 1911, *loc. cit.,* pp. 1171-1185.

16. *Gaceta oficial*, Mar. 13, 1911.
17. Wilson to Andrews, Sept. 20, 1911, *For. Rel.* (1912), p. 1173.
18. *Ibid.*, p. 1180.
19. *Ibid.*, p. 1184.
20. Andrews to Wilson, Oct. 9, 1911, *loc. cit.*, pp. 1186-1187.
21. Dodge to Knox, Nov. 29, 1911, *loc. cit.*, pp. 1193-1194.
22. *Idem* to *idem*, Mar. 5, 1912, *loc. cit.*, pp. 1198.
23. *Idem* to *idem*, Nov. 28, 1911, *loc. cit.*, pp. 1191-1192.
24. *Idem* to *idem*, Dec. 22, 1911, *loc. cit.*, pp. 1196-1197.
25. Eduardo Chiari to Dodge, Mar. 21, 1912, *loc. cit.*, p. 1199.
26. Wilson to Dodge, Apr. 8, 1912, *loc. cit.*, pp. 1200-1201.
27. Dodge to Knox, May 13, 1912, *loc. cit.*, pp. 1201-1202.
28. Panama, Sec. A. y O. P., *Memoria*, 1912, II, 446-483.
29. Eduardo Chiari to C. C. Arosemena, June 5, 1912, *loc. cit.*, I, xlix.
30. *Idem* to *idem*, Aug. 23, 1912, *loc. cit.*, I, l-li.
31. C. C. Arosemena to Eduardo Chiari, Aug. 26, 1912, *loc. cit.*, pp. li-lii.
32. Dodge to Knox, Aug. 20, 1912; Sept. 3, 1912, *For. Rel.* (1912), pp. 1203, 1205-1206.
33. *Idem* to *idem*, Jan. 14, 1913, *For. Rel.* (1913), pp. 1094-1095.
34. E. T. Lefevre to Dodge, Jan. 31, 1913, *loc. cit.*, p. 1098.
35. Dodge to Knox, Jan. 30, 1913, *loc. cit.*, pp. 1096-1097.
36. E. T. Lefevre to Dodge, Jan. 31, 1913; Knox to Dodge, Feb. 17, 1913, *loc. cit.*, pp. 1098-1099.
37. Dodge to Knox, Feb. 22, 1913, *loc. cit.*, p. 1100.
38. *Gaceta oficial*, Mar. 4, 1913; Price · to Bryan, Feb. 14, 1914, *For. Rel.* (1914), p. 1029; *The Canal Record*, VII (1914), 234; Panama, Sec. A. y O. P., *Memoria*, 1914, pp. 493-498.
39. Lindley M. Garrison, U. S. secretary of war, to Bryan, Apr. 4, 1914, *For. Rel.* (1914), pp. 1030-1031.
40. Bryan to Price, June 29, 1914; Lansing to Price, Oct. 15, 1914, *loc. cit.*, pp. 1032, 1034.
41. *The Canal Record*, VII (1914), 414; *BPAU*, XXXVIII (1914), 784.
42. *BPAU*, XXXVIII (1914), 468; XLI (1915), 474-476.
43. *Gaceta oficial*, Sept. 9, 1914; *Fitch Government Finances*, 1918, p. 314; Panama, Sec. H. y T., *Memoria*, 1916, p. xi; Morales to Bryan, Nov. 2, 1914, *For. Rel.* (1914), pp. 1034-1035; Morales to Lansing, July 28, 1916, *loc. cit.* (1917), p. 1180.
44. Panama, Sec. A. y O. P., *Memoria*, 1916, pp. v-viii; 1924, p. 20.
45. Morales to Lansing, July 28, 1916, *For. Rel.* (1917), pp. 1179-1180.
46. Price to Lansing, Aug. 13, 1916, *loc. cit.*, p. 1184.
47. Lansing to Porras, Dec. 22, 1916, *loc. cit.*, pp. 1180-1181.
48. Porras to Lansing, Dec. 26, 1916, *loc. cit.*, pp. 1181-1182.
49. Lansing to Porras, Jan. 4, 1917, *loc. cit.*, pp. 1182-1183.
50. Babson, *op. cit.*, pp. 90, 96.
51. *Gaceta oficial*, Jan. 6, 1917.
52. Panama, Sec. R. E., *Memoria*, 1918, pp. 129-151.
53. Porras to Lansing, Aug. 1, 1917; Lansing to Porras, Aug. 14, 1917, *For. Rel.* (1917), p. 1183.
54. *Gaceta oficial*, Feb. 9, 1917; Panama, Sec. A. y O. P., *Memoria*, 1918, pp. 6-7.
55. *Gaceta oficial*, Feb. 14, 1913.

56. Dodge to Knox, Jan. 8, 1913, *For. Rel.* (1913), pp. 1081-1083.

57. Dodge to Knox, Jan. 27, 1913, *loc. cit.,* pp. 1087-1088.

58. Knox to Dodge, Feb. 13, 1913, *loc. cit.,* pp. 1090-1091.

59. E. T. Lefevre to Dodge, Mar. 17, 1913, *loc. cit.,* p. 1094.

60. Price to Lansing, Dec. 21, 1916, *loc. cit.* (1917), p. 1185.

61. Polk to Price, Feb. 14, 1917, *loc. cit.,* p. 1186.

62. *Gaceta oficial,* Mar. 23, 1917; Aug. 21, 1919.

63. Newton D. Baker, U. S. secretary of war, to Lansing, Mar. 27, 1917, *For. Rel.* (1917), p. 1189.

64. Duncan to Price, Apr. 11, 1917, *loc. cit.,* p. 1190.

65. Garay to Price, June 15, 1917, *loc. cit.,* p. 1194.

66. Panama, Sec. A. y O. P., *Memoria,* 1928, pp. 141-143; *Gaceta oficial,* Feb. 24, 1919; Price to E. T. Lefevre, Nov. 1, 1919, Panama, Sec. R. E., *Memoria,* 1920, p. 112.

67. E. T. Lefevre to Price, Dec. 26, 1919, *loc. cit.,* p. 113.

68. Hazera to C. B. Hewes, U. S. chargé, July 10, 1920, *loc. cit.,* pp. 114-115.

69. Panama, Sec. A. y O. P., *Memoria,* 1928, pp. 141-143; Great Britain, Dept. of Overseas Trade, *op. cit.,* 1922, p. 21.

70. *BPAU,* L (1920), 667.

71. *Gaceta oficial,* Jan. 27, 1921; *Star and Herald,* Apr. 5, 1921; George Orr, U. S. consul at Panama, "Railway Mileage Republic of Panama," May 22, 1922, pp. 9-11, MS., in Columbus Memorial Library.

72. Long, *op. cit.,* pp. 147-151.

73. *Ibid.,* pp. 134-152; United Fruit Company, *Annual Report,* 1925, p. 18; Panama, *Compendio estadístico, 1909 a 1916,* p. 67.

74. República de Panamá, Sec. A. y O. P., *Especificaciones para el contrato de construcción del ramal de Ferrocarril Concepción-Puerto Armuelles* (Panama, 1926), pp. 1-32; H. D. Myers, U. S. vice-consul at Panama, "Extension of Chiriqui Railway Republic of Panama," June 26, 1926, pp. 1-6, MS., in Columbus Memorial Library.

75. *BPAU,* LX (1926), 929-930; *Commerce Yearbook,* 1926, II, 426.

76. *Commerce Yearbook,* 1930, II, 441; *BPAU,* LXIII (1929), 1059; Great Britain, Dept. Overseas Trade, *op. cit.,* 1929, pp. 14-15; Panama, Sec. H. y T., *Memoria,* 1930, pp. lxi-lxii.

77. Kepner and Soothill, *op. cit.,* pp. 166-170.

78. *Current History,* XXVI (1927), 311.

79. George von L. Myer, secretary of the navy, to Knox, Dec. 11, 1911, *For. Rel.* (1912), p. 1206.

80. Beekman Winthrop, acting secretary of the navy, to Knox, Dec. 13, 1911, *loc. cit.,* p. 1206.

81. Dodge to Knox, Dec. 21, 1911, *loc. cit.,* p. 1209.

82. *Idem* to *idem,* Dec. 26, 1911, *loc. cit.,* pp. 1209-1211.

83. Myer to Knox, Jan. 23, 1912, *loc. cit.,* pp. 1217-1218.

84. Dodge to Knox, Feb. 10, 1912; Feb. 14, 1912, *loc. cit.,* pp. 1218-1220.

85. Wilson to Dodge, Apr. 15, 1912, *loc. cit.,* p. 1233.

86. *Idem* to *idem,* May 13, 1912, *loc. cit.,* p. 1235.

87. Dodge to Knox, June 12, 1912; Ramón M. Valdés, Panamanian minister at Washington, to Knox, Nov. 26, 1912, *loc. cit.,* pp. 1235-1236, 1240.

88. 38 *U. S. Stat. at L.,* 560-569.

89. Henry Breckinridge, acting secretary of war, to Bryan, Aug. 26, 1913, *For. Rel.* (1914), p. 1036.

90. Josephus Daniels, secretary of the navy, to Bryan, Nov. 22, 1913, *loc. cit.*, pp. 1039-1040.

91. Price to Bryan, Jan. 16, 1914, *loc. cit.*, pp. 1040-1041.

92. Bryan to Price, Jan. 29, 1914, *loc. cit.*, pp. 1041-1042.

93. Price to E. T. Lefevre, Feb. 16, 1914, Panama, Sec. R. E., *Memoria*, 1914, pp. 219-221.

94. Bryan to Price, Apr. 29, 1914, *For. Rel.* (1914), p. 1042.

95. E. T. Lefevre to Price, Aug. 14, 1914, Panama, Sec. R. E., *Memoria*, 1914, pp. 223-224.

95. E. T. Lefevre to Price, Aug. 14, 1914, Panama, Sec. R. E., *Memoria*, 1914, 25, 1914, *For. Rel.* (1914), pp. 1044-1045.

97. Bryan to Price, Aug. 13, 1914, *loc. cit.*, p. 1046.

98. Panama, Sec. R. E., *Memoria*, 1914, p. 225.

99. Price to Bryan, Aug. 23, 1914, *For. Rel.* (1914), p. 1049.

100. *Idem* to *idem*, Sept. 2, 1914, *loc. cit.*, p. 1051.

101. *Cong. Rec.*, 69 Cong., 2 Sess., LXVIII, 1851-1852.

102. Panama, Sec. H. y T., *Memoria*, 1930, pp. 223-224.

103. *Ibid.*; *Estrella*, Jan. 1, 1931.

104. IBAR, *Monthly Bulletin*, XXI (1905), 505-507; BPAU, XLI (1915), 469; Harris, *op. cit.*, pp. 201-202; Panama, Sec. A. y O. P., *Memoria*, 1912, I, xx-xxii.

105. *Gaceta oficial*, Jan. 6, 1917.

106. Porras to Garay, May 23, 1919, Panama, Sec. R. E., *Memoria*, 1918, pp. 132-133.

107. *Idem* to *idem*, July 1, 1917, *loc. cit.*, pp. 144-146.

108. *Idem* to *idem*, July 10, 1917, *loc. cit.*, pp. 146-147.

109. Porras to Lansing, July 27, 1917, *loc. cit.*, pp. 147-148.

110. Lansing to Garay, Aug. 24, 1917, *loc. cit.*, p. 149.

111. Garay to Porras, Sept. 10, 1917, *loc. cit.*, p. 150.

112. Porras to Garay, Sept. 22, 1917, *loc. cit.*, pp. 150-151.

113. *BPAU*, XLVIII (1919), 125.

114. Curran, *op. cit.*, pp. 33-34.

115. *Gaceta oficial*, Feb. 26, 1920; Panama, Sec. A. y O. P., *Memoria*, 1920, p. ix.

116. Panama, Sec. A. y O. P., *Memoria*, 1922, pp. i-v; R. C. Hardman, "The Highway Program of Panama," in *The Pan American Magazine*, XXXVII (1924), 273-278.

117. Panama, Sec. A. y O. P., *Memoria*, 1922, p. v; Curran, *op. cit.*, p. 33; *Estrella*, Feb. 25, 1921; *Star and Herald*, Feb. 26, 1921.

118. Panama, Sec. A. y O. P., *Memoria*, 1924, pp. 1-3; BPAU, LVI (1923), 288-289, 609; *Kimber's Government Debts*, 1931, p. 942.

119. Panama, Sec. R. E., *Memoria*, 1924, pp. 71-74.

120. *Cong. Rec.*, 69 Cong., 2 Sess., LXVIII, 1848-1852.

121. *N. Y. Times*, Jan. 5, 1930, III, 8:4.

122. George M. Hanson, "Motor Car Roads in Panama," consular report, July 31, 1926, p. 1, MS., in Columbus Memorial Library.

123. Panama, Sec. A. y O. P., *Memoria*, 1924, pp. 3-4; Curran, *op. cit.*, p. 35.

124. *Kimber's Government Debts*, 1931, p. 944; *The Pan American Magazine*, XLII (1929), 210-211.

125. *Commerce Reports*, Sept. 15, 1930, p. 644.

126. *Moody's Government Securities*, 1934, p. 2657.

127. *BPAU*, LXV (1931), 556.

128. Norton, *op. et loc. cit.*, p. 32; *Panama American*, May 23, 1928.

129. *BPAU*, LXII (1928), 725; LXIV (1930), 304; *N. Y. Times*, Jan. 5, 1930, III, 8:4.

130. Statement to the writer by the Division of Latin American Affairs, Department of State, July 12, 1934.

131. *Cong. Rec.*, 69 Cong., 2 Sess., LXVIII, 1852.

132. South to Alfaro, Aug. 10, 1927, Panama, Sec. R. E., *Memoria*, 1928, p. 133.

133. *Idem* to *idem*, Aug. 9, 1928, *loc. cit.*, p. 132.

134. *The Pan American Magazine*, XLI (1929), 291.

135. *BPAU*, LXIII (1929), 615, 833; *Commerce Reports*, June 10, 1929, p. 642.

136. *Commerce Reports*, Apr. 8, 1929, p. 84; June 3, 1929, p. 584; *BPAU*, LXIII (1929), 615, 723, 1166; Governor of the Canal Zone, *Annual Report*, 1931, p. 113.

137. *Commerce Reports*, May 6, 1929, p. 329; May 13, 1929, p. 393; Aug. 5, 1929, p. 332.

138. Great Britain, Dept. of Overseas Trade, *op. cit.*, 1929, p. 15.

139. J. D. Arosemena to South, Apr. 22, 1929, Panama, Sec. R. E., *Memoria, Anexos*, 1930, II, 157-158; *BPAU*, LXIII (1929), 723, 833-834, 1267.

140. *BPAU*, LXVI (1932), 135.

CHAPTER IX

THE WORLD WAR

PRESIDENT Pablo Arosemena could not have realized that the world was soon to be plunged into the most colossal struggle in history when on October 5, 1910, he stated in his inaugural address:

The ties that bind us to the American Union shall be maintained with integrity, and the Treaty of November 18, 1903, shall be maintained without restrictions which might alter its purpose or deprive it of its wide scope. We shall be grateful and loyal to that great nation which, with its immense power, guarantees the independence of the Republic. We have a broad interest in the work on the canal, and I consider, in the remote event of its being threatened, that for its defense we Panamanians are the natural allies of the United States and it is our duty to join her soldiers under the Stars and Stripes.[1]

Despite the arbitration treaties of William Jennings Bryan, which Panama, along with many other governments, signed on September 20, 1913,[2] the nations of the earth were soon at each others throats as if possessed with the souls of primordial beasts. The little Republic of Panama was drawn with its gigantic protector into the maelstrom. Foreseeing a future war, the United States had asked and obtained permission in July, 1912, for its troops to reconnoiter on Panamanian soil, explaining that the Army should know of places where enemy forces might land in order to be prepared to repel them.[3]

Immediately after the beginning of the World War Panama and the United States signed a protocol to maintain their obligations as neutrals. This agreement provided:

That hospitality extended in the waters of the Republic of Panama to a belligerent vessel of war or a vessel belligerent or neutral, whether armed or not, which is employed by a belligerent power as a transport or fleet auxiliary or in any other way for the direct purpose of prosecuting or aiding hostilities, whether by land or sea, shall serve to deprive such vessel of like hospitality in the Panama Canal Zone for a period of three months, and *vice versa*.[4]

On November 19, 1914, the United States issued a proclamation forbidding any aircraft of a belligerent power to descend or ascend within the Canal Zone or to pass through the air spaces above the lands and waters of that territory. Under these rules the Canal Zone was declared to encompass the cities of Panama and Colón and their adjacent harbors.[5]

In January, 1915, warships of Great Britain and Japan anchored off Puerto Piñas and landed officers and men. Since the port was neither equipped for nor open to commerce the circumstances seemed suspicious. The rumors were that August Dziuk, a German subject and manager of a company holding concessions near the mouth of river Piñas, was in close touch with the German government and that he had erected a wireless station in Panamanian territory,[6] but these reports were apparently unfounded. When the Panamanian foreign office protested to the British and Japanese governments that the vessels had remained at Puerto Piñas five days in violation of international law, it was assured that the incident was caused by an accident to the machinery of one of the ships.[7]

In August, 1916, the Allied Powers included Panama in their proposal to exclude submarines from the regulations in relation to the admission of merchant vessels and warships into neutral waters. Panama declined, saying that compliance would be a violation of the Hague Convention. This reply caused some surprise, for the idea of the Allied Powers was similar to that advanced by the United States in its protest to Germany after the *Lusitania* disaster.[8]

The war undoubtedly welded Panama and the United States more closely together, but in no wise stopped the continuous friction between the two governments. On November 6, 1916, the *Asociación del Comercio* of Panama complained to Foreign Secretary Garay that the governor of the Canal Zone had named a commission to study the problem of transferring all laborers of the United States quartered in Panama and Colón to the Canal Zone.[9] On December 1 Minister Porras lodged a protest with the State Department, asking that the workers be left in the Panamanian cities and declaring that their removal would cause irreparable damage to Panamanian property owners who had constructed houses for the use of the laborers. He further stated that the contemplated action of the governor was not in accord with the policy outlined by Roosevelt in his letter of October 18, 1904, to Taft.[10] Lansing answered on February 15, 1917, that his government had studied the question carefully and would continue with its plans. The Canal Zone authorities, he explained, were of the opinion that the workers could be better controlled by American police. Also the employees were compelled to pay exorbitant rents and corresponding immoderate prices for the necessities of life, which resulted indirectly in a charge on the American government.[11] However, Porras was informed on April 20, 1917, that the matter was pending because Congress had made no appropriation for the project.[12]

On December 20, 1916, Minister Price sent President Wilson's latest peace plea to the Panamanian government.[13] Secretary Garay replied, promising co-operation and praising the endeavors of the American executive to end that "horrible hecatomb" in the following eloquent phraseology:

The altruistic attitude assumed by His Excellency, President Wilson, is worthy of the admiration and acknowledgment of all the nations of the world, belligerents as well as neutrals. Panama, in particular, applauds with enthusiasm his noble achievement, which is inspired with superior ideals of peace and justice, and receives with sympathy his commendable words which predicate respect to the rights and privileges of small nations and weak peoples against the transgressions and aggressions of the strong.

This Republic views with satisfaction the beautiful spectacle offered to the world by the Federal American Union in unfurling with courage the banner of peace and proclaiming, by means of the exchange of ideas at the present time, the undying desire for Justice and Right; and hopes that the benefits which should result from this wise policy may not have long to wait.[14]

Panama was included in the abortive attempt of Venustiano Carranza, president of Mexico, to build up sentiment in the Americas ostensibly for peace, but actually for the benefit of the Central Powers.[15] The Panamanian government indicated its ardent desire for the cessation of the war, but did not rise to the Mexican lure.[16] The Bolivian appeal of 1917 to the American nations for a declaration against submarine attacks on neutral merchant vessels found prompt and willing acceptance in Panama.[17]

On February 3, 1917, the Panamanian government was notified that, since Germany had decided to renew its submarine warfare, American participation in the European cataclysm appeared inevitable.[18] Secretary Garay replied that Panama would respect its obligations to the United States and would co-operate in the defense of the Canal.[19] On February 24 the National Assembly passed a resolution stating that Panama could not remain indifferent to any international conflict in which the United States engaged, and expressing a desire to co-operate with the American government with all forces and resources in the defense of the common interests and ideals of the two peoples.[20] On March 10 it authorized the president to reorganize the government, to increase the national police or to create a military force, to emit a one-half million *balboa* bond issue, to make regulations concerning the food supply, and to take steps toward employing the military forces of the republic with those of the United States in defense of Panama and the Canal Zone.[21]

Following the American declaration of war against Germany President Ramón M. Valdés issued a proclamation on April 7, 1917, declaring that if any other nation in the world were involved Panama would maintain strict neutrality, but that non-partisanship was impossible in a conflict in which the United States participated because that nation had guaranteed the independence and sovereignty of Panama and had constructed in Panamanian territory a work that had to be preserved for the development and progress of mankind. He stated that Panama would assist the United States in preventing hostile acts against the territory of the Canal Zone and urged all Panamanians to aid the American forces.[22] Two days later Panama cancelled the exequaturs of the German diplomatic agents accredited to it.[23] Thus the Republic of Panama took its place among the belligerent powers opposed to Germany, but its action was unique in that no formal declaration of war was issued. The Panamanian foreign office soon made it clear, however, that the executive proclamation was to be regarded as a declaration of war.[24] President Valdés congratulated the United States on April 6 for plunging into the war to save humanity,[25] and again the Panamanian government on April 11 expressed admiration for the course of Wilson. The adulation resounded with allusions to liberty, universal peace, justice, and right which America was to preserve and insure for the world.[26]

On April 3 the American minister and the governor of the Canal Zone conferred with the Panamanian government on war measures. The governor requested that upon a formal declaration of war by Panama all adult male Germans in Panamanian territory be delivered to the Canal Zone authorities. Valdés assented,[27] and on April 12 about thirty German subjects in Panama and Colón who were definitely suspected of improper activities were arrested. These prisoners and the crews of the German vessels interned at Cristóbal were incarcerated in an American government hotel on Taboga Island.[28] President Wilson regarded this with disfavor and stated that if the existing military force was insufficient to defend the Canal Zone he would have additional troops furnished.[29] The Swedish government soon protested that one of its subjects had been seized and imprisoned on Taboga Island. In order to allay Panamanian fears, Lansing cabled Price:

. . . you are authorized to advise the Panamanian Minister for Foreign Affairs that this Government will hold Panama harmless against loss on account of having heretofore interred persons in conformity with this Government's desire, provided this Government shall be kept informed of the proceedings of claimants and be satisfied that the Government of Panama resisted their claims in good faith.[30]

The United States immediately set up a censorship over the Panama office of the Central and South American Cable Company. Secretary Garay complained on April 10 that the office was within the jurisdiction of Panama and that the matter had not been treated diplomatically. He stated that the manifestations of loyal and friendly co-operation of Panama with the United States did not permit it to suppose for an instant that this had been done in deliberate disregard of the sovereignty of Panama. Undoubtedly it was an inadvertence or a simple lack of prudence to which he respectfully wished to call the attention of the Washington government.[31] Governor Chester Harding explained that the United States had no intention of exceeding its rights and that the censorship had been established on the basis that the cables landed in the Canal Zone and that it was for the protection of Panama, as well as the United States. The Panamanians were reminded that Minister Price had informed them as soon as the censorship was started.[32] Panama contended that neither these facts nor the Canal treaty gave the United States the right to establish a censorship in Panamanian territory, but granted permission for it as a military necessity. The Panamanian government felt that the incident indicated the urgent need for an agreement on matters of common interest and hoped that American action in this case would not be taken as a precedent.[33]

Considering the war period an opportune time for gaining a few concessions, Panama renewed its demand for customhouses in Balboa and Cristóbal. On April 20, 1917, Porras explained that this had not been pressed when the boundary convention of 1914 was negotiated because Governor Goethals had not known the extent of land needed for the administration of the Canal. He pointed out that the waterway had been completed for some time, and stated that his government was desirous of erecting its custom-houses.[34] Two months later Lansing replied that the United States did not deem a cession of territory for custom-houses necessary, but that Governor Harding had no objection to assigning offices to the Panamanian customs inspectors.[35] Panama reiterated its demand for the lots of land,[36] but was informed on November 16 that Harding had been instructed to give its officials office space in Balboa and Cristóbal. The State Department considered this more satisfactory and more in accordance with the needs of the republic.[37] Panama was far from satisfied and on January 17, 1918, again demanded the building space which it claimed under Article IX of the treaty of 1903. Porras stated that the acceptance of offices in American government buildings in the terminal ports did not invalidate Panamanian claims to areas for its own custom-houses.[38]

In accordance with a law of December 30, 1916,[39] and immediately after the American declaration of war, Panama appointed Eusebio A. Morales, Julio Arjona Q., and Jorge E. Boyd to act with Minister Porras in Washington for gaining the co-operation of the United States in highway, railway, radio, and agricultural developments.[40] The commission proposed that the Washington government furnish engineers to survey a route for a railroad from Colombia to Costa Rica and that the section between Panama City and David be built at once. Among the main highways suggested, that from Panama City across the Isthmus to Portobelo was probably the most important. The Panamanians wanted the two governments to share equally the expenses, and, in return, the United States might take over the railway in time of war and might use the roads at all times. These were to be administered by a board composed of an equal number of Panamanians and Americans. Panama hoped to get its part of the costs by a direct loan from the Washington government or through its co-operation.

On May 23 Minister Porras predicted failure, for conferences with officials of the War, Navy, and Agricultural Departments had given him no promising impressions. The United States appeared to think nothing of the railway project, but he thought some interest was indicated in the highways. He believed the request for radio stations was about the only one that had a chance of success. One example of the attitude of the American government was the answer of the Department of Agriculture on being informed that Panama needed highways for the development of interior husbandry. The Panamanians were told that no statement could be made on that subject because no expert on roads was present.[41] One June 30 the Washington government replied that the Panamanian proposals had been considered carefully, but could not be granted. In view of the fact that the principal object of the recommendations was to assist in the war, and that the highways and railroad could not be completed within several years, the United States dropped them from consideration. Radio stations at Puerto Obaldía, La Palma, and Punta Mala, and assistance in agricultural development by the giving of information were promised. Appreciation for Panama's willingness to co-operate was expressed.[42] This futile attempt indicated the success of all the efforts of the Panamanians toward taking definite action in co-operating with the Washington government. The United States had little need of the help of the Isthmians other than their loyalty and acquiescence in whatever it wished to do in their territory.

On November 5, 1917, the National Assembly met in special session to consider war measures. On November 20 the legislature validated all acts of President Valdés in connection with the conflict and declared that Panama had been in a state of war with Germany since April 7, 1917. The rights of German citizens under Article 47 of the constitution were suspended, and the president was authorized to co-operate in defense of the Canal, to prohibit commerce with the enemy, to foster agricultural development, and to borrow additional funds.[43] On November 21 a decree was issued requiring all subjects of Germany, Austria-Hungary, Turkey, and Bulgaria residing in Panama to register, to report to their registration officers at ten-day intervals, and to get government permission to travel more than fifteen miles from their respective places of abode.[44]

The United States informed Panama on December 8, 1917, that it had declared war on Austria-Hungary the previous day.

The National Assembly immediately voted to make the same declaration, and on December 12 President Valdés proclaimed the Republic of Panama in a state of war with Austria-Hungary.[45]

On April 2, 1918, Secretary Garay protested to Minister Price that the United States had established a *cuartel* for naval patrols on pier four in Panama City. Since Panama had given so many proofs of friendship with the United States, Garay found it inexplicable that this station had been set up within Panamanian jurisdiction and without consultation with his government. He complained:

> All nations, Mr. Minister, have the duty of zealously defending their sovereignty and the rights that derive from it, and acts such as this, which imply a disregard of that sovereignty, profoundly affect the national dignity and cannot but exercise regrettable influence upon the good relations which happily exist between our two governments.[46]

Price courteously answered that the *cuartel* had been established on property of the Panama Railroad Company and that the commander of the fifteenth naval district had secured the permission of the governor of the Canal Zone. The commander had not the slightest desire to offend the Panamanian government and assumed entire responsibility for the error.[47] Panama accepted the explanation and granted the right to maintain a patrol station for the duration of the war, but stipulated that the guards were to exercise no authority in Panamanian waters or territory other than in connection with American sailors.[48]

The United States started censoring mails in the Canal Zone shortly after declaring war, but did not ask for Panamanian aid until July 23, 1918, when permission to censor the mails of Panama City and Colón with the assistance of Panamanian authorities was requested.[49] Secretary Lefevre answered a month later that the censorship of mails would be a violation of Article 38 of the constitution, but that its provisions might be suspended in time of war. Since the existing emergency required drastic action, the secretary of government and justice had prepared a decree for the next National Assembly dispensing with that guarantee and establishing the censorship. Lefevre explained that it was but a repetition for him to state that Panama wished to aid in every way in order to impede the enemies of the United States and to assure better protection for the Canal Zone.[50] The censorship of mails passing through Balboa and Cristóbal was probably as effective as was necessary.[51]

The Germans interned by Panama were permitted to enjoy the luxuries of the American government hotel on picturesque Taboga Island for more than a year, depriving Canal Zone employees of one of their pleasure resorts. On April 11, 1918, the War Department ordered the prisoners transferred to New York and the abandonment of Taboga as an internment camp. Four days later Price informed the Panamanian government of the proposed removal. Lefevre asked for a formal notification and stated that he would respond after consulting the president and cabinet members. Since the interns belonged to Panama, he expected his government's jurisdiction to be recognized and respected. After conferring with the commanding officer of the Canal Zone, Price sent a formal note to the Panamanian government, stating that the removal of the Germans was a necessary military measure and expressing confidence that Panama would concur in the judgment of those responsible for the defense of the Canal. He then told the State Department that he anticipated no trouble from Panama other than insistence upon the recognition of its technical rights. The Canal Zone officials were of the opinion that Panama might be humored in time of peace, but that the determination of the United States should prevail in war.[52]

The Panamanian and American officials were able to reach an agreement whereby the interns were to be removed to the United States. The Washington government guaranteed that the legal status of the prisoners would not be changed, that the rights of the two governments would neither be altered nor forfeited, and that the note of June 21, 1917, by which the United States assumed responsibility, would not be modified. A promise was obtained that the Canal Zone officials would keep future interns on the Isthmus, for Panama was considering the arrest of additional Germans in reprisal for the internment of five Panamanian students in Germany.[53]

On June 12 the German government entered a formal protest through the Swiss chargé at Washington against the transfer of its nationals from Panama. The United States would be held responsible for all injury sustained for that reason.[54] Germany also complained to the Panamanian government through the Spanish vice-consul at Panama City, claiming that its subjects were interned in Panama and therefore were not within the jurisdiction of the United States. Notwithstanding these expostulations the prisoners were removed to the United States, and Taboga Island reverted to a recreation center for Canal Zone employees.[55]

On September 27, 1918, Attorney-General T. W. Gregory asked the State Department if the removal of the Germans from Taboga was justified by international law. Lansing replied that most of the prisoners had been taken from four German ships that had been in the port of Colón since August, 1914. These men had been taken to Taboga on February 3, 1917, under Articles VII and XXIII of the Canal treaty. The persons confined on April 12, 1917, were Panamanian interns for whom the United States assumed responsibility and Panama had raised no objection to their transfer to the United States. Articles I, VII, and XXIII of the treaty of November 18, 1903, removed all doubt as to the legality of the action. Lansing explained that no exact precedent for the exchange of civil interns between allies existed, but that prisoners of war were exchanged. He concluded:

On analogy and in principle, there seems to be no reason why civil interns, in the absence of treaty stipulation with the enemy, should not be transferred from one ally to another in the interest of the common cause while retaining their original status. In the present case the political ties between the United States and Panama which are much closer and stronger than between allies in ordinary circumstances, would tend to justify even greater freedom of transfer of interns.[56]

The explanation of the State Department did not solve the problem of the office of the attorney-general, which replied: "Our difficulty, however, arises from the question whether this Government, under its own laws, namely section 4047 of the Revised Statutes, has the power to intern an alien enemy resident in the Republic of Panama and brought into this country against his will." The conclusion had been reached that no legal basis existed for a presidential order of internment. The bringing of interns into the United States might not be a breach of international law, but the attorney-general intended to cancel their orders of internment and leave their disposition to the War Department.[57] The aliens were not returned to Panama until June, 1919.[58]

The matter of Panamanian interns was expected to be an issue in the conference concerning prisoners of war beginning in Switzerland between the United States and Germany on September 24, 1918. The American commissioners believed the Germans would attempt to hold the United States responsible for German subjects and property in Latin America and asked the State Department if counter claims might be advanced in regard to Americans in Turkey.[59] Lansing sent them a list of American cases in Turkey, but advised that the matter be broached only to deter Germany from making threats in regard to Latin America and only after consultation with the State Department.[60] The German delegates did propose that the United States urge Panama and Cuba to set their interns free and permit them to be repatriated. The Americans inquired if they might promise to suggest that Panama and Cuba treat all German civilians in accordance with the agreement reached by the United States and Germany in return for similar service in regard to citizens of the United States in Turkey and Bulgaria.[61] Lansing answered that the commissioners might agree in reference to Panama and Cuba, but to obtain some other concession because developments in Bulgaria and Turkey made it inadvisable to concede that Germany had any influence with them in the matter of American interests.[62]

The year 1918 was marked by considerable disorder and turbulence in the Republic of Panama. Vice conditions became so grave that Brigadier General R. M. Blatchford issued an order on May 29 prohibiting officers and men from visiting the territory of the republic. He charged the Panamanian government with connivance in the sale of drugs and adulterated liquors, in the existence of dishonest gambling, and in the prevalence of unrestricted prostitution.[63] President Ramón M. Valdés died on June 3 and was succeeded by Ciro L. Urriola.[64] After Urriola issued a decree postponing the municipal and national elections,[65] the United States sent troops into and assumed control of Panama City and Colón on the afternoon of June 29.[66] The Panamanian government protested bitterly but ineffectively.[67] The elections were held on scheduled time under the supervision of American soldiers.[68] Urriola and his successors made attempts to clean up Panama and Colón. The sale of liquor was restricted, opium traffic was prohibited, and sanitary conditions were to be improved.[69] But for many months the American Army men were not permitted to visit Panamanian territory for their alcoholic beverages and the enchantments of the *calle de prostitutas* and elsewhere.[70]

Not only did the United States assume jurisdiction over Panama City and Colón, but also sent a detachment of troops to David in the province of Chiriquí for the protection of American lives and property.[71] Despite the passionate protests of the Panamanian government against the military occupation of Chiriquí, the soldiers were not retired until August 16, 1920.[72] The Republic of Panama, however, remained loyal to the United States in the face of all dissension. One indication of its unswerving support was the suspension of business for fifteen minutes in the National Assembly on October 6, 1918, in order to permit Panamanian girls to solicit subscriptions for the fourth liberty loan.[73] Panama, Colón, and the Canal Zone purchased approximately $5,000,000 of the various American war issues.[74]

The war years witnessed the paving of the way toward the appointment of a fiscal agent and a police inspector from the

United States by the Panamanian government. After the matter was suggested in 1916 by the Washington government, the National Assembly on December 30, 1918, provided for a fiscal agent, and Addison T. Ruan was engaged for that post in 1919.[75] Law 51 of 1917 provided for two technical instructors for the Panamanian police, but failed to meet with public approval. Law 34 of 1918 authorized the employment of a foreign police inspector and empowered him to reorganize the police force of the republic.[76] Albert L. Lamb was selected in 1919,[77] and he had produced a fairly efficient force when the Panamanian-Costa Rican clash occurred in 1921.

The oldest and the youngest republics of the New World remained in the closest relations throughout the European struggle. When the war ended, the Panamanian government prepared to send a delegate to Versailles to sign the peace treaty. Some were inclined to ridicule this technical formality of that tiny nation which had followed the United States but had taken no active part in the hostilities. However, Panama considered the signing of the treaty a legal requisite indispensable for terminating the state of war with Germany and was signatory of the Treaty of Versailles. The little republic also broke away from the United States and became one of the charter members of the League of Nations.[78]

NOTES

1. IBAR, *Monthly Bulletin,* XXXI (1910), 889.

2. Panama, Sec. R. E., *Memoria,* 1914, p. xxxv.

3. Dodge to Chiari, July 18, 1912; Chiari to Dodge, July 20, 1912, *loc. cit.,* 1912, pp. 49-50.

4. *For. Rel.* (1914), p. 985.

5. 38 *U. S. Stat. at L.,* 2039.

6. Garay, *op. cit.,* pp. 7-8.

7. Panama, Sec. R. E., *Memoria,* 1916, p. lxiii-lxiv.

8. Garay, *op. cit.,* pp. 11-12.

9. Alfaro to Garay, Nov. 6, 1916, Panama, Sec. R. E., *Memoria,* 1918, p. 227.

10. Porras to Lansing, Dec. 1, 1916, *loc. cit.,* pp. 231-232.

11. Lansing to J. E. Lefevre, Feb. 15, 1917, *loc. cit.,* p. 234.

12. Lansing to Porras, Apr. 20, 1917, *loc. cit.,* p. 235.

13. Price to Garay, Dec. 20, 1916, *loc. cit.,* pp. 79-81.

14. Garay to Price, Dec. 26, 1916, *loc. cit.,* p. 81-82.

15. Percy Alvin Martin, *Latin America and the War* (Baltimore, 1925), pp. 521-541; C. Aguilar, Mexican foreign secretary, to Garay, Feb. 12, 1917, República

de Panamá, Sec. R. E., *Documentos relacionados con la actual Guerra Europea* (Panama, 1917), pp. 7-9; J. Fred Rippy, *The United States and Mexico* (New York, 1931), pp. 358-359.

16. Garay to Aguilar, Feb. 15, 1917, Panama, Sec. R. E., *Documentos relacionados con la actual Guerra Europea,* p. 9.

17. Plácido Sánchez, Bolivian foreign minister, to Garay, Feb. 17, 1917; Garay to Sánchez, Feb. 24, 1917, *loc. cit.,* pp. 9-10.

18. Price to Garay, Feb. 3, 1917, Panama, Sec. R. E., *Memoria,* 1918, p. 82.

19. Garay to Price, Feb. 7, 1917, *loc. cit.,* pp. 82-83.

20. Panama, Sec. R. E., *Memoria,* 1918, p. 3.

21. *Ibid.,* p. 4-5.

22. *Ibid.,* pp. 5-6.

23. *Ibid.,* p. 6.

24. Martin, *op. cit.,* p. 488.

25. Valdés to Wilson, Apr. 6, 1917, Panama, Sec. R. E., *Documentos relacionados con la actual Guerra Europea,* pp. 12-13.

26. Garay to Price, Apr. 11, 1917, Panama, Sec. R. E., *Memoria,* 1918, pp. 85-86.

27. Price to Lansing, Apr. 3, 1917, *For. Rel.* (1918), supplement 2, p. 232.

28. *Idem* to *idem,* Apr. 12, 1917, *loc. cit.,* p. 233.

29. Lansing to Price, Apr. 12, 1917, *loc. cit.,* p. 233.

30. *Idem* to *idem,* June 21, 1917, *loc. cit.,* pp. 233-234.

31. Garay to Harding, Apr. 10, 1917, Panama, Sec. R. E., *Memoria,* 1918, p. 295.

32. Harding to Garay, Apr. 19, 1917, *loc. cit.,* p. 296.

33. Garay to Harding, May 24, 1917, *loc. cit.,* pp. 297-298.

34. Porras to Lansing, Apr. 20, 1917, *loc. cit.,* pp. 154-156.

35. Lansing to Porras, June 21, 1917, *loc. cit.,* pp. 156-157.

36. Porras to Lansing, Sept. 2, 1917, *loc. cit.,* pp. 160-161.

37. Polk to Porras, Nov. 16, 1917, *loc. cit.,* p. 161.

38. Porras to Lansing, Jan. 17, 1918, *loc. cit.,* pp. 162-163.

39. *Gaceta oficial,* Jan. 6, 1917.

40. Panama, Sec. R. E., *Memoria,* 1918, pp. 131-132.

41. Porras to Garay, May 23, 1917, and enclosures, *loc. cit.,* pp. 132-140.

42. *Idem* to *idem,* July 1, 1917, and enclosures, *loc. cit.,* pp. 144-146.

43. Garay, *op. cit.,* pp. 36-38.

44. *BPAU,* XLV (1917), 834.

45. Price to Garay, Dec. 8, 1917; Garay to Price, Dec. 14, 1917, Panama, Sec. R. E., *Memoria,* 1918, pp. 87-88.

46. *Idem* to *idem,* Apr. 2, 1918, *loc. cit.,* p. 244.

47. Price to Garay, Apr. 27, 1918, *loc. cit.,* pp. 245-246.

48. Garay to Price, May 7, 1918, *loc. cit.,* pp. 246-247.

49. Greene to E. T. Lefevre, July 23, 1918, *loc. cit.,* p. 299.

50. E. T. Lefevre to Greene, Aug. 24, 1918, *loc. cit.,* pp. 300-301.

51. Garay, *op. cit.,* pp. 157-158.

52. Price to Lansing, Apr. 16, 1918, *For. Rel.* (1918), supplement 2, p. 234.

53. *Idem* to *idem,* Apr. 19, 1918, *loc. cit.,* p. 235; Panama, Sec. R. E., *Memoria,* 1918, pp. xiii-xiv; *Star and Herald* (Weekly), Aug. 8, 1924.

54. Carl P. Hübscher to Lansing, June 12, 1918, *For. Rel.* (1918), supplement 2, p. 235.

55. Lansing to Baker, June 18, 1918, *loc. cit.,* pp. 235-236.

56. Lansing to Gregory, Oct. 28, 1918, *loc. cit.,* pp. 239-243.

57. J. B. O'Brian, special assistant to the attorney-general, to Lansing, Nov. 19, 1918, *loc. cit.*, pp. 243-244.

58. *Star and Herald* (Weekly), June 30, 1919.

59. William G. Sharp, U. S. ambassador to France, to Lansing, Sept. 13, 1918, *For. Rel.* (1918), supplement 2, pp. 87-88.

60. Lansing to Pleasant A. Stovall, U. S. minister to Switzerland, Sept. 30, 1918, *loc. cit.*, pp. 93-94.

61. Stovall to Lansing, Sept. 28, 1918, *loc. cit.*, p. 93.

62. Lansing to Stovall, Oct. 9, 1918, *loc. cit.*, p. 96.

63. *Star and Herald* (Weekly), June 10, 1918.

64. *N. Y. Times*, June 29, 1918, 3:4.

65. *Star and Herald* (Weekly), June 24, 1918; Panama, G. y J., *Memoria*, 1918, pp. 305-307.

66. *Star and Herald* (Weekly), July 8, 1918; *N. Y. Times*, June 30, 1918, 8:5; Garay, *op. cit.*, pp. 59-60.

67. Urriola to Wilson, June 28, 1918, *N. Y. Times*, June 30, 1918, 8:5.

68. Buell, "The United States and Panama," *loc. cit.*, p. 416; *N. Y. Times*, July 6, 1918, 4:5; *Star and Herald* (Weekly), July 15, 1921.

69. *N. Y. Times*, July 11, 1918, 10:2.

70. *Ibid.*, Nov. 17, 1918, 3:6.

71. Panama, Sec. R. E., *Memoria*, 1918, pp. xxxviii-xxxix.

72. *Ibid.*, 1920, p. xxiii.

73. *BPAU*, XLVII (1918), 619. The fact might be noted that Panama, in comparison with the larger neighbors of the United States such as Mexico and Canada, played little or no part in the American food conservation program. Documents relating to Canada and Mexico are in The National Archives, United States Food Administration, FA 16HB-A1; FA 25H-A1; FA 25H-A2; FA 25H-A3; FA 25H-A4.

74. *BPAU*, XLVIII (1919), 138; *Star and Herald* (Weekly), Sept. 30; Oct. 28, 1918.

75. *BPAU*, XLVIII (1919), 708-709; XLIX (1919), 96; Garay, *op. cit.*, pp. 54-55; *For. Rel.* (1919), II, 679-688.

76. Garay, *op. cit.*, pp. 56-57.

77. *For. Rel.* (1919), II, 688-689; Panama, Sec. G. y J., *Memoria*, 1920, p. vii.

78. Garay, *op. cit.*, pp. 90-93; *Sen. Doc.*, No. 1063, 62 Cong., 4 Sess. (Ser. 6350), pp. 3149, 3163, 3329, 3539.

CHAPTER X

HOSTILITIES BETWEEN PANAMA AND COSTA RICA

PRESIDENT Belisario Porras little realized what he was to face in the near future when he expressed in his New Year message of 1921 confidence in the ability of his country to solve its own problems.[1] In less than two months the Panamanians were virtually at war with Costa Rica, and before the end of the year their dignity and self-respect had suffered at the hands of the Colossus of the North.

On February 21, 1921, Costa Rican troops arrived at Pueblo Nuevo de Coto, province of Chiriquí, in the disputed area on the Pacific and demanded the surrender of the village.[2] The police officials offered no resistance and immediately sent the news of the invasion to David, where it was relayed to Panama City.[3]

The Panamanian government straightway communicated with the American State Department. On February 24 Chargé José E. Lefevre conferred with Secretary of State Bainbridge Colby and other officials in Washington. The United States was placed in an embarrassing position, because Woodrow Wilson was to be succeeded within eight days by Warren G. Harding, and no policy could be formulated for fear that it would be inconsistent with the ideas of the incoming Republicans. Colby only attempted to pour oil on the troubled waters until March 4.[4]

Popular feeling flamed in Panama and Costa Rica, especially in Panama. On February 24 a Panamanian mob tore down and trampled under foot the coat of arms on the Costa Rican consulate in Panama City; the Costa Ricans retaliated in San José.[5] The Panamanian government organ, *Diario Nacional*, declared the invasion an attack on the sovereignty of the republic and a sufficient cause for war.[6] Because of the rumor that

Panama would be aided by American forces, Costa Rican sentiment flared up against the United States. Mobs broke out the windows of a United Fruit Company building in Limón.[7]   In the meantime recruits were streaming in for service in both republics.[8]

On February 25 President Porras issued a proclamation that the Costa Rican invasion should be met with force, and exhorted the Panamanians to forget their party differences in this *momento supremo* and unite for the maintenance of the national dignity.[9]   On the following day a decree suspended individual guarantees under the constitution, provided for a military force, called for volunteers between the ages of eighteen and forty, and summoned the National Assembly for a ten-day extraordinary session beginning March 1.   An order was then issued establishing a strict censorship.[10]   Porras was reported to have signed a declaration of war, but was withholding it pending developments.[11]

Coto was retaken without bloodshed on the morning of February 27.   The Costa Rican troops were captured, as well as reinforcements arriving on the *Sultana* later in the day. Four of the invaders were killed and nine wounded before the vessel surrendered.   The Panamanians had two wounded, but captured a sorely needed machine gun, twenty-five rifles, ammunition, and supplies.[12]

President Porras began to have internal troubles after the *Star and Herald* reported on February 28 that he had said: "War between Panama and Costa Rica over the question of the occupation of Coto would be an absurdity. . . . The idea that two neighboring Republics should enter war over a virtually unsettled district about the size of a United States county is repugnant to me."[13]   A committee of citizens immediately visited Porras and demanded his resignation.   Later that day a mob gathered before the presidential palace, and Minister Price, who was in conference with Porras, called for American troops.   Before the soldiers arrived the palace was attacked, but the disturbance was soon quieted.   The troops guarded the president throughout the night under the provisions of Article

VII of the treaty of 1903. In spite of a request from Porras for their withdrawal, the Americans remained in Panama nearly two weeks.[14]

On February 28 the State Department addressed notes to the belligerents, expressing strong disapproval of the methods being employed in regard to the boundary dispute. Colby stated that the matter should be settled, but without violence, which was not a proper means of arriving at a final agreement on an arbitral award. During the day he conferred with Chargé Lefevre and Ricardo J. Alfaro, a special envoy from Panama to Harding's inauguration, and again offered the good offices of the United States in the hope that the republics might reach an amicable understanding on the boundary line.[15]

On March 1 President Porras reviewed the recent events for the National Assembly, but did not mention declaring war. The Assembly proposed $50,000 for arms, the raising of an army by the president, and a $500,000 internal loan secured by the proceeds of the national lottery. These proposals became law on March 4, but the arms appropriation was raised to $100,000.[16]

On February 28 Secretary-General Eric Drummond instructed the political advisers of the Council of the League of Nations to investigate the Panamanian-Costa Rican trouble.[17] This produced no statement from the Washington government, but Senator William E. Borah declared that he assumed Drummond was "desirous of destroying the last vestige of the League." He stated that interference in the affair confirmed every American objection to the League and was "utterly violative of the Monroe Doctrine in its very essentials."[18]

The first correspondence with the League by the contending powers was a note of March 2 from Secretary Narciso Garay. This reviewed occurrences since February 21, denounced the aggression of Costa Rica, and stated that Panama had accepted the good offices of the United States.[19] On March 4 Drummond addressed identical notes to both governments reminding them of their obligations as League members and requesting information.[20] By that time the Panamanian note had reached the

Council in Paris, and the secretary-general answered, expressing regret at the outbreak and satisfaction that Panama had accepted the offer of American mediation.[21]

Fighting was renewed at Coto on March 1, when a third detachment of Costa Ricans arrived. That force, together with the *Estrella* and the *Esperanza,* was taken. About thirty Costa Ricans were killed, over a hundred prisoners captured, and nearly one hundred rifles added to the Panamanian equipment.[22] The numbers engaged were insignificant, but numbers are of little importance in such situations. Possible international complications, the course pursued by the United States, and the attitude of Latin America were of high consideration. According to an official Costa Rican report, only 115 men were sent to Coto.[23] The Panamanian forces were small and ill equipped, for Panama had no regular army.[24] The Panamanian losses were small; the foreign secretary reported to the National Assembly in 1922 that not a single Panamanian was killed in the entire struggle, exclaiming, "So certain is it that the Gods protect the innocent!"[25]

Costa Rica retaliated for the Coto defeats by advancing across the Sixaola River into the province of Bocas del Toro. Guabito was taken on the morning of March 4. The Panamanians retreated, and the Costa Ricans proceeded with the aid of United Fruit Company transportation and food to Almirante, which fell that afternoon. The town of Bocas del Toro was captured the following day.[26] This aggression resulted in another note from Garay to the League, protesting that these "acts of arbitrary violence" were "incompatible with the principles of a State" sheltered "under the aegis of the League of Nations."[27] President Porras issued a statement that the Panamanians did not oppose the invaders because of a desire to avoid damage to Americans, but if Costa Rica did not retire Panama would be compelled to use force to recover its territory.[28]

On March 5 the State Department received replies to the Colby note. The Costa Rican answer was unsatisfactory, but Panama was willing to accept the mediation of the United

States and asked for a declaration from the Washington government in regard to its understanding of its obligations to Panama in this case.[29] On the same day the new secretary of state, Charles E. Hughes, dispatched demands to both governments for the immediate suspension of hostilities. Costa Rica was urged to advance no further on the Pacific and to withdraw its troops from Bocas del Toro. He stated that his government recognized the boundary controversy as definitely settled by the White Award of 1914 and could not regard forcible measures by either party as justifiable.[30]

On March 6 the Panamanian press published a disavowal by President Porras of the White Award. The old contention that the chief justice had exceeded his powers was renewed, and he was charged with having given insufficient study to the question. Panama was disposed to accept American mediation provided Costa Rica withdrew to the left bank of the Sixaola and refrained from attacking Coto. Porras suggested that the matter be submitted to the A. B. C. Commission, the League of Nations, or a council of international law professors.[31] At the same time the Costa Rican minister at Washington, Octavio Beeche, stated that his government had notified the United States that it had no intention of seizing Panamanian territory, but merely proposed to obtain land which by treaties and arbitral awards rightfully belonged to it.[32] On March 7 Beeche informed Hughes that the Costa Rican forces would withdraw across the Sixaola and that no further advance would be made in Chiriquí. He expressed the firm conviction that the Porras-Anderson Treaty of 1910 and the White Award would be "respected and carried out in their entirety."[33]

Anti-American feeling was reported to be running high in Panama on March 7 because the Panamanian papers were not permitted to publish the Hughes notes and the interviews of President Porras with foreign correspondents. The general impression was that the United States had demanded the evacuation of Coto by Panamanian forces.[34] Costa Rica, however, appeared pleased with the attitude of the Washington government, which had virtually terminated the conflict, but some disappointment was evidenced that Coto had not been avenged.[35]

The Panamanian government explained to the League on March 8 that it was unable to accept the White Award. If this offended the United States and rendered it unfit to act as mediator, Panama would be prepared to submit the dispute to the *Corte Internacional de Arbitraje de La Haya* or to the *Corte Internacional de Justicia de la Liga de Naciones*.[36] Costa Rica informed the League that the mediation of the American government had practically ended the controversy.[37] Drummond replied on March 12 that he was pleased that Costa Rica had accepted the intercession of the United States and that he considered the dispute in the process of settlement.[38] He had already expressed appreciation for the Panamanian acceptance of the American offer.[39]

Garay informed Price on March 8 that the Panamanian military forces would be withdrawn from Coto, but that the civil and police authorities would remain. He explained that this was not to be interpreted as an acquiescence in the White Award, which the executive, the legislature, and the people had refused to accept since 1914. He complained that his country had been in friendly relations with "all the peoples of the earth, when suddenly, like a thunderbolt out of a clear sky, fell the unexpected and unjustified attack upon it by . . . Costa Rica." The Panamanian reserved the right to demand indemnity for damages and expenditures arising from the encroachment.[40]

The Washington government not only sent notes to the contending powers, but ordered the special service squadron under Rear Admiral Henry F. Bryan to protect American interests at Punta Burica and Bocas del Toro. The cruiser *Sacramento* was sent to Almirante, where the United Fruit Company had extensive developments. The American troops in the Canal Zone were also factors of some importance.[41]

On March 15 Secretary Hughes sent an elaborate argument to the Panamanian government. In answer to Panama's inquiry as to what the United States considered its responsibilities to be toward that country, Hughes stated that the American government would have to inquire into the merits of the controversy before it could perform its obligations. The extent of the sovereignty and hence the territorial limits of Panama would have to be determined before the United States could assume its duties under the Hay-Bunau-Varilla Treaty.

Hughes contended that the boundary question had two aspects: one involving the Pacific side of the central *cordillera* and the other the Atlantic littoral. He stated that the line on the Pacific side had been determined by the Loubet Award and had been accepted by both republics in the Porras-Anderson Treaty. He, therefore, considered it the unavoidable duty of his government to request Panama to relinquish jurisdiction over the territory on the Costa Rican side of the line defined by President Loubet and to transfer such jurisdiction to the government of Costa Rica in an orderly manner. Hughes tediously attempted to prove that Chief Justice White had not exceeded his authority in handing down his decision and urged Panama to take steps toward the appointment of a commission of engineers, as provided in the Porras-Anderson Treaty, in order that the boundary might be marked in accordance with the White Award.[42]

On March 19 President Porras appealed directly to President Harding, complaining that the demand for the acceptance of the White decision was painful and humiliating. Two successive legislatures and all municipalities of the republic had petitioned for a rejection of the award because the American jurist had "notoriously exceeded" his jurisdiction and had given Costa Rica more than it had asked for in 1900 and because the execution of the award would be a violation of the constitution. Porras pictured himself as addressing a magistrate who so loved justice and equity that Panama's cause would be better appreciated and that it might be classified among nations with self-consciousness and dignity. Harding was asked to use his "personal, political, and administrative influence" that the dispute might have a solution more in accord with justice and dignity. Porras concluded, "We Panamans are confident in your righteousness and we hope that that confidence will not be rewarded with disappointment."[43]   Harding replied immediately that he would be distressed extremely to believe that Panama had cause to feel wounded or to assume that the United States was unmindful of the "peculiarly friendly relationship" of the two nations, but he made it clear that the State Department had acted with his knowledge and approval and that the acceptance of the White Award was the unalterable position of the United States.[44]

The American note of March 15 was well received in Costa Rica and was characterized as "an admirable judicial document" and "an exemplary act of equity."   The Panamanian government called a special session of the National Assembly for March 28 to consider this ultimatum.[45]   Porras indicated at the first meeting that a refusal to accept the White Award might result seriously, for it might cause the withdrawal of the United States from the controversy.   The Assembly immediately began the consideration of an internal loan of $1,000,000 and the appointment of a commission of international lawyers to render a decision in regard to the demand of the United States.   The Panamanians planned to sell enough bonds to make impossible the discontinuance of the national lottery, which was to expire on July 1 and which was opposed by the Washington government.   Seven deputies were named to study the Hughes note and to consider a tentative answer that had been prepared by a committee of prominent citizens.[46]

Although the reappointment of Addison T. Ruan as fiscal agent was hailed as an indication of a conciliatory attitude on the part of the Panamanians,[47] the National Assembly unanimously approved the drafted rejection of the White Award and authorized Porras to retain three Panamanian and three foreign experts to fight against its execution.[48]   Chief among the foreigners engaged was the Cuban international lawyer, Dr. Antonio S. de Bustamante.[49]

On April 21 the State Department received the approved note which was a general résumé of the entire controversy. Panama's strong objections to the findings of Chief Justice

White were especially emphasized. The question of whether the United States was acting as a friendly mediator or as the guarantor of Panamanian independence was considered in the beginning. If the Washington government was acting as a protector the Panamanians should be guarded from Costa Rican encroachment. Since Costa Rica had rejected the Loubet Award and Panama had not accepted the White Award, the *status quo* arrangement had not ceased to exist. The fact that the guarantee of Panamanian independence in the treaty of 1903 was not limited caused the United States to be "jointly liable with Panama in the defence of all the rights and actions bestowed upon Panama by titles of dominion and immemorial possession." The first article of the Hay-Bunau-Varilla Treaty was not deemed to constitute the United States as "judge and arbitrator of the territorial rights and actions of Panama in relation to its neighbors," but simply made the American government "the guarantor of Panama's independence and integrity." The treaty involved no moral obligation on the part of the United States toward Panama, which had fearlessly and unhesitatingly entered the World War as America's ally and which had contributed more than any other nation to the prestige and power of the United States.

The fact was noted that Hughes had quoted a statement made by White that both republics had conceded it incumbent upon him to substitute a line "most in accordance with the correct interpretation and true intention" of the Loubet Award. This "entirely gratuitous statement" had "contributed greatly to the erroneous premises and misunderstanding upon which the opinion of the State Department was based," and the allegation was "entirely groundless so far as the Republic of Panama" was concerned. Further, Hughes had asserted that White had awarded Costa Rica a portion of territory claimed by Panama and Panama a section claimed by Costa Rica. This indicated a "noble impulse of equity" which did honor to the Washington government, but at the same time showed "its imperfect knowledge of the matter under discussion." A "more complete knowledge and a more exact understanding of the rights and position of Panama" undoubtedly would be followed by a "radical change in the mind and judgment of the State Department."

The Panamanians finally came around to using some American thunder against the position of the Washington government. The Republic of Panama, shielded by the security of international law, which equally sheltered all nations, had refused to accept the decision of Chief Justice White "with the same kind of and almost the same reasons" that had caused the United States to decline a judgment rendered in 1831 by the king of The Netherlands in a boundary litigation with Great Britain. The American minister at The Hague had then argued that the arbiter had departed from his powers in abandoning the boundaries of the treaty and in substituting for them a different line.

The suggestion of a settlement by plebiscites in each of the two zones was again advanced. Panama wanted the plebiscites conducted by commissioners from both of the contending governments, with the mediation of the United States.[50] Apparently no one expected this or the other proposals of the note to be accepted, for rumors of war spread quickly after the action of the National Assembly. Panama indicated that it was prepared to accept any consequences that might follow its determination to preserve Panamanian territorial integrity. Chargé Lefevre stated in Washington that if the United States refused Panama a new hearing, his government would await the next move of Costa Rica. If a crisis could be averted for a few months, he believed an amicable adjustment possible. But Panama would regard a forced evacuation of the Coto region without a full discussion of the boundary question as "an act of coercion." Panama continued preparations for *guerra* with Costa Rica, but the general understanding was that the United States would not tolerate war between the two republics over their frontier.[51]

The State Department gave Panama a lengthy answer on April 30, but presented little that had not been stated repeatedly since 1914. Hughes expressed surprise and regret at the contents of the Panamanian despatch and further clarified his stand on Article I of the Canal treaty by saying that the duty of the United States to maintain the independence of Panama required it to investigate "the merits of any controversies relating to the boundaries" of the republic in order to determine the true extent of its territory and obliged it to assure itself that Panama faithfully performed its international obligations. The line on the Pacific Coast could not be regarded as being in dispute, the chief justice had not exceeded his jurisdiction, and the request for plebiscites could not be granted. Hughes regretfully stated that the United States expected an immediate transfer of the Coto territory to Costa Rica and explained:

Unless such steps are taken within a reasonable time the Government of the United States will find itself compelled to proceed in the manner which may be requisite in order that it may assure itself that the exercise of jurisdiction is appropriately transferred and that the boundary line on the Pacific side, as determined in the Loubet award, and on the Atlantic side, as determined by the award of the Chief Justice of the United States, is physically laid down in the manner provided in Articles II and VII of the Porras-Anderson treaty.[52]

The situation remained unchanged throughout the month of May. The death of Edward D. White on May 18 received little attention.[53] The United States refused to recede from its position, and Panama was equally determined. The general indication was that Panama would exhaust all known diplomatic methods to prevent the execution of the adjudication. The *status quo* was maintained quietly in the disputed regions. The United States played a waiting game, and Costa Rica was content to leave the affair to the Washington government. The Republic of Panama, however, decided that matters might be handled more expeditiously in the United States. Toward the end of the month a committee headed by Narciso Garay arrived in Washington. After interviews with American officials Garay stated on June 12 that a memorandum was being prepared for submission to the State Department that would clarify the situation and show that the United States had an erroneous opinion of his government's attitude. He explained that Hughes had said he would welcome any information showing that Panama was justified in refusing to accept the White boundary. He commented that his mission was to correct a mistake and that he had come to Washington in the most friendly spirit.[54]

The United States held unwaveringly to the White Award. Nothing seemed capable of shaking its position. Hughes undoubtedly considered himself right in refusing to listen openmindedly to the fervent appeals of the Panamanians. However, the strengthening of Costa Rican good-will in order to counteract British oil influences there, was hinted at as one reason for American harshness toward Panama. One North American writer commented: "A strong smell of oil pervades the operatic warfare recently waged on the frontier of Costa Rica and Panama."[55] The Latin Americans apparently favored Costa Rica, and the United States might gain goodwill by similar support.[56] Microscopic Panama unfortunately happened to be the victim.

The attitude of the Central American republics appeared to incline toward Costa Rica. Guatemala, Honduras, and El Salvador were reported as contemplating declaring war against Panama if Costa Rica took that step. This might have been a part of the campaign to bring Costa Rica into the projected Central American Union.[57] Panama tried unsuccessfully to gain the sympathy and assistance of various Latin American republics. Missions were sent to Argentina, Brazil, and Chile to encourage them to ·take steps of a mediatory nature. The Washir ·on government was sufficiently concerned to dispatch a memorandum to the Argentine government defending its position. Argentina then informed the Panamanians it could act as a friendly mediator only if petitioned by both parties.[58]

Garay was reported to have broached the matter of holding plebiscites again on June 19. He stated that a settlement based on the White decision would entail permanent warfare between Panama and Costa Rica. However, Panama would submit without further parley if a group of impartial jurists would decide that White had not exceeded his jurisdiction. He could not understand why the United States had taken the position of the executor of the White Award, but realized that if the United States persisted Panama could only yield to superior power.[59] On June 25 Garay submitted a memorandum to the State Department that was chiefly a reiteration of the reasons for the rejection of the White Award.[60] On June 30 he visited the State Department and was told that the United States could not recede from its position. His suggestions that an American league of nations be formed for settling the dispute, that the United States force Costa Rica to accept the Panamanian view, or that the two contestants attempt to reach a new understanding through the *buenos oficios* of the United States were not acceptable to Hughes.[61]

The general impression was that the Washington government would give Panama until July 2 to submit, but Panama wanted more time in order to treat with Costa Rica. On July 7 Garay intimated that the time had been extended and that an adjustment would probably be reached because a "compulsory execution of the White award by the United States would create an impossible situation in Panama." He and Beeche then conferred unsuccessfully.[62] By July 21 the Panamanian was of the opinion that the Washington government had practically eliminated Costa Rica from the controversy. He suggested submitting to the Permanent Court of The Hague the question: "Is the White award within the terms of the Arbitral Compromise of 1910 and is or is it not valid for Panama?" This was, he believed, at issue between the United States and Panama rather than between Panama and Costa Rica. Garay hoped that deference for the sovereignty of his country and the cause of arbitration, so dear to the United States, would prevent a settlement by force.[63] Hughes answered on July 29 that Costa Rica was not out of the controversy and explained that his government had intervened solely because both parties had accepted its offer of mediation and the United States had guaranteed the independence of Panama. He hoped that the Panamanians would soon name their commissioner to lay down the boundary line.[64]

Garay then called the attention of Hughes to the obligation of Costa Rica as a member of the League of Nations to
submit the dispute to arbitration.   Since the United States had
made a true apostleship of arbitration, the secretary of state
was asked to urge Costa Rica to arbitrate.[65]   On July 30 Garay
again wrote that Panama could not accept the White Award
because it annulled that of Loubet, and reminded the Washington government that Article I of the Canal treaty did not
give it the right to determine the boundaries of Panama nor
the power to negotiate with another government over the limits
of Panama.[66]   On August 5 Hughes informed Garay that Costa
Rica had named its member of the demarcation commission and
had asked Chief Justice William H. Taft to appoint two more
in accordance with the provisions of the Porras-Anderson
Treaty.[67]   The Panamanian immediately protested to Hughes
and to Taft.[68]

On August 18 the State Department sent its final decision
to the Panamanian government indicating that every argument
of any importance had been covered, expressing regret that
Panama and Costa Rica had failed to arrive at a direct agreement, and stating that the Washington government did not
"feel compelled to suggest to the Government of Costa Rica
that it delay longer taking jurisdiction over the territory which
is now occupied by Panama and which was adjudged to belong
to Costa Rica by the terms of the Loubet award."[69]   In other
words, the time had come for Panama to surrender the disputed
area on the Pacific littoral to Costa Rica.

Panama made a gesture toward resistance, but a battalion of
marines was rushed from Quantico, Virginia, on the *Pennsyl-
vania* to the Canal Zone.[70]   President Porras cabled Garay for
an interpretation of the Hughes note of August 18.   Did it
mean that the United States would stand aloof, might hostilities
be renewed, was Panama to be permitted to use force to keep
Costa Rica out of Coto?   Porras stated that Panama would not
resist the demands of the United States, but would reject with
force any ultimatum from Costa Rica alone.[71]   Hughes answered bluntly that his government would not permit the re-

newal of warfare by Panama to prevent Costa Rica from taking possession of territory on the Pacific awarded to it by President Loubet.[72]

The Panamanian government announced on August 23 that the civil and police authorities had been ordered to retire from Coto. At the same time Garay was instructed to file a protest and leave Washington.[73] On August 24 President Porras charged that the United States had forced the surrender of Coto. Feeling ran high in Panama City and disturbances threatened. Porras protested that acts of violence had been perpetrated against his country and reserved the right to re-occupy Coto at the first opportunity. That night he signed a decree declaring a month of mourning in the republic for the loss of Coto.[74] On the same day the State Department announced that Chief Justice Taft had selected two Americans to act with the Costa Rican commissioner in marking the boundary line in accordance with the White Award.[75] Panama immediately advised the Washington government that it did not recognize the Taft appointments as valid.[76] Garay protested to Hughes that the dispatch of marines to the Isthmus indicated that force still ruled in the relations between nations and stated:

Panama is compelled to submit to its painful destiny, but in her own weakness finds sufficient energies to clamour to Heaven against the injustice and violence to which she has been subjected and to declare that while the hearts of Panamanians continue to beat in the world, she will maintain alive the profound wound inflicted against her dignity and pride and will look to the future with anxiety for the justice which she is now denied, confident that her day will arrive by the inexorable design of God.[77]

Hughes immediately answered that he hoped the people and the government of Panama would realize that the United States had acted in sincere friendship.[78] Minister Price informed the Panamanian government that Costa Rica would take possession of Coto about September 5.[79] Harding and Hughes were pictured as gratified at the action of Panama, which they regarded as another step toward the peaceful settlement of international controversies.   Costa Rica reiterated confidence in the United States.   Latin America criticized the intervention of the Washington government, and Panama was left in a bitter frame of mind.[80]   Colonel J. J. Morrow protested to the Panamanian government against the Porras mourning decree and the proposed closing of all places of business on Labor Day as an expression of sorrow for the loss of Coto.   He charged that these actions and the projected erection of a monument commemorating the Coto affair were anti-American propaganda and might lead to disturbances that would cause the American government to assume jurisdiction over the police forces of Panama and Colón.[81]   Secretary of Government and Justice Ricardo J. Alfaro replied that manifestations of hostility toward the United States would not receive the sanction of his government.[82] Thus the two peoples—Panamanians and Costa Ricans—who were naturally friends were left official enemies.[83]

In reviewing the events of the controversy, the editor of the *Nation* fittingly summarized the situation by saying that Secretary of State Hughes was correct in preventing war between Panama and Costa Rica, but he regretted that military force had been used to compel Panama to yield.   The methods of the Washington government were deprecated as follows:

Not without cause Latin-Americans regard the protective affection of the United States very much as the wise little frogs came to regard King Stork.   And some of them remembering the circumstances of Panama's creation, regard us as dubious upholders of the sanctity of treaties.   It pays to consider Latin-American opinion.   Besides it is never for the good of the soul of any people to be as God, dispensing justice to its weaker neighbors according to its own will.[84]

Through the friendly mediation of Chile, diplomatic relations were resumed between Panama and Costa Rica soon after the inauguration of President Florencio H. Arosemena in 1928,[85] and on October 6 they were congratulated by the United States.[86]   Since 1924 various protests have been made, and negotiations have been carried on intermittently between Panama and Costa Rica in an effort to find a basis for an amicable settlement, but thus far no definite results have been attained.[87]   In 1931 President Ricardo J. Alfaro signed a decree restricting the ownership of land by foreigners in a strip almost twenty miles wide along the Panamanian-Costa Rican frontier.[88]   During the past few years a movement has been under way whereby Panama may be able to recover some of its alleged losses and reach a final adjustment of the grievous boundary problem.[89]

Thus almost one hundred and twenty-five years of dissension has occurred over practically worthless territory, but value counts for little in matters of honor and politics such as this controversy involved.   Today Costa Rica has possession of both disputed areas, the Republic of Panama bitterly refuses to recognize the White Award, and the United States looks on and perhaps hopes for the best.   Fortunately, the territory on both sides has remained sparsely settled, except for the United Fruit developments on the Atlantic littoral, so that comparatively little local friction is engendered.[90]

NOTES

1. *N. Y. Times*, Jan. 3, 1921, 21:2; *Estrella*, Jan. 1, 1921.

2. *Estrella*, Feb. 25, 1921; Garay to Sir Eric Drummond, secretary-general of the League of Nations, Mar. 2, 1921; Alejandro Alvarado Quiroz, Costa Rican foreign secretary, to Drummond, Mar. 8, 1921, *The Official Journal of the League of Nations*, 1921, pp. 214, 217.   Hereafter cited as *OJLN*, 1921.

3. *N. Y. Times*, Feb. 25, 1921, 1:3; *Star and Herald*, Feb. 25, 1921.

4. *N. Y. Times*, Feb. 25, 1:3; Feb. 26, 11:1; Feb. 27, 7:1-2; Mar. 6, 1921, 1:8; *Star and Herald*, Feb. 25, 1921; *Estrella*, Feb. 25, 1921.

5. *N. Y. Times*, Feb. 25, 1:2-3; Mar. 2, 1921, 5:3; *Star and Herald*, Feb. 25, 1921.

6. *N. Y. Times*, Feb. 25, 1921, 1:2-3.

7. *N. Y. Times*, Mar. 8, 1921, 3:2.

8. *Ibid.*, Mar. 3, 6:1; Mar. 5, 10:2; Mar. 6, 2:1; Mar. 8, 1921, 3:2.

9. República de Panamá, Sec. R. E., *Controversia de límites entre Panamá y Costa Rica* (Panama, 1921), II, 41; *Estrella*, Feb. 26, 1921.

10. Panama, *Controversia*, 1921, II, 32-33; *Estrella*, Feb. 27, 1921.

11. *N. Y. Times*, Feb. 27, 1921, 1:1.

12. Panama, *Controversia*, 1921, II, 49-51; Garay to Drummond, Mar. 2, 1921; Quiróz to Drummond, Mar. 8, 1921, *OJLN*, 1921, pp. 214, 217; *Estrella*, Mar. 1, 1921.

13. *Star and Herald*, Feb. 28, 1921; *Estrella*, Feb. 28, 1921; A. S. Waddell, "Unsettled Boundary Disputes . . . ," in F. P. A., *Inf. Ser.*, V (1930), 496.

14. *N. Y. Times*, Mar. 1, 1:1, 3:3-4; Mar. 2, 5:2-3; Mar. 13, 1921, 14:1; *Estrella*, Mar. 1, 1921.

15. *N. Y. Times*, Mar. 1, 1921, 1:1, 3:3; *Star and Herald*, Feb. 28, Mar. 5, 1921; *Estrella*, Mar. 5, 1921.

16. Panama, Sec. R. E., *Memoria*, 1922, I, 320-321; *Estrella*, Mar. 2, 1921; Panama, *Controversia*, 1921, II, 285-286; *Star and Herald*, Mar. 5, 1921.

17. *N. Y. Times*, Mar. 1, 1921, 3:4-5.

18. *Ibid.*, 3:6.

19. Garay to Drummond, Mar. 2, 1921, *OJLN*, 1921, p. 214.

20. Drummond to Garay and Quiroz, Mar. 4, 1921, *loc. cit.*, p. 215.

21. Drummond to Garay, Mar. 4, 1921, *loc. cit.*, p. 215.

22. Panama, *Controversia*, 1921, II, 61-64; *Star and Herald*, Mar. 3, 1921; *Estrella*, Mar. 4, 1921.

23. Quiroz to Drummond, Mar. 7, 1921, *OJLN*, 1921, p. 217.

24. Panama, *Controversia*, 1921, II, 187.

25. Panama, Sec. R. E., *Memoria*, 1922, I, 319.

26. Garay to Drummond, Mar. 5, 1921, *OJLN*, 1921, p. 215; Panama, *Controversia*, 1921, II, 130-136; *N. Y. Times*, Mar. 5, 10:2; Mar. 6, 1:8; Mar. 7, 1921, 2:5; *Star and Herald*, Mar. 5, Mar. 6, 1921; *Estrella*, Mar. 17, 1921.

27. Garay to Drummond, Mar. 5, 1921, *OJLN*, 1921, p. 215.

28. Porras to John Foster Dulles of Sullivan and Cromwell, counsel for Panama, *N. Y. Times*, Mar. 5, 1921, 10:2.

29. *N. Y. Times*, Mar. 6, 1:6-8; Mar. 7, 2:5; Mar. 8, 3:1-2; Mar. 18, 1921, 2:3-6; *Star and Herald*, Mar. 6, 1921.

30. Note to Costa Rica, *N. Y. Times*, Mar. 8, 1921, 3:1.

31. *N. Y. Times*, Mar. 7, 1921, 2:4-5.

32. *Ibid.*, 2:5.

33. Beeche to Hughes, Mar. 7, 1921, *N. Y. Times*, Mar. 8, 1921, 3:1.

34. *N. Y. Times*, Mar. 8, 1921, 3:2.

35. *Ibid.*, Mar. 11, 1921, 3:6.

36. Garay to Drummond, Mar. 8, 1921, *OJLN*, 1921, p. 216.

37. Quiroz to Drummond, Mar. 8, 1921, *loc. cit.*, p. 217.

38. Drummond to Quiroz, Mar. 12, 1921, *loc. cit.*, p. 218.

39. Drummond to Garay, Mar. 9, 1921, Panama, *Controversia*, 1921, II, 162.

40. Garay to Price, Mar. 8, 1921, *N. Y. Times*, Mar. 11, 1921, 3:6; *Star and Herald*, Mar. 9, 1921; *Estrella*, Mar. 9, 1921.

41. *N. Y. Times*, Mar. 5, 10:2; Mar. 6, 1:8; Mar. 8, 1921, 3:2.

42. Hughes to Price, Mar. 15, 1921, *N. Y. Times*, Mar. 18, 1921, 2:3-6; *Estrella*, Mar. 19, 1921.

43. Porras to Harding, Mar. 19, 1921, *N. Y. Times*, Mar. 20, 1921, 1:1; *Estrella*, Mar. 20, 1921.

44. Harding to Porras, Mar. 19, 1921, *N. Y. Times*, Mar. 20, 1921, 1:1; *Estrella*, Mar. 20, 1921.

45. *N. Y. Times*, Mar. 23, 12:8; Mar. 26, 1921, 3:6; *Estrella*, Mar. 24, 1921.

46. *N. Y. Times*, Mar. 30, 1921, 6:2; *Estrella*, Mar. 29, 1921.

47. *N. Y. Times*, Apr. 1, 1921, 17:4-5.

48. Panama, Sec. R. E., *Memoria*, 1922, I, 352-353.

49. See Antonio S. de Bustamante, *Opinion; Panama-Costa Rica Boundary Controversy; Opinion* (Panama, 1921).

50. Panama, Sec. R. E., *Memoria*, 1922, I, 320-336; *Panama's Reply to the United States* (Panama, 1921).

51. *N. Y. Times*, Apr. 8, 1:2-3; Apr. 9, 14:2; Apr. 19, 1921, 19:4; *Estrella*, Apr. 19, 1921.

52. Price to Garay, Apr. 30, 1921, *N. Y. Times*, May 3, 1921, 1:3, 2:2-6; *Star and Herald*, May 7, 1921; *Estrella*, May 5, 1921.

53. *Estrella*, May 20, 1921.

54. *N. Y. Times*, May 30, 9:7; June 3, 17:7; June 8, 2:2; June 13, 1921, 15:6.

55. *The Nation*, CXII (1921), 390-391.

56. *N. Y. Times*, June 19, 1921, 3:7.

57. *Ibid.*, Apr. 15, 12:2; May 20, 14:7; May 29, 11:1; June 28, 17:6; July 1, 1921, 3:3; *Estrella*, Mar. 26, 1921, *Star and Herald*, Apr. 19, 1921.

58. *N. Y. Times*, July 21, 19:2; July 23, 1921, 7:3, 12:3-4; *Star and Herald*, May 19, 1921.

59. *N. Y. Times*, June 20, 1921, 15:4-5.

60. *Ibid.*, June 28, 1921, 17:6.

61. *Ibid.*, July 1, 1921, 3:3.

62. *Ibid.*, June 28, 17:6; July 1, 3:3; July 3, 14:5; July 8, 2:2; July 15, 1:2; *Estrella*, July 3, 1921.

63. Garay to Hughes, July 21, 1921, Panama, Sec. R. E., *Memoria*, 1922, I, 360-363.

64. Hughes to Garay, July 29, 1921, *loc. cit.*, pp. 365-367.

65. Garay to Hughes, July 29, 1921, *loc. cit.*, pp. 363-365.

66. *Idem* to *idem*, July 30, 1921, *loc. cit.*, pp. 367-368.

67. Hughes to Garay, Aug. 5, 1921, *loc. cit.*, pp. 368-369.

68. Garay to Hughes and Garay to Taft, Aug. 8, 1921, *loc. cit.*, pp. 369-372.

69. Hughes to Price, Aug. 18, 1921, *loc. cit.*, pp. 373-374; Price to R. J. Alfaro, *Estrella*, Aug. 20, 1921.

70. *N. Y. Times*, Aug. 22, 2:1; Aug. 23, 1921, 1:8; *Star and Herald*, Aug. 23, 1921; *Estrella*, Aug. 23, 1921.

71. Porras to Garay, Aug. 20, 1921, *N. Y. Times*, Aug. 24, 1921, 1:4.

72. Hughes to Price, Aug. 22, 1921, *loc. cit.*, 4:2.

73. *N. Y. Times*, Aug. 24, 1921, 1:4; *Estrella*, Aug. 24, 1921.

74. *N. Y. Times*, Aug. 26, 1921, 2:5; *Estrella*, Aug. 25, 1921.

75. *Ibid.*, Aug. 25, 1921, 15:1.

76. Panama, Sec. R. E., *Memoria*, 1922, I, 381-389.

77. Garay to Porras, Aug. 24, 1921, *Star and Herald*, Aug. 26, 1921.

78. Hughes to Garay, Aug. 26, 1921, Panama, Sec. R. E., *Memoria*, 1922, I, 381.

79. Price to Alfaro, Aug. 26, 1921, *loc. cit.*, p. 357.

80. *N. Y. Times*, Aug. 24, 1921, 4:1; Waddell, *op. et loc. cit.*, V (1930), 496.

81. *N. Y. Times*, Sept. 4, 1921, 7:5-8.

82. *Star and Herald*, Sept. 3, 1921; *Estrella*, Sept. 3, 1921.

83. Ricardo J. Alfaro, *Costa Rica y Panamá; en defensa de los que quieren paz y amistad* (Panama, 1927), p. 5.

84. *The Nation*, CXIII (1921), 251.

85. *BPAU*, LXIII (1929), 65.

86. *Press Releases*, Oct. 8, 1928.

87. *Current History*, XXX (1929), 1138; XXXI (1930), 1203; *N. Y. Times*, Mar. 15, 1928, 3:6; Feb. 18, 1930, 7:6; July 8, 1931, 11:4; Dana G. Munro, *The United States and the Caribbean Area* (Boston, 1934), p. 90.

88. *N. Y. Times*, Dec. 20, 1931, III, 6:5.

89. Statement to the writer, July 12, 1934, by the Division of Latin American Affairs, Department of State.

90. For documents printed in English which pertain to this chapter see *For. Rel.* (1921), I, 175-228.

CHAPTER XI

THE TREATY OF 1926

THE PANAMANIANS were not long in finding that John Hay and Philippe Bunau-Varilla had foisted upon them an exceedingly unsatisfactory treaty. They were the victims of a pact negotiated and signed on November 18, 1903, by an American who knew little of their interests and needs and by a Frenchman who probably cared less. The treaty was a matter of life and death to the Republic of Panama, but that nation was permitted only to consent to a document prepared thousands of miles away by a man whose eyes were lifted by the vision of $40,000,000 and accepted by another who, if he chanced to think of Panamanian welfare, only saw it reflected in the waters of the great Canal to be.

The United States, as previously noted, was beset immediately after taking possession of the Canal Zone with an uproar against its establishment of ports, tariffs, and postal services. The pacifying powers of Secretary of War William H. Taft were taxed to quiet the Isthmians. The Canal Zone commissaries, however, were not and probably never will be removed from the scroll of Panamanian lamentations. The business men of the Isthmus hardly waited for the ink to dry on the treaty before they were complaining that it implied that the United States might set up stores in the Canal Zone. They charged that the commissaries of the Panama Railroad and attendant smuggling already had caused great losses.[1] The American government opened its stores in due time, but limited sales to the gold roll (white) employees. In 1905 service was extended to all Canal Zone workers.[2] Undoubtedly the commissaries were absolutely necessary for the success of the Canal enterprise, and the United States was justified in opening them to all employees, for the cities of Panama and Colón were unable to supply the needs of the workers, and the articles they did furnish were priced unreasonably high.[3] Panama accepted this blow with good grace,[4] but asked that the stores handle only necessities.[5] On November 5, 1905, President Amador and a committee of business men, representatives of American interests prominent among them, visited Governor Charles E. Magoon for the purpose of reaching an agreement that would alleviate their sufferings at the hands of the Washington government. One of their foremost grievances was the commissary business.[6] To this complaint have been added numerous others as the relations of the two countries have become more complicated.

After Panama indicated that a new treaty was wanted to replace the Taft convention of 1904, the State Department agreed to begin negotiations in 1915. On September 24 Minister Price informed the Panamanian government that the secretary of state thought a committee of three should study the points for discussion and make recommendations for the treaty. The Canal Zone governor and Minister Price had been selected to represent the State and War Departments, and Panama was asked to name its single member.[7] Secretary Lefevre answered two months later that his government was not prepared to treat that important matter in the manner suggested. His department, he explained, had the points for treatment under consideration and would present them to the Washington government in time.[8] The outbreak of the war in Europe delayed negotiations until January 27, 1919, when President Porras appointed a committee to investigate the problems arising from the Hay-Bunau-Varilla Treaty. Toward the end of the year J. A. Arango, Luis E. Alfaro, Juan Navarro D., and Chargé José E. Lefevre were selected to negotiate with the American government for the removal of their alleged yoke.[9]

The commission eventually presented a memorandum to Governor Chester Harding enumerating the abuses that Panama wished eliminated. The United States was asked to prohibit the sale of luxuries in the commissaries because it was a violation of the treaty of 1903. A convincing protest was made in regard to the great amount of smuggling from the commissaries into Panama. The charge was that one-half the people of the cities of Panama and Colón used articles bought in the Canal Zone stores. The fact was that in 1918 the republic had a population twenty times as great as that of the Canal Zone, but imported less merchandise. The Panamanians wanted the sale of tobacco, one of the favorite contrabands, discontinued in the Army post exchanges and the silver roll (colored) employees prohibited from buying in the commissaries. The American government was to stop supplying articles that Panama was able to furnish ships passing through the Canal, to provide better facilities for Panamanian traffic with the vessels, and to permit two representatives of the commercial interests of both Panama and Colón to visit the boats in order to take care of prospective business. Further, the United States should return the great areas in Panama and Colón owned by the Panama Railroad, provide more adequate means of transportation for merchandise unloaded at Cristóbal for Panama City, improve storage privileges for Panamanians in the Panama Railroad warehouses, and increase the wharf space in Panama and Colón. The Washington government was asked to reduce water rates in Panama and Colón, to co-operate in highway building, to pay for the use of Panamanian telegraph lines, to determine and name the land necessary for Canal use, and to promise not to compete with Panama if it should build storage warehouses.[10]

Governor Harding replied on June 22, 1920, with a number of suggestions, but gave no real satisfaction. Nothing was to be done about sales to silver roll employees; the matter of luxuries, commissary trade with ships, and the restoration of lots owned by the Panama Railroad would be submitted to Washington; Panama might place representatives in the Canal Zone to call attention to illegal purchases in order to prevent smuggling. Harding thought Panama might reduce the import duty on tobacco so as to enable its merchants to sell that commodity at prices similar to those of the Canal Zone. He noted that the demand for lower freight rates and for improvement in the storage privileges had been withdrawn and that transportation facilities should be taken care of by the steamship companies. He approved the construction of Panamanian warehouses, but could give no assurance as to the policy of future Canal Zone administrations. The wharf space and water rate complaints had been smoothed over, but he could do nothing about the use of the telegraph lines. The territorial expropriation grievances would require settlement in Washington.[11]

The committee informed Harding on July 9 that Panama would place representatives in the Canal Zone, but that smuggling could not be prevented effectively as long as employees were permitted to make unlimited purchases in the commissaries. A reduction of the import duties on tobacco was impossible. The demand that silver roll workers be denied the use of the government stores, that the commissaries be prohibited from supplying vessels passing through the Canal, and that more satisfactory wharfage facilities be provided was repeated. The Panamanians had decided that the Panama Railroad should pay taxes on property within the cities of Panama and Colón and that it should bear a proportionate share of the water tariff. They wanted a definite statement that no warehouses would be built in the Canal Zone to compete with their proposed establishments. The committee admitted that all other points except the practice of the United States in condemning and seizing Panamanian territory for Canal use had been settled satisfactorily.[12] Harding merely acknowledged the note and promised to send it to Washington.[13]

As usual, nothing was accomplished and the matter dragged on into 1921. After Warren G. Harding's pleasant visit to Panama, Ricardo J. Alfaro was sent to the United States to attend his inauguration as president. Alfaro was also expected to gain a few material advantages, but hostilities broke out between Panama and Costa Rica on February 21, 1921, and he was so engrossed in defending his country from the State Department that little time was left for the principal object of his trip. He was able, however, to present a memorandum on April 2, making a strong plea for a new treaty that would remove a part of his nation's burden. The expropriation of

Panamanian territory was first and foremost among his complaints. Panama wanted the Panama Railroad to give up its lands in the cities of Panama and Colón, to pay water and sewerage charges and taxes on its Panamanian property, and to lower its freight rates. Complaints against luxury sales, commerce with ships, smuggling from the Canal Zone into Panama, and better transportation facilities from the terminal ports to Panamanian territory were renewed. Alfaro protested against the establishment of private commercial enterprises in the Canal Zone, charged that the United States was violating the provision of the Taft agreement of 1904 that related to invoices and manifests, and demanded cemetery space for Colón.[14]

On September 1, 1922, the State Department asked President Harding to recommend to Congress the abrogation of the Taft convention in order that negotiations might be undertaken for a new treaty with Panama. The explanation was made that it had been intended as a temporary arrangement to cover the period of the construction of the Canal and that it no longer provided an adequate basis for adjusting questions arising between the governments of Panama and the Canal Zone.[15] Harding, accordingly, secured the permission of Congress to annul the Taft agreement, but no date was set because of the desire to retain it until a new system of relations had been established tentatively by the projected treaty.[16]

The Panamanian government next presented a long protest to Secretary of War J. W. Weeks. In addition to the usual complaints, the charge was made that numerous persons and firms not connected with the Canal enterprise were being given commissary privileges and that Panama was being defrauded through the inefficient administration of the water systems of Panama and Colón. Payment of the $53,800 awarded by the mixed commission for the Malambo fire damages of 1906[17] and indemnification for the expropriation of Punta Paitilla in 1915 were demanded. Panama wanted a bridge or ferry across the Canal, the Canal Zone lands restored to the Panamanian farmers, and Gatún Lake cleared of dead trees so that it might be navigated to the agricultural developments that were being started along its shores. Objection was made to the depopulation of Panama and Colón by the removal of silver roll workers to government quarters at Balboa and to the practice of importing goods into Panama duty free by Canal Zone employees.[18]

On January 3, 1923, Minister Ricardo J. Alfaro made a strong appeal for new convention clarifying the Hay-Bunau-Varilla Treaty. He stated that the general opinion in 1903 had been that the United States would sign a treaty with Panama similar to the Hay-Herrán Treaty. To the utter surprise of the Panamanians many concessions had been made by Minister Bunau-Varilla that they had never imagined. True they were compensated somewhat by the guarantee of independence, but that stipulation had not been inserted for the exclusive benefit of Panama. Attention was called to the old grievance that the Panama Railroad Company operated

. . . commissaries, livery stables, garages, baggage transportation within the cities of Panama and Colon, dairies, poultry farms, butcheries, packing and refrigerating plants, soap factories, laundries, plants for roasting and packing coffee, sausage and canned meat factories, iron works, carpenter shops and cooperages, etc., besides its main and colossal business of collecting rents from the lots which it possesses in the cities of Panama and Colon.[19]

Alfaro stated that his government wished to sign some form of pact settling the points enumerated in the note of April 2, 1921. He explained that subjects of practically no importance to the United States might be matters of life and death to the Republic of Panama because of its small size and lack of development. Panama had no desire to enter the negotiations as a nation whose interests were antagonistic to those of the United States, but wished to co-operate in the operation and defense of the Canal and hoped that the Washington government would be actuated by the same spirit of cordial friendship that had inspired Roosevelt and Taft in 1904.[20]

After various conferences with the State Department and in answer to a note of October 15, 1923, Alfaro submitted an *aide-memoire* on January 4, 1924, in which he declared that the debate over the interpretation of the Canal treaty had led to no practical results. He asked that negotiations for a new agreement be opened upon the principles that the treaty of 1903 should not be construed by the United States so as to impose obligations that might hinder the welfare and development of Panama, and that the declared policy of the United States neither to apply that pact nor to operate the Canal in a manner prejudicial to Panamanian interests should be continued. He wanted the convention itself based upon the general idea that the Canal Zone should be occupied and controlled exclusively for the purpose of maintaining, operating, and protecting the Canal which was already constructed and made sanitary. Therefore, the Zone should not be open to the commerce of the world as an independent colony; Panama should be assured the development inherent with its geographical position; the operation, exploitation and the judicial, police, and administrative jurisdiction of the United States in the Canal Zone should not be interfered with; and the projected treaty should contain nothing that would lessen the prosperity, reduce the income, or diminish the prestige of the Republic of Panama. Alfaro then submitted the following thirty-two questions to be discussed:

1. Final determination of the lands necessary for the construction, maintenance, operation and sanitation of the Canal.

2. Acquisition of lands necessary for the protection of the Canal.

3. Expropriations of lands for the protection of the Canal.

4. Legal status of the Panama Railroad Company.

5. Lands in the city of Colón.

6. Payment for water and sewerage on the lands owned by the Panama Railroad Company.

7. General taxes on the lands owned by the Panama Railroad Company. Industrial activities of the company distinct from the exploitation of the railroad.

8. Freightages that the Panama Railroad collects.

9. Administration of the commissaries of the Panama Canal or the Panama Railroad Company.

10. Sales and service to the vessels that pass through the Canal.

11. Marine facilities in the port of Balboa.

12. Private enterprises established in the Canal Zone.

13. Legalization of the invoices and manifests of cargoes consigned to the merchants of Panama and Colón.

14. Cemetery for the city of Colón.

15. Maintenance of the order of depopulation dictated by the President of the United States in December, 1912, in conformity with the Panama Canal Act.

16. Warehouses of deposit.

17. Establishment of custom-houses in the terminal ports of the Canal for the examination of merchandise, baggage, and passengers consigned to or from the cities of Panama and Colón.

18. Passports.

19. Application of the Volstead Law.

20. Radio communications.

21. Aerial communications.

22. Sanitary jurisdiction in the cities of Panama and Colón and their ports.

23. Collection of the water and sewerage tax in the cities of Panama and Colón.

24. Communication between the cities of Panama and Colón and the remainder of the Republic.

25. Postal service.

26. Money.

27. Status and administration of the wireless stations in the territory of the Republic of Panama owned by the United States.

28. Extradition.

29. Exequaturs to the consuls who exercise their functions in the Canal Zone.

30. Santo Tomás Hospital.

31. Exercise by the officials of the United States of the rights and privileges stipulated to the said government by the Canal treaty and the contract celebrated with the Panama Railroad.

32. Coastal trade in relation to Article IV of the Canal Treaty.[21]

Secretary of State Hughes replied on January 11 that the United States was animated by the most friendly sentiments toward Panama and earnestly desired a satisfactory adjustment of the questions at issue. He declared: "It is not the desire of the Government of the United States to establish a commercial colony in the center of the territory of Panama, the economic competition from which would be a detriment to the prosperity and prestige of Panama." He explained that because of the uncertainty of the future his government had to reserve all rights granted by the treaty of 1903, but "would be pleased to receive and consider with the most careful attention the suggestions of the Government of Panama concerning the manner in which the United States could, by means of the non-exercise of a part of such rights, power, and authority, promote the prosperity and interests of Panama."[22]

On May 28, 1924, President Calvin Coolidge declared the Taft agreement of 1904 null and void after June 1, 1924.[23] Negotiations for a new treaty, however, had been initiated in Washington on March 17 by a committee composed of Ricardo J. Alfaro, Eduardo Chiari, Eusebio A. Morales, and Eugenio J. Chevalier. Questions for adjustment were grouped under lands, highways, sanitation, a cemetery for Colón, radio, and commercial privileges. One of the principal controversies that hindered the progress of the treaty was the insistence of the United States on the right to denounce Article IV, which contained the commercial clauses of the pact, at the end of fifteen years. Panama also was asked to sign a claims convention and to cede New Cristóbal, a part of Colón inhabited by Americans, to the Canal Zone. The Panamanians offered that district for the lots of land of the Panama Railroad in Colón, but the State Department peremptorily refused. They were denied the privilege of buying the property. They managed to get the area demanded reduced, but the State Department would not agree to all of their desires. Chiari returned to Panama in June to run for the National Assembly. Alfaro and Morales soon followed. Thus the discussions were suspended on August 5 after twenty-one sessions. An accord had been reached on the preamble and on articles one, three, five, seven, and nine to fourteen.

Toward the end of September President Porras and Minister John G. South renewed negotiations in Panama City. They were able to arrive at a tentative agreement, and discussions were renewed officially on June 18, 1925. The Panamanian commissioners and the State Department, however, were soon bickering over the land and commercial clauses. By December the Washington government had decided that the stipulations in regard to commerce might be made permanent, but that the demand for New Cristóbal could not be relinquished. Morales eventually carried the projected treaty to Panama, and the Panamanian government decided that it was better than nothing. He returned to Washington with proposals for modifications, and a definite agreement was reached in March, 1926. Morales and Alfaro were called home in June for further discussions which terminated in the unanimous acceptance of the treaty by the Panamanian cabinet. It was then signed on July 28, 1926, together with a claims convention providing for the arbitration of all matters which had arisen since November 3, 1903, between the governments of each country and the citizens of the other.[24]

The new treaty, in effect, restored the Taft agreement of 1904 and clarified part of the disputed points that had grown out of the Hay-Bunau-Varilla Treaty. The right of the United States to acquire additional land for Canal use was not restricted, but Panama was to be notified through diplomatic channels. Title was to pass to the United States at the time of notification, and the value of the property was to be determined by a member of the Panamanian supreme court and the judge of the Canal Zone district court. Whenever necessary, an umpire was to be named by the two governments. For New Cristóbal the United States made small concessions concerning the boundary between Colón and the Canal Zone and promised to build certain highways. The road from Panama City across the Isthmus would be completed from Alhajuela to Portobelo if Panama bore all of its cost except $1,250,-000. Both governments agreed to undertake various other bridge and highway developments, including a bridge across

Pedro Miguel Locks or a ferry on the Pacific side by the United States. Each was obligated to maintain the roads within its jurisdiction, but Panama was to spend at least $50,000 on maintenance under the supervision of its chief engineer and an engineer appointed by the United States. All highways were to be used freely except in time of war, and the system was to be completed within three years after the ratification of the treaty. The United States also was given the right to construct telephone and telegraph lines along all roads built.

Article IV provided that sales to ships should be continued, but that purchases from commissaries should be limited to employees of the American government, their families, and diplomats accredited to and designated by the Panamanian government. The United States agreed to continue its co-operation in preventing smuggling from the Canal Zone into Panama and to prohibit all private business from the Canal Zone other than that existing before July 28, 1926. With the exception of guests of the Canal Zone hotels, only persons connected with the Canal enterprise, their families, and their servants were to rent dwellings or to reside in the Canal Zone. The United States promised that no merchandise consigned to Panama should be landed at Balboa or Cristóbal without invoices and manifests legalized by Panamanian consular representatives, and that Panamanian merchants were to have the usual privilege of making sales to ships passing through the Canal. The article implied that the United States had the right to establish warehouses in the Canal Zone and that the hospitality of the Canal Zone hotels might be extended without restriction.

The reciprocal free exchange of goods, wares, and merchandise between the Canal Zone and Panama was continued by Article V, but no imports brought into the Canal Zone for sale in the commissaries or to ships, for distribution, or for re-exportation were to enter Panama without payment of duties. This clause did not apply to goods bought legally in the commissaries by American government employees who resided in the republic. The ports of Balboa and Cristóbal were to be free to all ships passing through the Canal, except for tolls and charges for the use of the Canal and duties on imports for consumption in the Canal Zone. The harbors of Panama and Colón were likewise free to ships passing through the Canal and to American government vessels engaged in Canal work. Panama was given space for the erection of custom-houses in the terminal ports, the reciprocal free passage of persons other than immigrants was guaranteed on the Isthmus, and the United States was accorded the use of the cities and harbors of Panama and Colón in cases of emergency in connection with shipping. The treaty, furthermore, modified the liquor convention of 1924[25] by authorizing the transportation of sealed and certified alcoholic beverages from one part of the republic to the other or from the terminal ports to Panamanian territory across the Canal Zone. The sanitary control of the United States over the cities of Panama and Colón was clarified and extended to cover any part of the republic threatened by an epidemic. No radio equipment except that owned by the United States and Panama could be imported, erected, or operated in Panamanian territory without the consent of the Washington government, and all private stations were to be subject to it. The United States was given the right to set up and maintain radio stations in Panama, and promised to keep them open to public business, but Panama was to retain sovereignty over their sites. Private aircraft and aviation centers on the Isthmus might be inspected by both governments, and planes owned by citizens of either might be operated in the Republic of Panama only with joint licenses issued by a board composed of representatives of the Washington and Panamanian governments. The monetary agreement between the two countries was broadened and included in the treaty. To the pretended dismay of the civilized world, the Republic of Panama agreed for the defense of the Canal to "consider herself in a state of war in case of any war in which the United States should be a belligerent" and to place Panamanian resources almost wholly at the disposal of the United States.[26]

Except for the provisions concerning liquor transit and high-way building the agreement did little more than give the Republic of Panama a treaty guarantee that the United States would continue its existing policies in the Canal Zone. Panama failed to get any limitation on the right of the United States to extend the Canal Zone as it chose, nor did it succeed in restricting the business of the commissaries to the necessities of the American government employees. Extradition, postal service, consular exequaturs, and the rights or abuses of the Panama Railroad were ignored. On the other hand, the United States gained a portion of the second largest Panamanian city and extended its treaty rights more clearly over sanitation, radio communication, and aviation. Also the provision that Panama should enter any war in which the United States engaged imposed a responsibility that might not have conformed with Panamanian obligations as a member of the League of Nations.

The American newspapers were unable to procure a copy of the treaty or any definite information as to its contents. Eventually it was submitted to the Senate Committee on Foreign Relations and to the Panamanian National Assembly in December, 1926,[27] but it was given to the world by a Cuban paper.[28] The treaty, more particularly the war clauses of Article XI, created an "international hubbub." The article was greeted as a violation of the Covenant of the League of Nations, but it actually recorded in black and white no more than a state of affairs which had been understood to exist since 1903. President Chiari stated that it would not alter the place of Panama in the League,[29] but it was decried as "an offensive alliance" that was a "new and extraordinary departure in Pan-American" relations. Panama was characterized as a creature of the United States with a government holding office under the shadow of American guns. One North American charged that the annexation of the Isthmus would be better than a law that the Washington government should have "the right to drag into a conflict the innocent people of the Republic of Panama, whose sole offense is that they live near the Canal."[30] Panama received generous praise in the United States. One paper pictured the treaty as a "proof of the friendly disposition of the Government and people of Panama," another stated that Article XI represented "a long advance over the previous attitude of Panama," and a third believed that it indicated that Panama was losing the attitude of being treated "too much as a vassal state, and too little as an independent nation."[31] Much violent opposition was aroused in Panama, and one article even threatened death to any member of the National Assembly who voted for ratification. The American Senate removed the injunction of secrecy from the treaty and started discussing it on January 18, 1927, but the National Assembly voted on January 26 to suspend further consideration of the convention and requested President Chiari to renew negotiations with the United States.[32]

The European press appeared to be most excited about the war clauses,[33] but much severe criticism was heard in Latin America. Secretary of State Kellogg was reported to have said that the unfavorable publicity in Europe was partly responsible for the failure of the treaty.[34] Panamanian newspapers immediately denied this.[35] The Mexican press charged that the Panamanian commissioners had been coerced by the State Department.[36] The clamor, contemptuously referred to by one Isthmian as *"Palabras, palabras y más palabras,"*[37] became so widespread that the Panamanian legations throughout the world issued the following statement at the order of the foreign secretary:

World press comments on the proposed treaty with the United States reveal a profound ignorance of our past relations with that country. It may properly be pointed out that before Panama joined the League we were bound to the United States by the treaty of November 18, 1903, which, though not stating it in detail, placed us in the peculiar position of being unable to remain neutrals in a conflict in which the United States could become involved. This was proved in 1917, when Panama declared war on Germany, twenty-four hours after the United States.[38]

Aged Philippe Bunau-Varilla took his pen in palsied fingers to defend the United States from the malignant shafts of its accusers. He stated that the new treaty did not modify that of 1903, but merely settled several of its details that needed definition. "To raise this great outcry about imperialism over what is simply an embodiment in fuller specifications of the terms of a general contract," he charged, "is sheer stupidity. If it is intentional, it is done in bad faith; if it is not intentional, it is due to ignorance." He explained that Article XI, "over which many ignorant commentators have spilled much ink and those sentimental spirits who are always prematurely mourning the death of liberty have shed many tears," was not a fearful exhibition of the American imperialism that was being dinned continually into the ears of the world and not an alliance destined to change the status of Panama within the League of Nations, but simply a repetition in somewhat more detail of Article I of the Hay-Bunau-Varilla Treaty.[39]

Eusebio A. Morales explained to the Eighth Assembly of the League of Nations in September, 1927, that Article XI had not been forced on Panama by the United States, but had been proposed by the Panamanian government as a demonstration of its solidarity with the United States in the defense of the Isthmus and had been accepted "with the lofty spirit and clear comprehension of mind that prompted Panama to present the proposition." He stated decisively that Panama had not surrendered the whole of its sovereign rights over the Canal Zone, and, consequently, had the privilege and duty of defending it. According to Morales, the war clause had no other significance than of offering Panamanian aid for the defense of Panamanian territory in which another country possessed vital interests. He hoped that the United States, "a just country, a lover of peace, and an enthusiastic supporter of international arbitration," would recognize the sovereignty of Panama in the future. He concluded that as a last resource that matter might be submitted to an impartial court for an equitable and final determination.[40] The State Department immediately made it clear that the League of Nations had nothing whatever to do with the control of the Canal Zone by the United States.[41]

The Panamanian government attempted to start negotiations for a new treaty, but accomplished nothing.[42] When complaints were made against the Canal Zone commissaries, the State Department bluntly stated in May, 1927: "When the ratifications of this treaty are exchanged, the question will be definitely settled."[43] By 1929, however, the Washington government had agreed to begin discussions for another treaty.[44] On August 12, 1930, Minister Ricardo J. Alfaro stated that the convention of 1926 had been undertaken in unfavorable diplomatic conditions and that in the more auspicious circumstances then existing the State Department was disposed to renew negotiations.[45] The claims convention was finally ratified by Panama on December 22, 1930, and was proclaimed on December 6, 1931. On December 17, 1932, it was modified by another convention which was proclaimed on March 30, 1933.[46] The treaty of 1926 has been discarded completely, and a new agreement has been reached between the United States and the Republic of Panama.

NOTES

1. Buchanan to Hay, No. 37, Jan. 18, 1904, Despatches, Panama, I.

2. Magoon to Amador, July 28, 1905, Panama, Sec. R. E., *Memoria*, 1906, pp. 273-276.

3. *Ibid.*; *Sen. Doc.*, No. 401, 59 Cong., 2 Sess. (Ser. 5097), I, 64.

4. Guardia to Magoon, Aug. 6, 1905, Panama, Sec. R. E., *Memoria*, 1906, pp. 276-277.

5. *Idem* to idem, Aug. 25, 1905, *loc. cit.*, p. 278.

6. Magoon to Root, No. 18, Nov. 9, 1905, Despatches, Panama, IV.

7. Price to E. T. Lefevre, Sept. 24, 1915, Panama, Sec. R. E., *Memoria*, 1916, pp. 157-158.

8. E. T. Lefevre to Price, Nov. 23, 1915, *loc. cit.*, p. 158.

9. Panama, Sec. R. E., *Memoria*, 1920, pp. 21-22.

10. *Ibid.*, pp. 22-28.

11. Harding to J. A. Arango, June 22, 1920, *Documents Relating to the Special Commission of the Republic of Panama before the Government of the United States* (Panama, 1920), pp. 6-8.

12. The commission to Harding, July 9, 1920, *loc. cit.*, pp. 11-14.

13. Harding to J. A. Arango, July 15, 1920, *loc. cit.*, p. 15.

14. Panama, Sec. R. E., *Memoria*, 1922, II, 194-203; Instituto Nacional de Panamá, *Documentos sobre la independencia del Istmo de Panamá* (Panama, 1930), p. 355.

15. *Sen. Doc.*, No. 248, 67 Cong., 2 Sess. (Ser. 7988), pp. 1-2.

16. C. Grand Pierre, "Panama's Demand for Independence," in *Current History*, XIX (1923), 128.

17. Panama, Sec. R. E., *Memoria*, 1918, p. xxxv.

18. *Memorandum de diversos asuntos que la República de Panamá desea arreglar con los Estados Unidos* . . . , pp. 5-16.

19. Alfaro to Hughes, Jan. 3, 1923, República de Panamá, Sec. R. E., *Documentos importantes relacionados con el tratado de 28 de julio de 1926* . . . (Panama, 1927), p. 36.

20. *Ibid.*, pp. 31-39.

21. *Idem* to *idem*, Jan. 4, 1924, Panama, Sec. R. E., *Memoria*, 1926, pp. 231-238.

22. Hughes to Alfaro, Jan. 11, 1924, *loc. cit.*, pp. 238-242.

23. "Panama," in F. P. A., *Inf. Ser.*, III (1928), 356; *Current History*, XX (1924), 488, 664.

24. Instituto Nacional, *op. cit.*, pp. 356-363, 439-464; *Press Releases*, Aug. 23, 1926; Panama, Sec. R. E., *Memoria*, 1926, pp. xxiii-xl.

25. 43 *Stat. at L.*, 1875; Governor of the Canal Zone, *Annual Report*, 1931, p. 113.

26. The treaty is printed in *Cong. Rec.*, 69 Cong., 2 Sess., LXVIII, 1848-1852; see also Fabián Velarde, *Analysis del nuevo tratado* (Panama, 1927), pp. 35-37.

27. "Panama," *loc. cit.*, p. 358; *Current History*, XXV (1927), 764; *Estrella*, Jan. 27, 1927.

28. *Star and Herald*, Dec. 28, 1926.

29. Richard Lee Strout, "The League and the Panama Treaty," in *The Independent*, CXVIII (1927), 95-96, 111.

30. "The Panama Treaty," in *The Nation*, CXXIV (1927), 6.

31. "Panama to Aid Us in War," in *The Literary Digest*, XCII (Jan. 1, 1927), 10.

32. *Current History*, XXV (1927), 920; *Estrella*, Jan. 27, 1927.

33. "Panama," *loc. cit.*, p. 359.

34. *N. Y. Times*, Aug. 25, 1927, 23:2.

35. *Ibid.*, Sept. 5, 1927, 7:7.

36. *Ibid.*, Aug. 28, 1927, 19:2.

37. Velarde, *op. cit.*, p. 35.

38. "Panama Balks at the New Treaty with Us," in *The Literary Digest*, XCII (Mar. 12, 1927), 16.

39. Philippe Bunau-Varilla, "Washington and Panama," in *The Living Age*, CCCXXXII (1927), 485-487.

40. Morales, *op. cit.*, II, 193-205.

41. *Current History*, XXVII (1927), 275-276; "Panama's Paradoxical Protest," in *The Literary Digest*, XCV (Oct. 1, 1927), 13.

42. "Panama," *loc. cit.*, p. 359.

43. *Press Releases*, May 14, 1927.

44. *Current History*, XXXI (1929), 582.

45. *N. Y. Times*, Aug. 13, 1930, 18:8.

46. *Gaceta oficial*, Jan. 13, 1931; *Press Releases*, Dec. 23, 1930; Hunt, *op. cit.*, pp. 835-843.

CHAPTER XII

PANAMA AND THE NEW DEAL

THE REPUBLIC of Panama went into the disastrous year of 1929 with an apparently promising future. Building construction and highway development were continued, the government reorganized its warehouse system, and the *Ferrocarril Nacional de Chiriquí* showed its first annual profit.[1] Panama City boasted of 4,000 automobiles, the entire country had a monetary circulation of $7,500,000, and the *Banco Nacional* had a capital and reserve of $2,000,000.[2] Excellent business conditions and importations of highway and railway materials caused Isthmian imports to reach a new height; exports were fair. Due in great measure to the large number of Canal Zone employees, the depression that followed the 1929 crash was late in reaching Panama, but the Panamanian government found itself in financial straits. The Chiari and Arosemena administrations had undertaken too ambitiously the development of the republic.

The Panamanians have never taken full advantage of the benefits to be derived from the Canal enterprise. The upper classes appear to be more interested in political and professional careers than in utilizing the commercial and industrial opportunities of their fortunate geographical position.[3] The business of Panama City and Colón was largely in the hands of Americans, Greeks, Chinese, Hindoos, Japanese, Italians, and other foreigners.[4] In fact, citizens of the United States have been accused of causing more trouble than Panamanians in the matter of agitation against the Canal Zone commissaries. Panama and Colón indicated in numerous ways the imprint of American influence. The people of Panama used 15,000,000 sticks of American gum annually, newspapers and shop signs were printed in English, one cabinet member admitted that he thought in English, the Panamanians had nineteen automobiles for every mile of highway, the Chinese legation labeled its official car in English, and the English-language motion pictures found no great handicap when presented in cosmopolitan Panama. The daughters of *altas familas* participated in sports, drove automobiles, and even worked. The Panamanians, men and women, were "wearing American clothes, driving American motor cars, eating American foods, drinking American drinks in American saloons and night clubs, and worst of all, from their point of view, speaking American."[5] The British consul informed his government that "in a place so Americanised as Panama" other nations could not hope "to attain more than a minor place in the market."[6]

In 1930 the Republic of Panama had a population of 467,-459; Colón and Panama City had grown from malarious villages into beautiful modern cities of 33,460 and 74,409 inhabitants, respectively. The Canal Zone added 39,467 to increase the total to more than half a million.[7] The school enrollment had risen from practically nothing in 1903 to nearly sixty thousand and 39.99 per cent of the Panamanians had become literate (*saben leer y escribir*).[8]

The revolution of January 2, 1931, disturbed economic conditions in Panama, but the operation of the Canal and construction work in the Canal Zone kept Panamanian suffering from becoming acute. The government suspended various public works, the banana market declined, and the cattle industry received a severe blow when the Canal Zone beef contract was awarded to a Cuban firm. Panama City had two thousand unemployed, but the construction of Madden Dam gave encouragement.[9] The presidential election of 1932 caused some disturbance, but the United States was not involved. The *Chiarist* or National Liberal party nominated Augusto Boyd, the Doctrinal Liberals chose Harmodio Arias, and the Reform Liberals selected Francisco Arias Paredes for candidate. After Boyd withdrew, Arias was elected comparatively quietly.[10] The Panamanian government immediately expressed appreciation to the State Department for the "opportune cooperation" of Canal Zone officials and for the "courteous, upright, intelligent and equanimous" assistance of Minister Roy T. Davis in the maintenance of public order and in promoting fairness in the election.[11]

Relations with the United States were improved somewhat in 1932 by a change in the liquor convention of June 6, 1924. A new agreement of March 14 provided that alcoholic beverages might be transported across Canal Zone territory and through Canal Zone ports if under seal and accompanied by proper certification from the Panamanian authorities.[12] Panama and Colombia also were reported to have established friendlier relations. The United States had attempted to get Colombia to recognize Panamanian independence and to provide for determing its boundary with Panama in the treaties of January 9, 1909,[13] but recognition was not accorded until the revised Thompson-Urrutia Treaty of April 6, 1914, went into effect on March 30, 1922.[14] Panama received its first Colombian minister in 1924,[15] and in 1932 had apparently agreed to a mixed commission for the demarcation of its boundary with Colombia.[16]

Panama began to feel the full effect of the world depression in 1932. The outcome of the presidential election gave some confidence, but the high tariff had a deterrent influence.[17] The financial situation became very difficult, but unemployment conditions were relieved slightly by the visit of the American fleet and by the construction work on the Madden Dam.[18] A rent strike in August threatened to provoke American intervention, but was settled in September.[19] By the end of the year the national debt was $19,257,968, and the government guaranteed $3,282,154 outstanding of the four *Banco Nacional* issues.[20]

The Republic of Panama was deep in the throes of the depression by 1933. Despite the campaign promise of President Arias that he would go into the streets with his hat in his hand "begging for money to keep up the interest and service on the public debt, rather than permit a default,"[21] all issues of the *Banco Nacional* were in default by January 1, and on May 15 the interest payments on the $12,000,000 loan of 1928 were suspended. Arias was forced to take stringent measures to prevent national bankruptcy. Merchantile stocks were exceedingly low except for Japanese goods, but the import duties were lowered for the encouragement of tourist trade, and the Panamanians agreed to use local products when possible.[22] On November 23 the government was able to announce a plan for the partial resumption of interest payments on the bonds of 1928.[23] The arbitration protocol of 1926, as modified by the convention of December 17, 1932, was carried into effect in 1933 by the settlement of 133 American and 55 Panamanian claims. On five awards citizens of Panama received $3,150, and Americans were given $114,396.25 on nineteen claims found valid.[24]

One Panamanian diplomat charged that the commercial and financial crisis in Panama was caused not only by the depression, but also by the Canal, which he claimed was a calamity for his country because it had "absorbed all the productive and commercial facilities of Panama, and, with the Saxon-American industrial companies," constituted "a terrible entity for the extraction of Panama gold," which had carried the Panamanians to the "door of general misery."[25]

The Panamanians feared that the credit and currency policy of the Roosevelt administration would aggravate their economic condition.[26] They became especially incensed over the sale of 3.2 per cent beer in the Canal Zone. On August 17 *El Diario* stated that Panama might sever diplomatic relations with the United States. President Arias immediately explained: "There is no basis of fact in the story. All questions pending between Panama and the United States have been or are being discussed frankly and openly and in an amicable manner."[27] The beer matter caused further trouble when the Canal Zone governor answered a protest against its sale. The foreign secretary indicated that he hoped the governor would not be called upon to express another opinion concerning the diplomatic relations of the two governments.[28]

President Arias eventually decided to make a personal appeal to Washington for the relief of Panama. The Panamanian unemployed had increased to fifty thousand, a large part being discharged Canal Zone laborers.[29] Other points for discussion were the Canal Zone commissaries, sovereignty over New Cristóbal, and radio control.[30] Arias arrived in Washington on October 9, 1933,[31] and after several conferences with the American government he and President Roosevelt issued a joint statement that the Hay-Bunau-Varilla Treaty now covered only "the use, occupation and control by the United States of the Canal Zone for the purpose of maintenance, operation, sanitation and protection of the Canal" and that Panama as a sovereign nation was entitled "to take advantage of the commercial opportunities inherent in its geographical situation as far as . . . [might] be done without prejudice to the maintenance, operation, sanitation and protection of the Panama Canal by the United States which is earnestly desirous of the prosperity of the Republic of Panama." The United States promised to consider sympathetically any request from Panama for solution by arbitration of any important question of a purely economic nature which did not affect the maintenance, operation, sanitation, and protection of the Canal. The United States agreed to exercise special vigilance to prevent contraband trade in articles purchased in the commissaries, to prohibit sales of "tourist" goods by the commissaries for disposal on ships passing through the Canal, and to regulate other sales by the commissaries to ships "with the interest of Panamanian merchants in view." The agreement further stipulated:

The services of the United States hospitals and dispensaries in the Canal Zone will be limited to officers and employees of the United States Government and of the Panama Railroad Company and their families, excepting only in emergency cases; admission to the restaurants, clubhouses and moving picture houses in the Zone will be similarly restricted.

The United States also intends to request of Congress an appropriation to assist in repatriating some of the aliens who went to the Isthmus attracted by the construction work of the Canal and have now come to constitute a serious unemployment problem for Panama.

The clause binding lessees or contractors of the restaurants to purchase their provisions from or through the Commissaries will be abrogated. The United States Government furthermore is prepared to make the necessary arrangements in order that Panama may establish at the terminal ports of the Canal houses and guards to collect duties on importations destined to other portions of Panama and to prevent contraband trade.[32]

The Panamanian people were jubilant over the success that they had prayed for daily since the departure of their chief.[33] Franklin D. Roosevelt became one of their heroes. The first Roosevelt had helped them secure their independence; the second had revived it for them. Arias was hailed as a good-will ambassador for the United States, and on his return to Panama on October 28 he received one of the greatest ovations in Panamanian history.[34] The joint agreement was speedily carried out by the Canal Zone government. The Canal club houses were closed early in November to all persons except American government employees, and sales by the commissaries of goods other than sea and ship stores to vessels passing through the Canal were prohibited. The announcement was made that lunch rooms and restaurants under private contract would be discontinued as soon as practicable.[35] This accord, however, was too early to take care of the annual rental of the Canal Zone. After the United States reduced the gold content of the dollar Panama refused to accept the $250,000 payment in 1934.[36]

President Roosevelt repaid the visit of Arias in July, 1934, while on his way to the American possessions in the Pacific. The relations of the two governments became considerably more friendly. Throughout the summer plans were formulated for a treaty to replace the unratified convention of 1926. Late in the year Panamanian commissioners arrived in Washington, and formal negotiations were initiated on November 5. Among the numerous points that were to receive consideration were the Canal annuity, radio control, commissary sales, the Panama Railroad lots in the cities of Panama and Colón, repatriation of West Indian laborers, sovereignty over the Canal Zone, expropriation of territory, and the right of the United States to intervene in Panama. The demands of the Panamanians aroused the ire of old Philippe Bunau-Varilla, who wrote on December 2, 1934: "Sense of gratitude seems to be entirely absent in the leadership of this little republic which owes its life to my initiative and to the protection I was happy enough to obtain for it from the United States President Theodore Roosevelt."[37]

Negotiations were continued from November 5, 1934, through 1935. The Panamanians returned to the Isthmus to consult their government in August, 1935, but came back and resumed discussions on October 22. In accordance with the "good neighbor policy" of President Roosevelt, the differences between the two governments were debated thoroughly and frankly, and an attempt was made "to eliminate, insofar as possible, all causes of friction and all grounds of legitimate complaint on the part of Panama, without sacrificing any rights deemed essential by this Government [the United States] for the efficient operation, maintenance, sanitation and protection of the Canal."[38] The result was the signature on March 2, 1936, by Secretary of State Cordell Hull, Assistant Secretary of State Sumner Welles, Minister Ricardo J. Alfaro, and Minister on Special Mission Narciso Garay, of the following agreements:

(1) A general treaty revising in some aspects the convention of November 18, 1903, between the United States and Panama. This treaty is accompanied by sixteen exchanges of notes embodying interpretations of the new treaty or agreements pursuant thereto;

(2) A convention for the regulation of radio communications in the Republic of Panama and the Canal Zone, accompanied by three supplementary exchanges of notes;

(3) A convention providing for the transfer to Panama of two naval radio stations, and

(4) A convention with regard to the construction of a Trans-Isthmian Highway between the cities of Panama and Colón.[39]

The agreements were not made public by the State Department, but their contents are generally known. The United States acknowledged the independence of the Republic of Panama by abolishing the guarantee of Panamanian sovereignty and freedom contained in Article I of the Hay-Bunau-Varilla Treaty. The "so-called Panamanian Platt amendment," the right of the United States to intervene in the cities of Panama and Colón and their adjacent harbors and territories for the preservation of order, was also abrogated. Hereafter co-operation and equal responsibility will replace the unilateral predominance exerted by the United States in its Isthmian affairs. The two countries are to take joint action, after mutual consultation, in the event of a conflict that might endanger the security of Panama or the safety of the Canal.

The treaty proclaims the principle that the benefits of the Canal must be primarily for the two nations that made it possible. The United States, accordingly, promises to co-operate in the prevention of contraband trade, to restrict the privilege of buying in the Canal Zone commissaries, to impose specific restrictions for regulating their sales to ships and tourists passing through the Canal, and to limit the use of clubs, theaters, laundries, cleaning establishments, hospitals, dispensaries, and restaurants of the Canal Zone to its employees. Persons not connected with the operation or administration of the Canal are not to rent dwellings or to live in the Canal Zone. All private commercial, industrial, and business enterprises not concerned with the operation of the Canal are to be prohibited from territory under the jurisdiction of the United States.

The Canal Zone is to be closed to the commerce of the world in order that it will not be a trade agency in competition with the Republic of Panama. Panamanian merchandise and produce are to have free entry into the Canal Zone. The treaty makes provision for the establishment of Panamanian customs houses at the terminal ports of the Canal for the examination of passengers and merchandise destined for Panama. The use of the port facilities of the Canal Zone for foreign commerce is permanently guaranteed to the Panamanians. Article IX of the treaty of 1903 is abolished, and the right to collect tolls from merchant ships in the ports of Panama City and Colón, even though they later pass through the Canal, is restored to Panama. The free transit between the Canal Zone and the Republic of Panama is to be limited only by the right of the Isthmian government to control immigration through the ports of the Canal. The United States is no longer to enjoy the facilities of the ports of Panama City and Colón without restriction, but may use them only in cases of emergency.

The United States recognized the fact that the Canal has been constructed and that the provisions of the original treaty now pertain only to the maintenance, operation, sanitation, and defense of the Canal. The treaty declares that Panama has complied with its obligation to permit the American government to use all lands and waters necessary for the construction of the Canal and surrenders the right of the United States to expropriate without restriction additional land for Canal use. Hereafter the United States may acquire jurisdiction over Panamanian territory by negotiation and purchase, but will no longer be able to exercise sovereignty over new expropriations. A slight adjustment is to be made in the boundaries of the Canal Zone in order that Colón and the remainder of the republic may be joined and that the United States may have a corridor from the Zone to the Madden Dam.

The United States renounced its monopoly of trans-Isthmian land communications. When the agreements are ratified Pamama may build a highway across the Isthmus linking its two most important cities, Panama and Colón. The right of Panama to all air waves within the jurisdiction of the Canal Zone and the republic proper for radio communication and the regulation of wireless is recognized upon a basis of strict equality and reciprocity. The two radio stations at La Palma and Puerto Obaldía, which are already in the possession of Panama, are granted to it formally by one of the conventions.

The grievance of Panama over the reduction of the gold content of the American dollar is to be adjusted to its satisfaction. The Canal annuity, the acceptance of which has been refused since 1934, is to be increased from $250,000 in gold to 430,000 *balboas*. The value of the *balboa* is fixed to equal the designated gold dollar of the present time. Thus Panama will receive approximately $7,500 more in gold each year than was paid before the Roosevelt administration. These provisions are to be retro-active to February 26, 1934, when the first payment in devalued currency was tendered and refused.[40]

The agreements were sent by plane to Panama immediately after their signature. The press reported that a special session of the National Assembly might be called to ratify them, but their consideration was left for the administration of J. D. Arosemena, who was elected president on June 7. President Arias issued a statement praising President Roosevelt and asking for a "fair and impartial judgment" of the treaty. He believed that by its ratification the "asperities would be smoothed over, the sovereignty and dignity of Panama re-affirmed, economic questions adjusted, and, finally the rights that Panamans have always considered sacred would be vindicated."[41]

The press comment on the new agreements has been rather favorable, but hints have been made that the United States was weakening its right to defend the Canal. One paper remarked: "As one Roosevelt assisted at the birth of the Republic of Panama, it is appropriate that another Roosevelt should officially recognize its rise to manhood among the nations." Theodore Roosevelt had freed Panama from Colombia, and now Franklin D. Roosevelt was "untying Panama—in part, at least —from *Miss Columbia's* apron-strings."[42] The dominant factor in the negotiation of the treaty, an American writer declared, was the belief "that the defense of the Canal could best be assured by a policy of joint responsibility, based on genuine mutual understanding and co-operation." Since the United States and Panama were equally interested in safeguarding the Canal, a sincere attitude "on the part of Panama would be more valuable for Canal defense than formal treaty pledges exacted at the cost of resentment and hostility."[43] Another commentator stated: "The new treaty, added to the payment made Colombia . . . goes about as far as legal devices can to heal the last wounds inflicted by the elder Roosevelt's impetuous method of clearing the way for the building of the Isthmian canal." He further said: "The contribution which the conclusion of such a treaty may make to the success of the forthcoming general American peace conference at Buenos Aires is obvious."[44] However, rumors have been spread that the Committee on Foreign Relations of the Senate has rejected the treaty because of the clauses pertaining to the defense of the Canal.

The treaty and the conventions were ratified on December 23, 1936, by Panama.[45] They may be placed in effect early this year, but the Panamanians will not be satisfied. As in the case of all other questions, there are two sides to the general controversy between the United States and Panama— my side and the wrong side. American government officials look upon the administration of the Canal Zone as proper and necessary; the Panamanians view it as "a great feudal enterprise" and "a brutal monopoly." The Americans point to the immense benefit that Panama has derived from the activities of their government; the Panamanians regard the administration of the Canal Zone as a cankering sore that continually drains their life blood. In the heart of their country is a government set up by a foreign power; a government that has been described as "scarcely socialism; rather it is bureaucracy raised to perfection. The Canal Zone is a benevolent dictatorship, a feudal paradise, not an organic functioning entity shaped by the active intelligence of its citizens."[46]

Thirty years of irritating grievances have been the result of the Hay-Bunau-Varilla Treaty. Could the situation have been otherwise? Probably it would have been but for the lack of tact on the part of numerous American officials. Many irritations will remain to clutter diplomatic channels between the two countries. Many points cannot be settled as the Panamanians wish; many others can be adjusted amicably. The consolidation of the posts of American minister and Canal Zone governor would hardly solve the problem of Panamanian-American diplomatic intercourse, but something might be gained by prohibiting direct communication between the Canal Zone government and the Panamanian foreign office. The Isthmians must work out their own destiny; they must strive to develop their possibilities as a trade center. But the fact is and will remain that Panama is "a sovereign nation only in so far as her sovereignty does not clash with the ideas of the elder statesmen of the State, War, and Navy Building at Washington."[47]

More than thirty years of progress and enlightenment, more than thirty years of smouldering dissatisfaction have followed four centuries of turmoil, strife, and misery. Fortunate, unfortunate Panama!

NOTES

1. *Commerce Yearbook*, 1930, II, 441; Panama, Sec. H. y T., *Memoria*, 1930, pp. lxi-lxii; *Gaceta oficial*, Sept. 20, 1929.

2. Guillermo Colunge (ed.), *La República de Panamá en la Exposición Ibero-Americana de Sevilla*, 1929 (n. p., n. d.), pp. 50-53.

3. Escobar, *op. cit.*, p. 147.

4. Reid, *op. et loc. cit.*, p. 58.

5. *N. Y. Times*, Mar. 2, III, 7:1; July 7, 1930, 12:2-3.

6. Great Britain, Dept. of Overseas Trade, *op. cit.*, 1929, p. 11.

7. República de Panamá, Dirección General del Censo, *Censo demográfico, 1930* (Panama, 1931), I, 7, 19, 108; U. S. Department of Commerce, Bureau of the Census, *Panama Canal Zone . . . Inhabitants* (Washington, 1930), p. 3.

8. *BPAU*, LXV (1931), 97-98; Panama, *Censo demográfico, 1930*, I, 11.

9. *Commerce Reports*, Jan. 5, p. 25; Feb. 9, p. 349; Aug. 3, p. 271; Sept. 7, 1931, p. 586; Jan. 4, 1932, pp. 10-11.

10. *Current History*, XXXV (1931), 436, 586; XXXVI (1932), 214-215, 589; *Press Releases*, June 6, 1932; *N. Y. Times*, June 8, 9:3; June 9, 1932, 9:2.

11. R. J. Alfaro to H. F. Alfaro, June 7, 1932, *Press Releases*, June 11, 1932.

12. *Press Releases*, Mar. 26, 1932.

13. *Sen. Doc.*, No. 1063, 62 Cong., 2 Sess. (Ser. 6350), pp. 239-247.

14. *For. Rel.* (1914), p. 148; *Current History*, XX (1924), 664; *Sen. Doc.*, No. 348, 67 Cong., 4 Sess. (Ser. 8167), III, 2538-2541.

15. *BPAU*, LVIII (1924), 1071.

16. *Ibid.*, LXVI (1932), 440.

17. *Commerce Reports*, July 4, 1932, p. 13.

18. *Ibid.*, Apr. 4, pp. 11-12; Mar. 7, 1932, p. 537.

19. *Ibid.*, Sept. 3, p. 383; Oct. 1, 1932, p. 3; *Current History*, XXXVII (1932), 88.

20. *Foreign Commerce Yearbook*, 1933, p. 225; *Moody's Government Securities*, 1932, pp. 2660-2661.

21. *N. Y. Times*, May 22, 1932, III, 8:3.

22. *Ibid.*, Aug. 13, 1933, IV, 13:2; *Current History*, XXXIX (1933), 86.

23. *Moody's Government Securities*, 1934, p. 2658; *N. Y. Times*, Nov. 23, 1933, 31:2-3, 37:7-8.

24. *Gaceta oficial*, Jan. 13, 1931; *Press Releases*, Dec. 23, 1930; Hunt, *op. cit.*, pp. 9, 19, 835, 841.

25. *N. Y. Times*, Jan. 8, 1933, IV, 2:2.

26. *Ibid.*, May 12, 1933, 25:1.

27. *Ibid.*, Aug. 18, 1933, 8:5; *Current History*, XXXIX (1933), 86.

28. *N. Y. Times*, Mar. 30, 1933, 11:2.

29. *Ibid.*, Oct. 18, 1933, 22:1.

30. *Current History*, XXXIX (1933), 346.

31. *N. Y. Times*, Oct. 10, 1933, 23:8.

32. *Press Releases*, Oct. 21, 1933; Sociedad Panameña de Acción Internacional, *Panama-United States Relations* (Panama, 1934), pp. 3-4.

33. *N. Y. Times*, Oct. 4, 1933, 10:4.

34. *Ibid.*, Oct. 22, 1933, II, 3:6; *Current History*, XXXIX (1934), 465.

35. *N. Y. Times*, Dec. 10, 1933, IV, 8:5; *Current History*, XXXIX (1934), 465.

36. *N. Y. Times*, Mar. 2, 3:3; Mar. 3, 19:2; Mar. 7, 1934, 18:5; "The Panama Republic's Demand for Gold," in *The Literary Digest*, CXVII (Mar. 17, 1934), 45.

37. Bunau-Varilla to the editor, *N. Y. Times*, Dec. 20, 1934, 22:6.

38. *Press Releases*, Mar. 2, 1936.

39. *Ibid.*

40. Gaston Nerval, "Panama Treaty Promises Rectification of Errors," in *The Sunday Star* (Washington, D. C.), May 10, 1934, p. D-3; *N. Y. Times*, Mar. 3, 1936; 1:3, 14:3-4. The treaty and the three conventions were published in the *Panama American*, Mar. 3, 1936.

41. *N. Y. Times*, Mar. 3, 1936, 14:3-4; *Panama American*, Mar. 3, 1936.

42. "Panama Man-sized at 32," in *The Literary Digest*, CXXI (Mar. 14, 1936), 7.

43. "New Treaty with Panama," in *Current History*, Apr., 1936, pp. 78-79.

44. "Acting the Part of the 'Good Neighbor'," in *The Christian Century*, LIII (Mar. 18, 1936), 420.

45. *Panama American*, Dec. 22, 23, 24, 1936; *Star and Herald*, Dec. 22, 23, 24, 1936.

46. Carleton Beals, "Revolt in Panama," in *The Nation*, CXLI (July 24, 1935), 99-101; "Correspondence Beals on Panama," *loc. cit.*, CXLI (Sept. 4, 1935), 270-273.

47. Jorge J. Blanco, "Portrait of a Sovereign State," in *The American Mercury*, XXVI (1932), 54.

BIBLIOGRAPHY

I. Manuscripts

United States, Department of State.
Consular Letters from Aspinwall (Colón), vols. 18-19 (1900-1906).
Consular Letters from Panama, vols. 24-27 (1901-1906).
Instructions, Panama, vol. 1 (1903-1906).
Despatches from Panama, vols. 1-5 (1903-1906).
Notes from the Department to the Panamanian Legation, vol. 1 (1903-1906).
Notes from the Panamanian Legation to the Department, vol. 1 (1903-1906).
Columbus Memorial Library, Pan American Union, Washington, D. C.
Geo. M. Hanson, U. S. consul at Panama City, Motor Roads in Panama, July 31, 1926.
Wm. S. Howell, Jr., U. S. chargé at Panama City, Roads and Road Construction in the Republic of Panama, October 22, 1924.
H. D. Myers, U. S. vice-consul at Panama City, Extension of Chiriquí Railway Republic of Panama, June 26, 1926.
Geo. Orr, U. S. consul at Panama City, Railway Mileage Republic of Panama, May 22, 1922.

II. Government Publications

Costa Rica, República de.
Documents Annexed to the Argument of Costa Rica before the Arbitrator Hon. Edward Douglass White Chief Justice of the United States under the Provisions of the Convention between the Republic of Costa Rica and the Republic of Panama, Concluded March 17, 1910. Rosslyn, Va., 1913. 4 vols.
Secretario de Relaciones Exteriores, *Documentos relativos al conflicto de jurisdicción territorial con la República de Panamá y sus antecedentes.* San José, 1921.

White, Edward Douglass, *Fallo arbitral del Chief Justice de los Estados Unidos de América en la controversia de límites de las Repúblicas de Costa Rica y Panamá.* San José, 1914.

Great Britain.

Department of Overseas Trade, *Report on the Commercial and Economic Situation in the Republic of Panama . . . and Costa Rica . . . .* London, 1921-1931.

League of Nations.

Official Journal of the League of Nations. 1920-1934.

Panama, República de.

Arbitration before the Honorable Edward D. White Chief Justice of the Supreme Court of the United States of Differences between the Republic of Panama and the Republic of Costa Rica; Additional Documents Submitted on behalf of the Republic of Panama, May 18, 1914. N. p., n. d.

Comisión Investigadora Electoral, *Informe de la comisión electoral de la provincia de Bocas del Toro.* Panama, 1908. (Reports were printed for all provinces.)

Dirección General de Estadística, *Compendio estadístico descriptivo de la República de Panamá con los datos sinópticos del comercio internacional de 1909 a 1916.* Panama, 1917.

Documents Relating to the Special Commission of the Republic of Panama before the Government of the United States. Panama, 1920.

Gaceta oficial. 1904-1934.

Instituto Nacional de Panama, *Documentos históricos sobre la independencia de Panamá.* Panama, 1930.

Memorandum de diversos asuntos que la República de Panamá desea arreglar con los Estados Unidos por considerar que varias actividades de la Compañia del Ferrocarril y Canal de Panamá no se conforman con las estipulaciónes del tratado existente entre los dos países y le causan además graves perjuicios al desarrollo de su comercio y sus intereses. Panama, 1923.

Panama-Costa Rica Boundary Controversy; Panama's Reply to the United States. Panama, 1921.

Secretaría de Agricultura y Obras Públicas.

Boletín de estadística. 1907-1929.

Censo demográfico, 1930. Panama, 1931. 2 vols.

Especificaciones para el contrato de construcción del ramal Ferrocarril Concepción-Puerto Armuelles. Panama, 1926.

Ferrocarril de Panamá a David; documentos referentes a la licitación para la construcción de un ferrocarril con ramales de Panamá a David en la República de Panamá; detalles, pliegos de cargos, especificaciones. Panama, 1911.

Memoria. 1906-1932. (Title varies.)

Secretaría de Gobierno y Justicia.

Memoria. 1906-1932. (Title varies.)

Secretaría de Hacienda y Tesoro.

Memoria. 1906-1932. (Title varies. The 1924 volume is translated into English.)

Secretaría de Relaciones Exteriores.

Controversia de límites entre Panamá y Costa Rica. Panama, 1914-1921. 2 vols.

Documentos importantes relacionados con las negociaciones del tratado de 28 de julio de 1926 tomados de la memoria de relaciones exteriores presentada a la Asamblea Nacional. Panama, 1927.

Documentos relacionados con la actual Guerra Europea. Panama, 1917.

Memoria. 1906-1932. (Title varies.)

United States of America.

Commerce Department.

Bureau of the Census, *Panama Canal Zone, Virgin Islands (U. S.) Guam, and American Samoa; Number and Distribution of Inhabitants.* Washington, 1930.

Bureau of Foreign and Domestic Commerce.

Commerce Yearbook, 1924-1933. Washington, 1924-1934.

Curran, Frank B., *Motor Roads in Latin America.* Washington, 1925. (Trade Promotion Series, No. 18.)

Foreign Commerce and Navigation of the United States, 1902-1933. Washington, 1903-1934.

Foreign Commerce Yearbook, 1933. Washington, 1934.

Harris, Garrard, *Central America as an Export Field.* Washington, 1916. (Special Agents Series, No. 113.)

Hasley, Frederic M., *Investments in Latin America and the British West Indies.* Washington, 1918. (Special Agents Series, No. 169.)

Long, William Rodney, *Railways of Central America and the West Indies.* Washington, 1925. (Trade Promotion Series, No. 5.)

Trade Directory of Central America and the West Indies. Washington, 1915. (Miscellaneous Series, No. 22.)

Trade Information Bulletin,

No. 281. Washington, 1922.

No. 503. Washington, 1927.

No. 657. Washington, 1929.

No. 707. Washington, 1930.

No. 767. Washington, 1931.

No. 810. Washington, 1932.

Weekly Consular and Trade Reports, Mar.-June, 1910.

Daily Consular and Trade Reports, July, 1910-Dec., 1914.

Commerce Reports, 1915-1934.

Congress. (Figures in parentheses represent serial numbers.)

Congressional Record, 56 Cong., 1 Sess. to 73 Cong., 2 Sess.

Houses Documents.

50 Cong., 1 Sess., No. 8 (4565).

58 Cong., 3 Sess., No. 226 (4853).

House of Representatives, Committee on Foreign Affairs, *The Story of Panama; Hearings on the Rainey Resolution before the Committee on Foreign Affairs of the House of Representatives.* Washington, 1913.

Senate Documents.

58 Cong., 2 Sess., No. 32 (4587).

58 Cong., 2 Sess., No. 51 (4587).

58 Cong., 2 Sess., No. 208 (4591).

59 Cong., 1 Sess., No. 429 (4919).

59 Cong., 2 Sess., No. 401 (5097-5100). 4 vols.

62 Cong., 3 Sess., No. 1063 (6350).

63 Cong., 2 Sess., No. 474 (6582).

67 Cong., 2 Sess., No. 248 (7988).

67 Cong., 4 Sess., No. 348 (8167).

Isthmian Canal Commission, *The Civil Code of the Republic of Panama and Amendatory Laws Continued in Force in the Canal Zone, Isthmus of Panama, by Executive Order of May 9, 1904.* Washington, 1905.

Malloy, William M., *Treaties, Conventions, International Acts, and Agreements between the United States of America and Other Powers, 1776-1909.* Washington, 1910. 2 vols.

Panama Canal Zone, Governor, *Annual Report,* 1914-1935. Washington, 1915-1936.

State Department.

Hunt, Bert L., *American and Panamanian General Claims Arbitration under the Conventions between the United States and Panama of July 28, 1926, and December 17, 1932.* Washington, 1934. (Arbitration Series, No. 6.)

Papers Relating to the Foreign Relations of the United States, 1902-1921. Washington, 1903-1936.

Press Releases, 1924-1936.

The Statutes at Large of the United States of America. Washington, 1850-1934.

III. Books and Pamphlets

Alfaro, Ricardo J., *Costa Rica y Panamá; en defensa de los que quieren paz y amistad.* Panama, 1927.

Alfaro, Ricardo J., *Límites entre Panamá y Costa Rica.* Panama, 1913.

Allen, Merritt Parmelee, *Sir Henry Morgan, Buccaneer.* New York, 1931.

Anderson, C. L. G., *Old Panama and Castilla del Oro.* Washington, 1911.

Anderson, Luis, *El laudo Loubet; contribución al estudio de la cuestión de límites entre Costa Rica y Panamá.* San José, 1911.

Anonymous, *"I Took the Isthmus"; Ex-President Roosevelt's Confession, Colombia's Protest and Editorial Comment by American Newspapers on "How the United States Acquired the Right to Build the Canal."* New York, 1911.

Anonymous, *Memorandum on the Change of Government in the Republic of Panama—January 2, 1931.* N. p., 1931.

Babson, Roger W., *The Future of South America.* Boston, 1915.

Bancroft, Hubert Howe, *History of Central America.* New York. 1882-1887. 3 vols.

Bourne, Edward Gaylord, *Spain in America, 1450-1580,* "The American Nation: a History," III. New York, 1904.

Bullard, Arthur, *Panama; the Canal, the Country and the People.* New York, 1914.

Bunau-Varilla, Philippe, *Panama; the Creation, Destruction, and Resurrection*. New York, 1914.

Bustamante, Antonio S. de, *Panama-Costa Rica Boundary Controversy; Opinion*. Panama, 1921.

Casas, Bartolomé de las, *Historia de las Indias*. Madrid, 1927. 3 vols.

Core, Susie Pearl, *Trails of Progress or the Story of Panama and Its Canal*. New York, 1925.

Colunge, Guillermo, ed., *La República de Panamá en la exposición Ibero-Americana de Seville, 1929*. N. p., n. d.

Dampier, William, *A New Voyage round the World*. London, 1703. 3 vols.

Dimrock, Marshall E., *Government-Operated Enterprises in the Panama Canal Zone*. Chicago, 1934.

Dunn, Robert Williams, *American Foreign Investments*. New York, 1926.

Eder, Phanor James, *Colombia*. London, 1913.

Escobar, Felipe J., *El legado de los próceres; ensayo histórico-político sobre la nacionalidad Panameña*. Panama, 1930.

Exquemelin, Alexandre Olivier, *The History of the Buccaneers of America; Containing Detailed Accounts of Those Bold and Daring Freebooters; Chiefly along the Spanish Main, in the West Indies, and in the South, Succeeding the Civil Wars in England*. Boston, 1856.

The Federal Reporter . . . , 1880-1924. St. Paul, 1880-1925. 300 vols.

Freehoff, Joseph C., *America and the Canal Title, or an Examination, Sifting and Interpretation of the Data Bearing on the Wresting of the Province of Panama from the Republic of Colombia by the Roosevelt Administration in 1903 in Order to Secure Title to the Canal Zone*. New York, 1916.

Gage, Thomas, *A New Survey of the West-Indies: or, the English American His Travels by Sea and Land: Containing a Journal of Three Thousand and Three Hundred Miles within the Main Land of America*. London, 1677.

Garay, Narciso, *Panamá y las guerras de los Estados Unidos*. Panama, 1930.

Gisborne, Lionel, *The Isthmus of Darien in 1852; Journal of the Expedition of Inquiry for the Junction of the Atlantic and Pacific Oceans*. London, 1853.

Graell, C. Arrocha, *Historia de la independencia de Panamá; sus antecedentes y sus causas, 1821-1903*. Panama, 1933.

Guardia, Santiago de la, *La intervención fiscal Americana en Panamá*. Panama, 1917.

Hakluyt, Richard, *The Principal Navigations Voyages Traffiques & Discoveries of the English Nation Made by Sea or Overland to the Remote and Fartherest Quarters of the Earth at Any Time within the Compasse of these 1600 Yeeres*. Glasgow, 1914, 12 vols.

Haring, Clarence Henry, *Trade and Navigation between Spain and the Indies in the Time of the Hapsburgs*. Cambridge, 1918.

Hart, Frances Russell, *The Disaster of Darien; the Story of the Scots Settlement and the Causes of Its Failure, 1699-1701*. Boston and New York, 1929.

Haskins, W. C., ed., *Canal Zone Pilot; Guide to the Republic of Panama and Classified Business Directory*. Panama, 1908.

Henao, Jesús María, and Arrubla, Gerardo, *Historia de Colombia para la enseñanza secundaria*. Bogotá, 1926.

Humbert, Jules, *Histoire de la Colombie et du Vénézuéla des origines jusqu'a nos jours*. Paris, 1921.

Insh, George Pratt, *The Company of Scotland Trading to Africa and the Indies*. New York, 1932.

Jane, Cecil, trans. and ed., *Select Documents Illustrating the Four Voyages of Columbus, Including Those Contained in R. H. Mayor's "Select Letters of Christopher Columbus,"* 2 vols., "Works Issued by the Hakluyt Society," LXX. London, 1933.

Johnson, William Fletcher, *Four Centuries of the Panama Canal*. New York, 1906.

[Johnstone, Mrs. Christian Isobel], *Lives and Voyages of Drake, Cavendish, and Dampier; Including an Introductory View of the Earlier Discoveries in the South Sea and the History of the Bucaniers*. New York, 1932.

Kepner, Jr., Charles David, and Soothill, Jay Henry, *The Banana Empire; a Case Study of Economic Imperialism*. New York, 1935.

Kimber, Albert W., ed., *Kimber's Record of Government Debts and Other Foreign Securities, 1921-1933*. New York, 1921-1933. A continuation of *The Fitch Record of Government Debts, 1916-1920*. New York, 1916-1920.

Markham, Clements R., trans. and ed., *Narrative of the Proceedings of Pedrarias Dávila in the Provinces of Tierra Firme or Castilla del Oro, and the Discovery of the South Sea and the Coasts of Peru and Nicaragua; Written by the Adelantado Pascual de Andagoya,* "Works Issued by the Hakluyt Society," XXXIV. London, 1865.

Markham, Clements R., trans. and ed., *Reports on the Discovery of Peru,* "Works Issued by the Hakluyt Society," XLVII. London, 1872.

Martin, Percy Alvin, *Latin America and the War.* Baltimore, 1925.

Means, Philip Ainsworth, *The Spanish Main, Focus of Envy, 1492-1700.* New York, 1935.

Méndez, Pereira Octavio, *Mi contestación al Dr. Alfredo L. Palacios.* Panama, 1926.

Merriman, Roger Bigelow, *The Rise of the Spanish Empire in the Old World and in the New.* New York, 1918-1934. 4 vols.

Munro, Dana G., *The United States and the Caribbean Area.* Boston, 1934.

Nuttall, Zelia, trans. and ed., *New Light on Drake; a Collection of Documents Relating to His Voyage of Circumnavigation, 1577-1580,* "Works Issued by the Hakluyt Society," XXXIV. London, 1914.

Ortega B., Ismael, *La jornada del día 3 de noviembre de 1903 y sus antecedentes.* Panama, 1931.

Palmer, B. W., *The American Banana Company.* Boston, 1907.

Parks, E. Taylor, *Colombia and the United States, 1765-1934.* Durham, 1935.

Pereyra, Carlos, *Francisco Pizarro y el tesoro de Atahualpa.* Madrid, n. d.

Pérez Sarmiento, José Manuel, *Manual diplomático y consular Colombiano.* Bogotá, 1927.

Pim, Bedford, *The Gate of the Pacific.* London, 1863.

Porras, Belisario, *A Lesson in Civics Which Should Remain Eternally Present in the Minds of All Panamanians.* Panama, 1924.

Porter, John Sherman, ed., *Moody's Manual of Investments; American and Foreign; Government Securities,* 1934. New York, 1934.

Richman, Irving Berdine, "The Spanish Conquerors; a Chronicle of the Dawn of the Empire Overseas," *The Chronicles of America Series*, II. New Haven, 1921.

Rippy, J. Fred, *The Capitalists and Colombia.* New York, 1931.

——————, *The United States and Mexico.* New York, 1931.

Roberts, George E., *Investigación economica de al República de Panama.* Panama, 1933.

Roberts, W. Adolphe, *Sir Henry Morgan, Buccaneer and Governor.* New York, 1933.

Santander, Callejas B., *Resumen político de la administración del Dr. Manuel Amador Guerrero, 1904-1908.* Panama, 1933.

Scruggs, William L., *The Colombian and Venezuela Republics; with Notes on Other Parts of Central and South America.* Boston, 1900.

Sociedad Panameña de Acción Internacional, *Panama-United States Relations.* Panama, 1934.

Sosa, Juan B., and Arce, Enríque J., *Compendio de historia de Panamá; text adoptado oficialmente para la enseñanza en las escuelas y colegios de la nación.* Panama, 1911.

Soto, Foción, *Memorias sobre el movimiento de resistencia a la dictadura de Rafael Núñez, 1884-1885.* Bogotá, 1913. 2 vols.

Star and Herald, printed at, *The Panama Massacre; a Collection of the Principal Evidence and Other Documents, Including the Report of Amos B. Corwine, Esq., U. S. Commissioner, the Official Statement of the Governor and the Depositions Taken before the Authorities, Relative to the Massacre of American Citizens at the Panama Railroad Station on the 15th of April, 1856.* Panama, 1857.

Tomes, Robert, *Panama in 1855; an Account of the Panama Rail-Road, of the Cities of Panama and Aspinwall, with Sketches of Life and Character on the Isthmus.* New York, 1855.

Ulloa, Antonio de, *A Voyage to South America, Describing at Large, the Spanish Cities, Towns, Provinces, &c. on that Extensive Continent.* London, 1760. 2 vols.

United Fruit Company, *Annual Report,* 1900-1934. N. p., n. d.

Valdés, Ramón M., *La independencia del Istmo de Panamá, sus antecedentes, sus causas y sus justificación.* Panama, 1903.

Vega, José de la, *La federación en Colombia (1810-1912).* Madrid, n. d.

Velarde, Fabian, *Análisis del nuevo tratado.* Panama, 1927.

Villegas, Sabas A., *The Republic of Panama, Its Economic, Financial, Commercial, and General Information.* Panama, 1917.

Wafer, Lionel, *A New Voyage and Description of the Isthmus of America.* London, 1704.

Weatherhead, W. D., *An Account of the Late Expedition against the Isthmus of Darien, under the Command of Sir Gregor McGregor together with the Events Subsequent to the Recapture of Portobelo, till the Release of the Prisoners from Panama; Remarks on the Present State of the Patriot Cause, and on the Climate and Diseases of South America.* London, 1821.

Winkler, Max, *Investments of United States Capital in Latin America.* Boston, 1929.

Wood, William, *Elizabethan Sea-Dogs; a Chronicle of Drake and His Companions,* "The Chronicles of America Series," III. New Haven, 1921.

Wright, I. A., trans. and ed., *Documents Concerning English Voyages to the Spanish Main, 1569-1580,* "Works Issued by the Hakluyt Society," LXXI. London, 1933.

IV. NEWSPAPERS, PERIODICALS, AND SPECIAL ARTICLES

1. Newspapers.

    New York Times. 1903-1936.

    Star and Herald (Panama City). This paper is in the Library of Congress, but the file is not complete. Part of it is weekly, part is daily, and part of it is *La Estrella de Panamá.* Various copies, many of them included in minister's despatches from Panama to the State Department, have been used of the *Panama Morning Journal,* the *Panama American, El Tiempo,* and *El Diario.*

2. Periodicals.

    Canal Record. Ancón, Canal Zone, 1908-1933. vols. 1-26.

    Current History. New York, 1914-1936. vols. 1-44.

    The Hispanic American Historical Review. Baltimore, 1918-1922; Durham, 1926-1936. vols. 1-16.

    The Nation. New York, 1865-1936. vols. 1-141.

    The Pan American Magazine. New Orleans, 1900-1931. vols. 1-44.

    International Union of American Republics.

Monthly Bulletin. Washington, 1902-1908. vols. 15-26.

Bulletin. Washington, 1908-1910. vols. 27-30.

Bulletin of the Pan American Union. Washington, 1910-1936. vols. 31-70.

Revue de L'Amérique Latine. Paris, 1922-1932. vols. 1-23.

3. Special Articles.

"A British Rubber Ghost in Panama," in *The Literary Digest*, LXXXIX (June 26, 1926), 13.

"Acting the Part of the 'Good Neighbor'," in *The Christian Century*, LIII (Mar. 18, 1936), 420.

"American Investments in the Western Hemisphere," in Foreign Policy Association, *Information Service*, III (1928), Appendix.

"Correspondence Beals on Panama," in *The Nation*, CXLI (Sept. 4, 1935), 270-273.

"Expansion of Banking in Panama," in *The Pan American Magazine*, XLI (1928), 246-247.

"New Treaty with Panama," in *Current History*, April, 1936, pp. 78-79.

"Panama," in Foreign Policy Association, *Information Service*, III (1928), 354-359.

"Panama Awaits the Ax," in *The Nation*, CXXIX (1929), 133-134.

"Panama Balks at the New Treaty with Us," in *The Literary Digest*, XCII (Mar. 12, 1927), 16.

"Panama Follows Suit, Revolution," in *Outlook and Independent*, CLVII (1931), 48-49.

"Panama Man-Sized at 32," in *The Literary Digest*, CXXI (Mar. 14, 1936), p. 7.

"Panama's Paradoxical Protest," in *The Literary Digest*, XCV (Oct. 1, 1927), 13.

"Panama to Aid Us in War," in *The Literary Digest*, XCII (Jan. 1, 1927), 10.

"The Panama Republic's Demand for Gold," in *The Literary Digest*, CXVII (Mar. 17, 1934), 45.

"The Panama Treaty," in *The Nation*, CXXIV (1927), 6.

"Revising Our Caribbean Policy," in *The New Republic*, LXV (1930-1931), 286-287.

"Unrest in Panama," in *The New Republic*, LXV (1930), 33-34.

Anderson, Chandler P., "The Costa Rica-Panama Boundary Dispute," in *The American Journal of International Law*, XV (1921), 236-240.

Beals, Carleton, "Revolt in Panama," in *The Nation*, CXLI (1936), 99-101.

Blanco, Jorge J., "Portrait of a Sovereign State," in *The American Mercury*, XXVI (1932), 54-61.

Brown, Vera Lee, "Contraband Trade: A Factor in the Decline of Spain's Empire in America," in *The Hispanic American Historical Review*, VIII (1928), 178-189.

Buell, Raymond Leslie, "New Latin American Revolts Test Our Recognition Policy," in *The New York Times*, Jan. 11, 1931, IX, 5:1-3.

Buell, Raymond Leslie, "Panama and the United States," in *Foreign Policy Reports*, VII (1932), 409-426.

Bunau-Varilla, Philippe, "Washington and Panama," in *The Living Age*, CCCXXXII (1927), 484-487.

Calhoun, Crede Haskins, "How Panama Paid Off Its Debts," in *Current History*, XIV (1921), 298-299.

Fox, L. C., "High Financing in Panama," in *The Nation*, CXXVIII (1929), 684.

Hackett, Charles W., "The Delimitation of Political Jurisdictions in Spanish North America to 1535," in *The Hispanic American Historical Review*, I (1918), 40-69.

Hardman, R. C., "The Highway Program of Panama," in *The Pan American Magazine*, XXXVII (1924), 273-278.

Kinnaird, Lucia Burk, "Creassy's Plan for Seizing Panama, with an Introductory Account of British Designs on Panama," in *The Hispanic American Historical Review*, XIII (1933), 46-78.

Lewis, Samuel, "The Cathedral of Old Panama," in *The Hispanic American Historical Review*, I (1918), 447-453.

Loosley, Allyn C., "The Puerto Bello Fairs," in *The Hispanic American Historical Review*, XIII (1933), 314-355.

Nerval, Gaston, "Panama Treaty Promises Rectification of Errors," in *The Sunday Star* (Washington, D. C.), May 10, 1934, p. D-3.

Norton, Henry Kittredge, "Why Britishers in Panama?" in *The World's Work*, LIX (1930), 29-32.

Pierre, C. Grand, "Panama's Demand for Independence," in *Current History*, XIX (1923), 128-130.

Reid, W. A., "Busy Days in Panama," in *Bulletin of the Pan American Union*, LXIV (1930), 53-62.

Rippy, J. Fred, "Political Issues in Panama Today," in *Current History*, XXVIII (1928), 226-227.

Rodríguez, Angel D., " 'American Powers in Panama,' " in *Current History*, XIV (1921), 300-302.

Roosevelt, Theodore, "How the United States Acquired the Right to Dig the Panama Canal," in *The Outlook*, XCIX (1911), 314-318.

Salandra, Dominic, "Porto Bello, Puerto Bello, or Portobelo," in *The Hispanic American Historical Review*, XIV (1934), 93-95.

Strout, Richard Lee, "The League and the Panama Treaty," in *The Independent*, CXVIII (1927), 95-96.

Thayer, William Roscoe, "John Hay and the Panama Republic from the Unpublished Letters of John Hay," in *Harper's Magazine*, CXXXI (1915), 165-175.

Vásquez Hernández, Publio A., "La personalidad internacional de Panamá," in *Boletín de la Academia Panameña de la Historia*, año I (1933), 463-626.

Waddell, Agnes S., "Unsettled Boundary Disputes in Latin America," Foreign Policy Association, *Information Service*, V (1930), 483-500.

Winkler, Max, "America, the World's Banker," in Foreign Policy Association, *Information Service*, III (1927), special supplement, No. 3, pp. 57-74.

Winkler, Max, "Prosperity and Foreign Investments; a Summary of U. S. Foreign Investments in 1929," in *Foreign Policy Reports*, VI (1930-1931), supplement, pp. 1-22.

Woolsey, Lester Hood, "The Sovereignty of the Panama Canal Zone," in *The American Journal of International Law*, XX (1926), 117-124.

INDEX

A. B. C. Alliance, 85; Commission, 210

Acción Comunal, 90

Aerial communication, 162, 232; discussion of, 183-185; regulation in World War, 191; treaty of 1926, 236

Aizpuru, Papi, 75

Alfaro, Horacio F., election supervision, 75-76; territorial expropriation, 157-158

Alfaro, Luis E., 226

Alfaro, Ricardo J., assumes presidency, 90-91; attends Harding inauguration, 154, 208, 228; boundary dispute, 208, 221, 222; hostilities between Panama and Costa Rica, 228; negotiation of treaty of 1926, 228-229, 230-234, 240; signs treaty of 1936, 248; territorial expropriation, 154-155

Alfonso XII, King of Spain, 119

All America Cables, Inc., 100

Allied Powers, 191

Amador, Raúl, 54

Amador Guerrero, Manuel, 36, 70, 79, 226; activity in independence movement, 13-16; administration threatened by army, 48-60; boundary dispute, 122-125; disbands army, 57-59; highway development, 181; invites U. S. election supervision, 65-66; fails to attend Obaldía inauguration, 72; Liberal protests against administration of, 69; presented with protest against Taft order, 26; protests against Taft order, 26; welcomes Taft, 39

Amalgamated Sugar interests of Utah, 172

American Banana Co., 121, 124

American Foreign Banking Corp., 101

American Lumber Co., 99

American Trade Developing Co., 97, 101

Anderson, Luis, boundary dispute, 125-131

Andrews, W. W., 165, 169

Annuity, amount, 12, 18, 104, 144; influence on trade balance, 113; payment refused, 247; pledged for bond issues, 105-106, 107, 108, 110, 170-171, 172; treaty of 1936, 250-251

Arango, José Agustín, 226; appointed to organize Panamanian government, 16; boundary dispute, 127; opinion on Hay-Herrán Treaty, 12

Argentina, 217

Arias Paredes, Francisco, 243

Arias, Harmodio, appointed secretary of government and justice, 90-91; assumes presidency, 91; denies will sever relations with U. S., 245; elected president, 243; joint statement with Franklin D. Roosevelt, 246-247; measures to avert national bankruptcy, 245; praises Roy T. Davis, 91; praises Franklin D. Roosevelt, 251; promises continued debt payment, 110, 244; visits U. S., 245-247

Arias, Ramón, 70

Arias, Ricardo, 37; appeals to U. S. for election supervision, 71-72; presidential possibility, 74; sent to U. S. to invest canal payment, 104; territorial expropriation, 145

Arias, Tomás, 30, 34, 35, 37, 53; admits port question settled, 36; appointed to organize Panamanian government, 16; asked to supply postage stamps for Canal Zone, 24; boundary dispute, 122-123; Bunau-Varilla letter concerning ports, 35; odious to Liberals, 48, 50; protests against Taft order, 25, 28-29; protests against lack of respect of U. S. for Panama, 36; resigns as secretary of foreign affairs and war, 51

Arjona, Aristides, 170, 178

Arjona Q., Julio, 196

Army of Panama, 42, 65, 79, 85, 209; disbanded, 57-60, 78, 84; personnel of, 52; threatens Amador administration, 48-60

Arosemena, Carlos C., boundary dispute, 129-131; railway development, 164-165, 167, 169, 171

Arosemena, Florencio H., 242; abrogates wireless decree of Aug. 29, 1914, 180; appoints economic commission, 109; attempts reforms, 109; elected presi-